BARGAIN
FEVER

BARGAIN FEVER

How to Shop in a Discounted World

Mark Ellwood

PORTFOLIO / PENGUIN

PORTFOLIO / PENGUIN
Published by the Penguin Group
Penguin Group (USA) LLC
375 Hudson Street
New York, New York 10014

USA | Canada | UK | Ireland | Australia | New Zealand | India | South Africa | China
penguin.com
A Penguin Random House Company

First published by Portfolio / Penguin, a member of Penguin Group (USA) LLC, 2013

Library of congress cataloging-in-publication data
Ellwood, Mark.
Bargain fever : the new shopping rules of getting more and paying less / Mark Ellwood.
pages cm
Includes bibliographical references and index.
ISBN 978-1-59184-580-5
1. Shopping.   2. Consumer education.   I. Title.
TX335.E45 2013
640.73—dc23
2013019045

Printed in the United States of America
3   5   7   9   10   8   6   4   2

Set in ITC Giovanni Std
Designed by Alissa Amell

For my parents, Derek and Joan

Contents

BARGAIN
FEVER

Introduction

My name's Mark, but I'm surprised my parents didn't call me Mark-down. Bargains have loomed large throughout my life. Growing up in London, I remember my mother's coupon stash. It was stored in an old Turkish delight box, clear plastic and brittle, that sat on the kitchen counter, just level with a child's eyes. Always stuffed with ripped-out coupons, their ragged edges meant that the lid could never quite close; the box gave off a sugary whiff of rosewater that made deals, quite literally, delicious. My mother is from Scotland; were bargain-hunting an Olympic sport, her countrymen would win gold, silver, and bronze (and probably melt them down for their value). Tartan tightfistedness is the butt of constant British jokes. Insulating windows with double panes is a booming business in Scotland, they say, because it stops the children from hearing the ice cream truck when it comes around.

In my mother's case, the determination to root out price adjustments is arguably her favorite hobby. She regularly returns items so she can, instead, rebuy them on sale. The staff at the refund counter at Marks & Spencer, the British department store, greet her by name with the warmth of an old friend. That same urge for a deal first emerged in me when I was a teenager, trawling for music in local record stores (RIP, HMV). I would drive from suburb to suburb on a single-minded search: to find the rare new releases that had been marked down to spike their chart placements. Nothing was as thrilling on a Saturday afternoon as finding a 7-inch single, half price at 99p. The fact that I'd spent more on gas to get to the store than I'd saved on The Cars didn't ever cross my mind.

Sales kept me solvent throughout university, when I was shipped in as a temp to staff the biannual extravaganzas at the tony British department store Harrods. It was a stressful gig, mostly because then-owner Mohamed Al-Fayed would prowl the shop floor sniffing out infractions of the staff policy (sitting, removal of jackets, or talking to colleagues) and firing miscreants on the spot. I kept my mouth shut, and my job, through several Januarys and Julys.

Soon after college, I moved to New York City, where I've spent the majority of my adult life. After arriving, I passed most Saturdays ambling around the aisles of Century 21, the discount megastore housed in an old bank just a few feet from what's now Ground Zero. I devised a system to sift through the haphazard racks of designer bargains (hint: Buy anything you see and like in every size, take that haul home, and just return the rejects). If I wasn't scoring deals at Century 21, I was lurking in the Strand bookstore. It's had a spiffy makeover since, but in the 1990s the Strand was still a dark, dusty place that smelled of old things, both books and New Yorkers. The racks in the basement were its treasure trove: full of publishers' review copies, illicitly offloaded by critics. I could buy brand-new hardcovers at half price.

Yet it was ducking into the boutique branch of Bloomingdale's in New York's Soho recently that made me professionally curious about all things cut-price. The store is just minutes from my apartment, and I wanted to buy some deck shoes. I was ready to snap up a snazzy pair in white when the perky sales assistant wandered over to chat. Unprompted, when I asked the price, she offered a spot out-of-towners' discount. Some of the chain's stores slash 10 percent off for tourists, she told me. Thank goodness I've held on to the occasional plummy British vowel. It was a gleeful moment, an unexpected deal that clinched the sale. The thrill was ruined a week later when I found the same pair of deck shoes nearby downtown at one of those stores where the sign in the window screams: CRAZY SALE—ALL SHOES 50% OFF. Just seven days later, at this new, just-started blowout sale, they were half price. Ten percent seemed like an insult. I kicked myself—with those shoes. But I still bought a pair in another color because the deal was too good to resist.

It was a landmark moment. My experience with those shoes left me wrong-footed. Clearly, bargains were now no longer restricted to niche stores, clearance periods, or grubby basements. Buying without a discount almost felt foolish, rather than fair. Frankly, I wondered, why would anyone ever pay full price again?

Just Deal with It

I started to notice deals everywhere. The nagging impulse to search for a code before checking out online. The stamping of a coffee card—where ten espressos will trigger a free drink—is like 10 percent off. Sneaking out of work a little early, or arriving a little late, because of a special one-day sale. Browsing at a brick-and-mortar store for a new TV before bettering the price with a dot-com deal. Shrugging at a 50% OFF sign, unimpressed, and instead waiting for that discount to tumble to 70 percent. Groupon, coupon-cutting, or asking, ever so gently, "Is that the best you can do?" Bargain hunting was inescapable and exciting, at least to my Scottish side.

In some cases, the spread of sales seemed sensible. Coffee shops co-opted the idea of a bar's happy hour to jolt sales in the slower afternoon period, as Manhattan's 'wichcraft did by selling drinks 50 percent off between 3 and 6 p.m. on weekdays. Few would criticize the restaurant in LA that offered a 5 percent discount to every diner who was willing to check his or her cell phone at the door, either. As the economy has slowed, most canny Americans sloughed off any shame over coupons; in a survey, more than a quarter admitted that they'd even used them on a date. So pervasive has the small slip of paper's—or chit's—pop culture profile become that underemployed megamom Kate Gosselin's next gig after her reality show imploded was blogging for a couponing website as its celebrity spokesperson (though her abrasiveness quickly cost her that job, too). Think of how Geico built its entire brand not on a Cockney-accented gecko but on a simple slogan: "Save 15 percent or less in fifteen minutes." Similarly, rival Progressive's perky spokesbot Flo long seemed unable to open her mouth without chirping "Discount!"*

The symptoms of such salesmania continued to spread. Take, for example, retailers starting markdowns the day before Black Friday, coining a

* Flo, played by improv vet Stephanie Courtney, beat the Pillsbury Doughboy to be named favorite ad mascot ever in a recent *Entertainment Weekly* poll (the gecko went out in the third round, bested by Tony the Tiger). "I just channel the friendliest person I could imagine," Courtney explained. "It's sort of like my mom to the tenth power. She's one of these ladies who is a perennial optimist."

new name for Thanksgiving—that's Gray Thursday, please. Even this wasn't always enough, as I heard stories of families delaying Christmas expressly to snap up gifts more cheaply. More than just a response to straitened economic times, there was a palpable pride in cut-price shopping that overrode any stiffened sense of tradition. One woman told me, all aglow, that she weighted boxes with sugar, then wrapped them, stunt-present style, until the real treats arrived a day later and 50 percent off. Another single mom opted to leave her young sons a note from Santa, apologizing that he couldn't make it to their house the night before and saying he'd asked her to take them shopping on his behalf. These women may have gloated over such reindeer games, but their clique has been rapidly expanding: December 26 is trending to be the third-biggest selling day each year, after Black Friday and the Saturday before Christmas.

Other statistics I unearthed were even more staggering. The number of Americans who would purchase clothes only on sale went up from 16 to 23 percent in the four years after 2007; that's nearly a quarter of the population. Even 1 percenters weren't immune to the call of the sale; among Americans earning $150,000 or more, that number doubled, from 10 to 20 percent.* In 2006, only one in three shoppers found a "70% OFF" sign credible; six years later, almost two thirds of people would buy in and believe such a markdown. Most tellingly, though, I found that retailers sold 40 to 45 percent of their inventory at some kind of promotional price in 2011. Ten years earlier, they had sold just 15 to 20 percent of stock that way. In just a decade, sales of sales more than doubled.

No wonder businesses have started to rely on bargains to spoofish— sometimes even dangerous—extremes. It's become a frantic game of markdown one-upmanship. Was it kosher for New Jersey's Seton Hall University to offer top-GPA types up to two-thirds off annual tuition, a discount of around $21,000?

When an Ohio animal shelter offered an 85 percent reduction on its cat adoption fee, there was only one catch: It clawed out a discount from

---

* In January 2012, globe-trotting garmento Philip Green (estimated personal net worth more than $6 billion) was reportedly spotted in Miami tantruming that the 25 percent off sign in one store didn't apply to its entire stock. He probably could have charged the mall itself, fixtures and all, to his Amex Black card.

$70 per cat to $20 for two cats with the proviso that its price cut applied only to the obese kitties, like 23-pound Zeke.

Black Friday might as well refer to the bruises that result from the scrum-like scrambles that have defined it in recent times. In one year alone, there was pepper spraying, Tasering, and shooting of customers, none of it by the police. One of the fiercest examples of shopper-on-shopper violence was, ironically, between a herd of mothers and daughters hopped-up on marked-down yoga gear.

What does it all mean, other than suggesting that gridiron gear is a suitable shopping outfit during sale time? This accelerating avalanche of bargains marks a seismic shift in the way we shop. It has fundamentally changed our relationship with stores. Markdowns have become a daily concept, no longer the exception but the norm. Full price is a quaint, retro notion rapidly losing any meaning. Living in *Let's Make a Deal*, people don't only want a deep discount, they *expect* it, and won't settle for anything less. There's never been a better time to be a buyer: empowered, informed, entitled. We won't return to a meek acceptance of retail's rules again. Wielding the pricing gun for the first time, shoppers call the shots. So what caused this pandemic, a bargain fever that turned ordinary Americans into the mall-walking dead?

Shopping 3.0

Contemporary life resembles a 3-D SkyMall catalog. This is the era of TV shows built entirely around our acquisition of too much stuff: *The Price Is Right* is a ratings footnote compared to bona fide prime time hits like *Hoarders* or *Storage Wars*. While one chronicles the dark side of our compulsion to acquire, the other turns it into sport. The same more-is-more impulse drives supersizing, whether foot-long hot dogs or Big Gulp drinks. It doesn't affect just fast food, but fast fashion, too, which birthed the phenomenon of hauling: teen girls binge-buying cheap clothing at the mall, then rushing home to upload YouTube clips showcasing their bulimic spree. They're more interested in the tally than the taille. America may have always celebrated conspicuous consumption, but something is different now. Choice has morphed into excess.

Indeed, products are proliferating at *Star Trek* speed. Supermarkets after World War II stocked an average of 3,750 items; by the end of the twentieth century that number had increased more than tenfold, to 45,000. In 1994, the total of UPCs for consumer products—in other words, things that could be sold at a store by scanning them—was just over five hundred thousand. Less than ten years later, it had reached almost seven hundred thousand. In 1980, there were six major blue jean brands in America; thirty years on, that number was eight hundred and climbing. We have enough excess possessions to birth not just a TV show about self-storage but also a booming industry. In 2012, there were 2.3 billion square feet of storage space in this country, and more added since. One in ten US households was renting some kind of unit, an increase of 65 percent since the late 1990s. Retail space increased at an average net rate of 4 percent over the same period, regardless of economic downturns or surges.

None of this would be problematic but for a sticky detail. The American population's average annual growth rate since 1980 has hovered around 1 percent; in 2011, it dropped to its lowest ever to 0.7 percent. These two contradictory forces create an era of oversupply and underdemand. This is the reason another fitting name for bargain fever could be Too Much Stuff Syndrome.*

In a new retail equation, ultimate power has shifted to the shopper for the first time. The tsunami of bargains presages the beginning of a third phase in retail—call it *shopping 3.0*. The first, spanning the century after the Industrial Revolution, foregrounded producer power: demand outstripped supply while distribution was complex and pricey. Shoppers outside major cities like New York or Chicago were hostage to manufacturers, and weathered both take-it-or-leave-it pricing and less choice.

The second phase, lasting approximately forty years, emerged from the ashes of World War II. Eisenhower's interstate highways made transport easier while suburbs boomed. It was the retailers' turn to dominate, and they did, a golden era of marketing when a great ad could turn any new

---

* Retail guru Robin Lewis has long been concerned about the effect of such over-expansion, noting how Lazard Frères was already reporting that there was twice as much retail space as demand warranted in the 1980s. "There is just too much stuff sloshing around the globe," Lewis told me.

product into a household name. Take Alka-Seltzer, which plink-plonk fizzed its way into every bathroom cabinet in the country. In the TV show *Bewitched*, what other job could shorthand how debonair and modern a man Darrin was but advertising executive? The shopping center was a cultural bellweather, a place of both yearning and spending, from concerts by Tiffany to seniors on walking loops, and bored mall rats. There was a chummy familiarity, almost a trust, between sellers and shoppers. Sure, there were deals, but their quantity was restricted; the bargains were limited to the minimum needed to keep ordinary Americans as placid as lotus-eaters. We took what we were given, and we were grateful for it.

The turn of the millennium marked the start of phase three, shopping 3.0. This new chapter has been Sadie Hawkins Day at the mall, a role reversal where overstocked stores must wait anxiously on the edge of the retail dance floor as potential customers prowl the room. Discounts have become the default, powered by the new (old) mantra, "Is that the best you can do?" Shoppers banding together to collude and wheedle a bulk deal from a seller, literally leveraging buying power, is the basis of the millennial phenomenon, Groupon.

The Internet has helped torpedo the power of mass advertising, so beloved a tactic in that second phase. It has also made prices transparent, via comparison engines that act much like warp-speed digital personal shoppers, and birthed businesses such as eBay. Such operations taught ordinary Americans that price tickets were not put there by the great printer in the sky, and reminded them of the thrill of negotiating a bargain. As a plus for newbies, online buyers can haggle remotely, via automation, and therefore embarrassment free, avoiding the markdown stare-down. Sellers— whether a hotel, a shoe shop, or a supermarket—are forced to slash numbers to stand out from the widening roster of competitors that crop up with each new Google search.

Under this new paradigm, shopping has become a daily Dutch auction, where retailers must drop their prices until a picky shopper raises his or her paddle and opens their wallet. Equal parts empowered and economically pinched, consumers can now demand markdowns, more like retail hackers than buyers. One business, Shopper Gauge, has even emerged to help stores better cater to such finicky customers. It uses security footage as the basis of a new kind of analysis to track whether someone who lingered in front of a given item ever bothered to buy it. The system is programmed to discount false positives from staff in uniform, for example, and bundle a group shuffling together as a family outing, as it flags those who linger for eight seconds or more (a mark of engagement) and then cross-references such numbers with how many sales of the browsed item were registered during that hour. If fifteen shoppers lingered for eight seconds, but only four sales were made, the company will flag that disparity so that adjustments can be made; boosting the bargain from 25 percent to 30 percent, for example. In other words, Shopper Gauge instructs shops to kowtow to consumers rather than the other way around. It's soft-soaping, not hard-selling.

Distributors were the decision makers in retail's first era, while shops held sway in phase two. In shopping 3.0 the power is in the hands of buyers for the first time. Who can resist squeezing, ever so gently?

The Bargain Bible

Bargains are the highest-profile evidence of the paradigm shift that's taken place in retail since the turn of the twentieth century. Those "50% OFF" stickers are proof that there's never been a better time to be a shopper, and there's no longer any reason to ever pay full price. This book will explore why deal hunting has gone from being a sign of indigence to one of intelligence, and explain how seeking out discounts became a badge of pride rather than a scarlet letter of shame. *Bargain Fever* will help you earn an A in Bargains 101, whether dipping into the crazy world of coupon addicts or finding out how large a spot discount Pottery Barn might offer you just for asking nicely (15 percent, in fact).

To start our journey, it's vital to understand two questions: Why do bargains work so effectively on even the savviest shoppers? And, as stores see their power ebbing, what tactics will they use to try to retain a modicum of control? The answer to both begins with a trip to a mall in upstate New York one Thursday night in late November. It's freezing, so don't forget your gloves.

1

Your Brain on Sales

*How an All-Natural "Buyagra" Makes Deals
Irresistible, the Power of Price Consultants,
and the Real Reason Target's Logo Is Red*

In less than two hours, shopping's newest bargain rubicon will be crossed for the first time: Black Midnight. Stores like the Target in Clifton Park will open as early as possible on Friday after Thanksgiving, 2011, to offer a marathon of markdowns. Bundled up against the cold, a crowd of three hundred or more lingers patiently in line, making it seem more like a busy summer Saturday than the middle of a chilly winter night. There's a buzz in the air, and crumpled circulars are passed around like contraband: 46-inch TVs for $298 (a $250 saving), $40 gift cards with every iPod touch, and a Nikon camera for less than half price at $99.

But these Spenderellas have no idea why they're really here, heeding the siren call of a sale rather than sleeping off the turkey torpor like the rest of us. Each shopper was stirred by an irrational, but instinctive, response: the surge of a chemical in their brains that is nature's bargain hormone, buyagra. Why else would anyone be standing in the freezing cold outside a suburban mall at 10 p.m. on Thanksgiving night?

Peggy Castle, a stout brunette, is first in line. She is typical of these extreme deal hunters, a veteran of door busting who arrived just after 5 p.m. Sitting in a lawn chair, swaddled in a parka, her only concession to fashion is a jaunty Coach headband. "Last year, I slept in Walmart all night to get a thirty-two-inch TV for my son," she says. "I brought a tent and they were kind enough to let us in so I slept in Home and Garden." Her voice is sandpaperier than Marge Simpson's. "Nothin' would have stopped me, I'm not even kiddin' ya. Nothin'." This year's mission: a $157 netbook computer for her soon-to-be son-in-law. Another bargaineer waiting in line with us held her Thanksgiving dinner a day early, on Wednesday, so she could focus completely on shopping tonight. Target's staffers, handing out treasure map–like guides, have stage whispered the quantities of loss-leading deals like those 46-inch TVs to calm the jittery crowd. But just in case that backfires, a smattering of security is dotted around the store's perimeter. Most are off-duty cops on the store's payroll, and their presence is vital to prevent the stampedes that have become as traditional as turkey and family rows during the holiday.

There's a similar scene just one hundred yards or so across the parking lot, where another cadre of midnighters clusters outside of Kohl's. This is a smaller crowd (just seventy-five or so) and mostly moms in the middle (-age, -class, -income), lured by one of the five hundred early bird specials touted on its circular. The mood here is more infectious than anxious, and the women trade tips as they chat. There's a festive edge to their sense of shopping clout. "They hide things around the store, you know," confides soccer mom–like Kelly Ballard. "We know that from last year. A GPS on sale? It might be tucked into the kids clothing." Another Spenderella tallies her potential haul like a mathlete with a Mastercard, stacking different discounts together for maximum impact: charge card, VIP card, Kohl's cashback dollars ("It's fifteen dollars Kohl's cash for every fifty dollars you spend, instead of just ten dollars"). "The prices are cheaper than the Internet," she raves.

This crowd needs more entertaining than policing, so Kohl's has hired a two-story bus decked out as a makeshift cupcakery. Neon lights humming, it's completely empty. Kelly Ballard scoffs. "You drink coffee, you gotta pee eventually, and where you gonna?" She shrugs.

Such singlemindedness is a tip-off to her mental state, flooded with bargain-seeking hormones. She and her fellow shoppers are hopped up on discounts, brains flushed much the way they would be after a hit of cocaine or crystal meth. They're suffering true bargain fever. This febrile state of mind is sparked by a well-known but misunderstood chemical: dopamine. This "buyagra" triggers every time a great deal appears, hardwiring us to respond to bargains. In fact, for a surprisingly large number of Americans, dopamine is, quite literally, impossible to resist.

Blame It on the Brain

The brain is the Kim Kardashian of the body: high-profile and high-maintenance, with a true purpose that we still can't quite understand. What's certain, though, is how it evolved: much like a pearl, with layers accreting over time around a grain of sand. In a human brain, the equivalent to that grain of sand, buried deep at its center, is the striatum. A region that governs basic functions such as sex, food, and survival, it's also one of the areas most susceptible to the effects of dopamine.

Dopamine is a neurotransmitter, a chemical that acts like an e-mail message sending instructions between various areas of the brain. For every message marked URGENT, the striatum is a prime target. Dopamine is a compound so basic that it's found in the brains of snails, reptiles, and fish. Even honeybees rely on the buzz of a dopamine doppelganger as a neurotransmitter. For a long time scientists assumed that dopamine was a "hedonic," a kind of feel-good juice released whenever we detect something pleasant. But about twenty years ago, science realized it had misunderstood dopamine's true mission almost entirely. The chemical was far more crucial to our brain's operations than anyone had realized. Its role was also far more complicated.

Wolfram Schultz led this discovery. Now a scientist at the University of Cambridge in England, Schultz is kind eyed and square jawed, and speaks softly with a crisp German lilt. In his study, Schultz monitored the brain activity of monkeys while a simple sequence was carried out. A light was flashed, a few seconds passed, then some apple juice was squirted into the monkey's mouth. During this experiment, Schultz chanced on two surprising facts about dopamine. First, that once a monkey had learned the sequence, this chemical surged in the brain when the light flashed, rather than when the juice was squirted. In other words, the monkey was actually responding to the anticipation rather than the reward.

More intriguing, after repeating the experiments for a while, Schultz was surprised to discover that the best way to maximize dopamine in the monkey's brain was with a shock squirt of juice, without the light as a warning. Dopamine, he concluded, wasn't feel-good juice after all. Instead, it flagged unexpected bonuses—whenever we're happily caught off guard, say, or something turns out better than planned.

The findings were bolstered by a similar experiment involving rats, in which a rat was dropped for several days into a maze containing Fruit Loops hidden under a toy. Every time the experiment was run, the rat's behavior remained unchanged; he'd chow down on the cereal with gusto. What happens in his brain, though, is very different. On day one, discovering that unexpected food for the first time, dopamine spritzes liberally, celebrating and marking the bonus. Five days later, that same hormone is all but absent; the rat takes the cereal for granted. In other words, dopamine is the chemical equivalent of an aha moment (Pax, Oprah Winfrey). Order a slice of chocolate cake in a restaurant and there'll be little dopamine released in your brain. But if that café spontaneously produces a slice complete with a candle on your birthday, dopamine neurons will spurt.*

The something-for-nothing setup of a bargain on Black Midnight affects our brain in a similar way. Anything that costs less than might be expected activates that flow of dopamine. Indeed, it's akin to cocaine's

---

* This isn't dopamine's only role in our brains; it's also one of the chemicals that codes movement. As such, it's dopamine that dies off in Parkinson's patients, who demonstrate a lack of affect and motivation—in other words, are all but immune to the urge that drives shoppers to the mall on Black Friday. The commonest treatment for Parkinson's involves compounds known as dopamine agonists, artificial replacements that break down into dopamine once they reach the brain. Around 20 percent of patients who take such pills experience some kind of compulsive behavior, including extreme shopping—one man spent $100,000 on QVC and its ilk in a single month. Indeed, in France a fifty-one-year-old patient sued one of the dopamine agonist drugmakers; the married father of two claimed that the pills had turned him not only into a compulsive online gambler but a gay sex addict whose risky behavior had led to his being raped. All of which makes you feel a lot less fretful about that Black Friday splurge, at least.

euphoria, which is also dopamine driven; those narcotics trick the brain into releasing it roughly fifteen times faster than usual. This chemical—which Schultz calls "the best reward system the brain has"—not only spotlights an unexpected pleasure but motivates us to seek out that feel-good moment again.

Imagine a total stranger walks up to you on the street and hands you a thousand-dollar check that can be cashed at any bank. The first time you go to your local branch and exchange it for greenbacks, dopamine will deluge your striatum. Now let's say Mr. Moneybags keeps popping up across town, never in the same place twice but always with that thousand-dollar check. On his one hundredth appearance, as he hands you that check, the brain's reaction has modulated, much like the rat in the maze or the juiced-up monkeys. The surprise isn't the money itself but the man with the check. Dopamine's response migrates from simple payoff (cashing the check) to anticipation (the sight of the generous stranger). Put another way, if you found a bargain at a store last Thanksgiving, your brain will be bubbling with that wallet-opening hormone before midnight even strikes. As long as you chance on a great deal again (as Target, Kohl's, and co all but guarantee), the cycle will keep repeating. This is another reason, in addition to oversupply, that the past decade has seen an acceleration of discounts. It now takes deeper and more frequent markdowns to achieve the same retail high.

If dopamine is triggered so reliably at the sight of a shopping steal, how does anyone manage to emerge from a store without snapping up every bargain on offer? Thankfully, there's a trip wire in our brain that takes the form of a chemical tussle between three distinct regions. The nucleus accumbens, the insula, and the dorsolateral prefrontal cortex (call it the DLPFC—all the experts do) all react to that tsunami of dopamine. Together, they decide whether or not we should act on dopamine's prompting.

The nucleus accumbens and insula are both buried in the center of the brain, close to or part of the striatum. Their location is a tip-off that they were early to evolve, making them likely to play roles in visceral or gut reactions. Both have multiple functions but, broadly speaking, the

nucleus accumbens has a teenage-like fondness for immediate gratification, while the insula has a spinster's readiness to register disgust.

The DLPFC, one of the brain's outermost layers, is very different; rare
in animals, it's correspondingly challenging and expensive to study. The
greater the number of layers in a brain, the more senior an animal's
position in the evolutionary food chain. Only high-level primates such
as rhesus monkeys or apes have this region, which is lacking in com-
moner lab subjects such as rodents. The DLPFC is assumed to be a high-
functioning system that weighs the pros and cons in actions. It's involved
in short-term memory, delayed gratification, and all-round calming
down. One team of researchers tested this hypothesis by applying mag-
netic stimulation to various parts of the DLPFC in subjects. They demonstrated that by boosting the left side of this section, the subjects showed
an increase in impulsiveness; while strengthening the right side made
the volunteers' caution cast-iron hard (pity the poor patsies in that study
who likely now have no problem working out which way is north on the
journey home).

One kooky experiment best explains how our brains both weather
and process that dopamine deluge. Researchers used an fMRI brain scanner to monitor twenty-six men and women while they were shown eighty
products, everything from Godiva chocolates to a Harry Potter box set.
Participants could choose to buy any item using monies provided by the
researchers. They were shown each product for a few seconds, then a
price of between $8 and $80 flashed onto the screen. The researchers
explained that these were discount prices, without specifying the actual
discount percentage from the retail price (reductions were up to 75 percent). The experiment was intended to examine how the brain assesses
pricing, and especially discounts.

Their findings uncovered a distinctive sequence. Take a Harry Potter
devotee, going Hogwarts-wild over the sight of a beloved box set. That
surprise appearance was an ideal dopamine trigger. At the first surge, the
nucleus accumbens flared with excitement; its level of activity in direct
relation to how much a subject desired the treat. Then, when a price appeared next to those books, the brain activity shifted to the insula. It's
the brain's Debby Downer—a stoic processor of chronic pain or disgust

(*How much is it? Can I afford it?*). If the price of the item was lower than expected—*Just twenty bucks for all seven books? Wow!*—blood then surged to the headmaster-like DLPFC. The DLPFC tallied the pluses and minuses of the splurge. It was this region, researchers suggested, that made the final purchasing decision. If there was too much blood flow to the insula, the volunteers didn't buy; the brain's gut reaction had dismissed the product as not a good enough deal. But if there was a surge to either of the other areas, they snapped up the cut-price treats. The absolute price was irrelevant. Each of the three areas, the nucleus accumbens, insula, and DLPFC, activated in proportion to whether the subjects considered an item a good deal or a bad deal. So consistent did that pattern seem to be that the researchers could accurately predict purchasing decisions from the activity observed in these three distinctive regions.*

If every brain were identical, of course, our reaction to that "50% OFF" sign would be equally consistent. So why are some people, like our Black Midnight Spenderellas, more willing to camp out overnight for a good deal than the rest of us? The answer comes down to DNA. In most brains, a dopamine dump is quickly broken down by an enzyme known as COMT. However, a genetic quirk that affects one in four Caucasians renders COMT less effective than it should be. In the brains of the people with this gene mutation, dopamine lingers far longer than nature intended, making them more trigger-happy than normal when bargain hunting. As dopamine spurts like a party popper, the brain has to clean up the chemical streamers. For most of us this happens at power vacuum–like speed, but anyone with this variant of COMT has the equivalent of a hand broom.

Among this group, then, dopamine can short-circuit the DLPFC's ability to exert control over our actions. Instead, overdosed with the hormone, the brain allows the striatum and, especially, the nucleus accumbens to wrestle primacy away. In shopping terms, that makes those bargains—already a dopamine-producing delight—almost irresistible. As Yale neurobiology professor Amy Arnsten put it, "It's losing that part

* Some scientists are chary about simplifying the brain in such a Freudian manner, turning the nucleus accumbens, insula, and DLPFC into little more than physical manifestations of the id, ego, and superego. But there's certainly compelling evidence for much of this thesis.

of you that says, 'Do I really need this? Can I afford this? Yes, it's a good deal but is it a good deal for me?'" Even those with the non-variant COMT enzyme can suffer a similar fate; stress inhibits the DLPFC's power, too, along with our willingness to defer to its reasoning. This is the reason that stores try to pressure shoppers with time-sensitive deals: each frisson of pressure makes it harder for reason to retain hold. Struggling with hundreds of other sharp-elbowed shoppers, tussling over the same doorbuster deal, makes that low price even harder to resist.* (All the more reason to make a list and check it twice before chancing any pre-Christmas bargains.)

If dopamine is "buyagra," the chemical and physiological reason that sales are irresistible to the human brain, then dopamine and *money* are as combustible a combination as Burton and Taylor. Certainly, stores rely on such vulnerability every day. But when it comes to sales or bargains, there's a problem. As we've seen, dopamine encodes a learned response. In other words, once Peggy Castle and her fellow Spenderellas discover that Walmart offers the best Black Friday bargains, they'll remember and return. However, if sales are too frequent and aggressive, that dopamine shock of a sale dissipates. When shoppers expect a price to be lowered, the surprise is gone, along with that wallet-opening feel-good juice. That is, unless you can trick the brain. Tens of millions of research dollars have been funneled into finding out the best way to engineer sales-minded sleights of hand. It's a last gasp attempt by stores to flex their dwindling control. If you think you can outsmart such retail skullduggery, read on.

It's Saturday, early summer. You're close to budget for the month, but a new branch of Best Buy opened up in your town—just as your TV has malfunctioned for the fourth time in four weeks. How handy, then, that the electronics megastore is staging a giant sale on Samsung flat screens with 30 percent off each model: a 32-inch for $499, a 40-inch for $699, and a 46-inch for $899. It's such a great deal, you couldn't possibly pass it up. Six hundred ninety-nine dollars later, there's barely room in

---

* One recent study charted how women's heart rates beat faster at the whiff of a deal than at a picture of Ryan Gosling or a pricey pair of shoes; one woman's pulse quickened to 187 BPMs—that's racier than on a roller coaster—when she was offered the chance to save around $1.30 on a bottle of shower gel.

the trunk for the giant cardboard box. *Sold*. Heading back to the mall, you stroll past The Children's Place, where there's a sign blaring: ENORMOUS MEMORIAL DAY SALE. It's a handy reminder; one of your colleagues just had a baby and it would be rude not to buy her a trinket. A triple pack of onesies is reduced from $12.95 to $7.77. *Sold*. You should really go home for lunch, but you're curious to check out Panera Bread's new menu. Apparently, it now sells a lobster roll—way too pricey at $16.99 for a sandwich—but the $6.59 soup-and-salad deal is a bargain. It's basically like saving ten dollars and the smell of fresh-baked bread is making you even hungrier. *Sold*. Nordstrom is next door, the department store that bests its rivals on quality and service. Just inside you spot a $110 MICHAEL Michael Kors maxi dress that will be so versatile for the hot months ahead, and the workmanship is top-notch. It would be silly to leave it on the rack. *Sold*. On your way out of the mall, you walk past the red Target logo. It's just too cute, that red, black, and white Sale sign with a picture of Bullseye the dog. Just ten minutes to browse, you tell yourself, as the deals are so good. The rack of sunglasses, all just $12.99, aren't on sale, but you could do with a spare pair to keep in the car. *Sold*. Driving home toward the freeway, Walmart and Costco are looming. They jog a guilty memory—you should have brought the grocery list on the fridge—so you detour quickly to see if anything catches your eye. Walmart has a twelve-pack of Heinz ketchup for $36.17, and Costco's bulk order of paper towels is just $19.08. *Sold*. Total tally from the trip: $891.60, plus gas and sorry-I-splurged gift to defuse your spouse's fuming after seeing the credit card bill. Call it a round $1,000 that you spent on a day when you didn't even intend on opening your wallet.

Take heart, though, because none of this was your fault (especially for the one in four with the iffy COMT gene). Each store was using a different discounting trick to trigger the dominoes of dopamine in your brain. It was an episode of *Wipeout* at the mall, except every obstacle didn't dunk you, but rather derailed you into spending money. Only in the last two decades has this new retail landscape emerged, its architects members of that booming but shadowy new industry: price consulting. Their jobs wouldn't exist were it not for the explosion of interest in the field of a renegade academic discipline known as neuroeconomics.

The Bird in the Hand, the Funhouse Mirror, and the Cab in a Rainstorm

Human beings make stupid decisions around money, as the authors of buzzy books like *Freakonomics* and *Predictably Irrational* have explained so adroitly. Putting a tax rebate into a savings account instead of using it to pay down high-interest debts is illogical, but commonplace. Why has *Deal or No Deal*, a game without skill or strategy centered simply on the suspense of watching someone open some boxes, become a global TV megahit, seen everywhere from Albania to Vietnam? Even feeding a one-armed bandit relies on much the same suspension of smarts. It's all thanks to our irrational relationship with money, a flaw that neuroeconomists have made their mission to understand and exploit.

Three crucial tenets of this field help explain why sale signs are so dopamine boosting. The first is what neuroeconomists call loss aversion, a fancy name for the Bird in the Hand rule. Time and again, experiments have shown that the human brain feels greater pain and anxiety over losing money than excitement at gaining it. In other words, we'd rather stick with what we have than chance even rational risks.

Take a set of volunteers who've arrived at a lab one morning to be greeted with a crisp hundred-dollar bill. Each is now one hundred dollars richer, unexpectedly (cue: warming spritz of dopamine). But ask those very same participants to gamble that money on a coin toss a little later—they can win ten dollars on heads, but must surrender ten dollars on tails—and few, if any, will agree. Up the ante to fifteen dollars won and only ten dollars lost and still most resist. Though the worst that gamble can leave them is ninety dollars richer than they were before they walked into the lab, loss aversion is too powerful to overcome.

Safeguarding our pocketbooks in this way is so visceral an impulse that the rational, DLPFC-style brain is overridden by this impulse. One price consultant often runs a spontaneous real-world experiment when addressing a conference or meeting full of sharp-suited execs. He'll offer such money-juggling titans a choice between receiving a onetime payment of $4,000 or gambling fifty-fifty on receiving $10,000. Logically, the latter is a far better offer, yet every time the overwhelming majority chooses the former. The price consultant will point this out to the throng, pause, and then pose a second conundrum. Fictitious debt forgiven, there's a fresh challenge: each person can either forfeit $3,500 or gamble fifty-fifty on losing $8,000 or nothing at all. Again, most will choose the latter: the illogical but more loss-averse option. The Bird in the Hand rule is that our pain at foregoing cash is so acute that it overrules the logic of winning it.*

The second key theory of neuroeconomics is the reference point, which acts as a kind of fiscal funhouse mirror warping our perceptions and perspectives around money. An old experiment concerning salaries best illustrates this. Volunteers were offered two similar situations. In one, they could opt to earn $35,000 in an office where every other staffer's salary was $38,000; in another, their salary would be just $33,000 but their peers would earn only $30,000. It's a no-brainer to a computer, but to a human brain, this puzzle is agonizing. Eighty-four percent of people, quite rationally, chose the former, since they would be earning more money. Even so, 62 percent said that they would be *happier* in the latter case—earning less in absolute terms, but more than their peers. The fiscal Funhouse Mirror reminds us that the value of money is surprisingly relative. When we look at numbers, whether salaries or prices, we consider them in context, weighing up fairness or advantage. In bargain terms, it's the power of the "WAS!/NOW!" sticker.

The third theory of neuroeconomics that helps decode the power of a sale is the idea of transaction utility. *Utility* is a familiar term in conventional economics, too: It denotes the value of something to an individual. If every slice of pizza costs the same regardless of toppings, picking pepperoni because it's your favorite indicates it has more utility, or value, to you. But neuroeconomics further unpacks the idea to look at what it calls transaction utility. Think of this as the Cab in a Rainstorm principle. Simply put, the same taxi is more valuable (or at least valued) when it's stormy than on a sunny day.

---

* We're loss averse about more than just cash. Every Sunday a team that gains a slight lead in an NFL game will tweak its tactics to safeguard that advantage. No longer are they playing to win, but rather playing *not to lose.*

Imagine one Saturday at the mall, you're waiting in line to buy a polo shirt at a store and a passerby confides that Macy's has the same item but reduced from $25 to $15. Most people would ditch the line and scurry over to the department store to save $10. Later that same day, you're on line again, this time to buy a seated lawn mower for $525. Another helpful stranger pitches in and says it's $10 cheaper at Home Depot next door. Few people would bother to make the change this time, though rationally the saving is identical ($10, enough to buy a season's worth of weed killer). This is the perfect example of transaction utility for a neuroeconomist: the $10 discount has relative, rather than absolute, value. To humans, so deliciously irrational, $10 can be worth more or less depending on the circumstance.

Another classic study that also illustrates this theory tasked volunteers to picture themselves on a hot beach with a friend. This friend was offering to go and fetch a bottle of ice-cold water, but the friend was facing a quandary: two places selling water, both of them a similar, long hike away. One was a swanky five-star resort's beach bar, the other a ramshackle island hut. Before setting off, the volunteers were asked a question. The friend needed to know the maximum they were prepared to pay for a bottle of H_2O, since its price would differ between bars (tough to replicate the experiment today, since we'd just text and ask). At the tony spot, the volunteers would be willing to pay an average price of $2.65; at the grimy hut, they would stump up only $1.50. That difference is completely illogical. Indeed, to a classical economist the idea of paying a varied price is nonsensical. The product was the same (ice-cold bottled water) and would be drunk in the same place (a fictitious lawn chair miles from civilization); in theory, the venue where it was purchased would be irrelevant. Again, a bottle of water isn't just a bottle of water. Value exists in context, and is far from absolute.

There's a difference between transaction utility (the Cab in a Rainstorm) and acquisition utility, the term neuroeconomics applies to that more traditional idea of cost, as in the pizza and pepperoni example. Take Mr. Bill Dollar and his wife, Penny. She's thrilled after spending the day at the mall, since she's coming home with a beautiful punch bowl. Penny's giddy with excitement (and dopamine), trilling that the bowl was reduced from $600 to $150. Bill grumblingly reminds her how long it's been since they hosted any kind of party where it could be used. Both of them are assessing the punch bowl's value, or utility, but they're doing so in different ways. Mr. Dollar is focusing on acquisition utility, syncing the price with its usefulness—cost per use, in other words. Mrs. Dollar, on the other hand, is obsessed with how much she's saved. Driving home, Penny was muttering "Six hundred dollars, six hundred dollars, six hundred dollars." She's energized by the fact that the actual price she paid is lower than her reference point. Hers was a good deal, illustrating what's technically known as positive transaction utility. And whether it's a price cut for Penny or Fruit Loops cereal for a rat in a maze, *positive transaction utility* is the term neuroeconomists use for the moment dopamine squirts into the brain.

.99 Problems: The Five Secrets of Price Consulting

Such experiments may be merely intriguing to ordinary Americans, but price consultants have made a career—and many millions—out of them. They leverage our irrational relationship with money to help maximize retailers' profits, the ultimate antagonists in shopping 3.0. Knowing their tricks, though, it's easy to spot them every time they're applied.

For centuries, pricing was simple. Since the advent of accounting ledgers in medieval times, vendors had adhered to a cost-plus pricing model: noting how much it cost to acquire an item, adding on a standard margin, and offering it to the market at that price. This was arithmetic.

Retailers shuffled away from this approach in the 1890s. British economist Alfred Marshall, credited with inventing the supply and demand curve, noted that capitalism wasn't just about cost or supply but about the customers' wants and needs. Yet prices didn't truly detach from cost until American economist Theodore Levitt published his *Mad Men*–era screed *Marketing Myopia* several decades later. Levitt's essential insight was that customers don't buy ¼-inch drill bits, they buy ¼-inch holes. A company's job is to solve their customer's real need, rather than simply sell them something. Such a revelation encouraged retailers to push the margins with the lip-biting optimism of a tax-deducting entrepreneur. This was alchemy.

Price consulting became a career per se in the mid 1980s, thanks to Hermann Simon, a wily ex-professor of economics in Germany. Simon was obsessed with the idea of "willingness to pay." He and his upstart cohorts wanted to dismantle retail's old structure and rebuild it without regard to cost-plus pricing. On behalf of a client, they asked themselves three questions, all of them aimed at maximizing a company's profits: Who is the customer? What do they need? How much are they willing to pay to solve that need? Using their answers, Simon and his colleagues invented value-based pricing, essentially transaction utility in practice. Don't start with manufacturing costs, Simon said, but with the customer and what they value about a certain product. Today, price-consulting savants break down exactly how much the demand for a good or service yo-yos in sync with its price tag (a concept known as *price elasticity of demand*), then help businesses adjust accordingly. The brinkmanship is akin to an everyday auction, pushing prices as high as the market will bear. With the excess that characterizes manufacturing today, though, such machinations have become even more complex.

The industry-wide Professional Pricing Society was founded in 1984, but saw the fastest uptick in membership in the first decade of the twenty-first century, from around six hundred people to four thousand or so worldwide. Most of its members specialize in what's euphemistically called *price optimization*. It's better to think of it as a game of What Can We Get Away with Charging for That? Of course, once price is unmoored from cost, it does two things simultaneously: It boosts margins while allowing suppliers to offer discounts with far less impact on their income.

One supermarket study in the 1990s showed how easy it is for consultants like these to play with price. Interviewers stationed at cash registers asked shoppers for their receipts and staged an impromptu pricing pop quiz. Few, if any, of the shoppers were as price aware as they might have assumed, largely unable to rattle off the cost of a sixteen-ounce bottle of ketchup, for example. Rather, they largely trusted that an endcap was the standard location for sale items and they blithely (and blindly) relied on that truism.

By the late 2000s, almost every price tag had been "optimized." Consultants earn hefty fees to decide whether to charge 99 cents or $1 for that toothbrush (99 cents, without question, but we'll get to that). They leave their DNA on every recommended retail price (RRP), including discounts. Over the last few decades, price consultants have developed five gimmicks that are used every day in every store and mall across America. Each is a fail-safe way to trigger a dopamine rush—unless, of course, you stymie the reaction by spotting the trick first.

Think back to that imaginary $1,000 trip to the mall. Price consultants' trick number one was in effect at Panera, with its $16.99 lobster sandwich. That menu was value engineered using the reference point. Commentators snarked when the 1,400-franchise chain introduced this pricey sandwich in summer 2009 at the nadir of the Great Recession. But it was a masterstroke of menu writing. An absurdly expensive treat became an anchor price, throwing everything else on the list into bargain relief. (An added bonus for the company: Panera's margin is higher on costlier items, so the chain is glad to serve up an occasional lobster roll to the hungry and foolish.) An entire article in *The New York Times* was devoted to breathlessly charting the rise of the $40 entrée. What went unacknowledged, of course, was the passel of menu consultants (yep, that's an industry, too) who was gently nudging those prices up for reasons other than quality. "It's menu engineering: make sure you have an outrageously priced $125 hamburger and right next to it, the item you want to sell, the one that has the highest margin, and might be priced at $21," scoffs one price consultant. An ultra-luxury item that's absurdly overpriced isn't intended to sell but rather shift your reference point artificially northward, reframing full-price items as soi-disant bargains.

Price consultants rely on what they call *mental accounting*, our tendency to portion out funds in our heads and earmark them for different uses, like dinners, movies, or clothing. Make a steak seem cheaper than expected by using a high-priced decoy, and it's a positive utility shock to the brain that triggers dopamine. Less was deducted from that invisible account in your mind than expected. Minutes later, of course, that rush has coaxed you into splurging on a dessert using "left over" money.

Think of these illogically expensive items as the pricing equivalent of a cheerleader's frumpy friend; Plain Jane amps up the hotness of the rest of the clique simply by being there and making them seem more appealing. Just like that homely hanger-on, no one is supposed to want these items—but if they do, it's an amusing bonus. High-priced decoys edge a reference point upward and guarantee a dopamine rush over a far greater number of items.

It isn't just restaurants that rely on that trick, of course. Pick a fashion brand—Coach maybe, or J.Crew—and then ask a sales assistant what the priciest item is in the store. Likely, the answer will be surprising. Maybe it's the J.Crew Collection spaghetti strap sequined dress ($650) or a Globetrotter suitcase ($1,750). Coach has a smattering of bags for $1,200, like the Caroline, a truly beautiful pleated and gathered leather satchel. Most of the stock at both retailers, however, is $500 or less. Similarly, look at the layout of any department store's furniture section: good chance there's a sumptuous and pricey sofa in the center, quickly noticed and admired by everyone. Its purpose is solely to make everything else look more affordable. If Neiman Marcus didn't pad its holiday catalog with outlandish treats, such as a lifetime pass on American Airlines for $3 million, customers wouldn't be able to appreciate how much of a bargain that pair of Swarovski-studded Manolo Blahniks truly are.

Reference points are also the reason a so-called manufacturer's suggested retail price (MSRP) exists on cars or electronics; the stores seem cheap in comparison with the MSRP. It's the same with advertised reference prices (ARPs)—the power of that "WAS!/NOW!" sticker. And it's why original prices are proudly touted during markdown season, right there on the same tag. Once we mull buying that lobster sandwich or the sequined dress at J.Crew, our anchor price shifts upward and—presto— the rest of the stock triggers a gentle spritz of bargain buyagra.

Trick number two of price consulting is evident in the trio of TVs you spotted at Best Buy on that fictional mall jaunt. This is Goldilocks pricing, where the most effective bargains are not always the cheapest item in the store. At that imaginary Best Buy, those three Samsung TVs were marked down by 30 percent: a 32-inch for $499, a 40-inch for $699, and a 46-inch for $899. What no blue-shirted staffer would tell you is how uneven of an order the store has placed. Two of those TV sizes are little more than set-dressing, as the store will probably sell a few 32-inch models, and perhaps one or two of the largest option. Together, though, the least expensive and the most expensive help funnel shoppers toward the just-right option: the 40-inch TV (which is likely to offer the healthiest margin of all and will be ordered in dramatically larger quantities).

Goldilocks pricing, also called *versioning,* uses the reference point in a different way: It identifies a target item and then bookends it with similar offerings that make it both a bargain (cheaper than that 46-inch TV) and better quality (that 32-inch is for skinflint Luddites). Offering just a pair of similar items, shoppers will be drawn to the cheaper one. Present a trio instead, though, and they will gravitate to the mid-priced option. Goldilocks pricing underlies the old three-class carriage system on trains, and why gas is displayed in triplicate.

Look at the appliance departments at Sears or Lowe's or Home Depot and count the trios. The real difference in features among the items, especially the house-brand models, will be surprisingly slight, but it will be the mid-priced option that is being subtly promoted at every store. High-end stock-keeping units (SKUs) add as much credibility as revenue to any category. Prices for phones at Best Buy Mobile are displayed the same way, in threesomes: the New Family Plan, the 2-Year Upgrade Plan ("That LG Nitro HD 3 is just $49.99 . . ."), and the Regular Price without contract (". . . unless you opt to buy it without contract, then it costs $649.99"). Of course, restaurants use the threefer model to manage supplies and avoid spoilage on unused food. Imagine a menu that has a chicken entrée for $15 and a fish alternative for $19. That $4 seems significant, so there will be a skew toward the cheaper option. But add a $45 porterhouse steak to the menu and the $4 seems negligible.

Perhaps the most masterful example of versioning is that of Procter & Gamble's diapers. In 1978, seventeen years after launching Pampers, P & G faced a dilemma. Sure, its revolutionary disposable diapers were so far more convenient than traditional cloth nappies, but shoppers perceived the new-fangled disposables as pricey in comparison to the muslin cloth ones. So the company turned to versioning, and created a premium sister brand, Luvs, that would put Pampers in the middle, between its sibling disposable and the bargain muslins. It repositioned Pampers to the just-right price. Unsurprisingly, sales skyrocketed and the brand became a household name. By the 1990s, with cloth diapers now a charming anachronism, P & G was facing a different problem: warehouse clubs. How could it supply this booming retail market while resisting reductions in the price of Pampers? The solution was simple. Luvs was no longer needed as a premium decoy, so in 1994 it was rebooted as a cheaper alternative to Pampers.

Trick number three that price consultants use at every mall is disarmingly simple. Remember that sign outside The Children's Place on our $1,000 trip, the one screaming "ENORMOUS MEMORIAL DAY SALE"? Price consultants realized very quickly that marking items down isn't enough to stoke a dopamine rush in unsuspecting shoppers. Stores must also remind shoppers of the deal at every opportunity, whether or not those prices have actually changed.*

Jargoneers call the DISCOUNT!, BARGAIN!, REDUCTION! signs *information cues*. Over and over, studies have shown how impactful they can be on what is actually bought. Two professors teamed up to look at the power of flagging sales via a clothing catalog. In three separate and simultaneous print runs, the pair priced the same dress at $54, $49, and $44 to see which would sell better. Customers randomly received one of the three catalogs and the researchers waited to see which price would prove a best seller. The $49 was the winner—probably, as we'll see, thanks to the trigger of that ending-in-nine figure. In the next print run, though, they tweaked the three catalogs. The prices remained $54, $49, and $44, but an ON SALE flash was added next to all three prices. In this round, sales data was split equally among the trio. So our brains respond to being told something is a bargain regardless of whether or not it truly is.

MIT's Duncan Simester, one of the professors from this initial study,

---

* One Morgan Stanley retail researcher who tracks specialty stores chuckled when he compared The Children's Place Memorial Day prices with prices a week earlier. He found them all identical, albeit the items were still on sale.

became obsessed with the idea of bargain response and widened his research from catalogs to real-world retail. He partnered with a chain of convenience stores, tweaking prices of various commodity items in eighteen of its outlets in one city. To iron out variables, Simester used almost two hundred different products for the experiment. These were then divided into three different groups, varying from store to store. Take a bottle of shampoo, for example; in the control group of shops, it was sold in the same way at the same price as before. In a second group, the price was reduced by 12 percent, but no indication of that change was made. In the final group of stores, though the price remained the same, a perky red-and-yellow LOW PRICE sticker appeared on the shelf. In this experiment, Simester's results were telling: The quietly discounted group sold just over 17 percent more units than the control. But the group with the LOW PRICE sticker also had increased sales, in this case by 3.4 percent. That profit uptick cost the store nothing more than the price of printing a few flimsy sheets of paper. It's a reminder to double check the true discount any time you're nudged by a splashy sign to pick up a supposed special offer in the grocery store.

Thanks to its iconic logo, Target scores a bull's-eye when it comes to trick number four, designed to maximize the sale of bargains. Why are so many store logos, especially those known for good value—J. C. Penney, Target, Macy's—red? And why, when department store S. S. Kresge launched its discount offshoot Kmart, did it swap out its signature green for red? Red is, quite literally, an eye-catching color. It's the longest wavelength so, because of a glitch in how our eyes process color, anything red appears closer than it is. It jumps out at us from the landscape, and demands attention. Some scientists suggest this is a holdover from early primates using the shade as a clue to the ripeness of fruits—clearly, if this were the case, prehistoric monkeys would not have been as fond of bananas as their contemporary counterparts.*

Chris McManus, professor of psychology at University College London, has found that the first and second color words to evolve in every

---

* When the postal service was invented in the United Kingdom, mailboxes were originally green, but so many people complained that they were bumping into these strange new metal contraptions that they were repainted scarlet.

language have been *black* and *white*. But when or if a third color appears, it is—always and without exception—*red*. McManus suggests that this lexical quirk has important implications for how the brain interprets red, both consciously and subliminally. The longer the word for a color has been in use, he believes, the greater the number of associations, meanings, and nuances it can acquire. In this way, the color itself gains more impact. In other words, since we've been using the word for red far longer than that for, say, purple, it's embedded more deeply into our psyche. Thanks to both history and physiology, we notice a bright red sale sign more quickly and with greater interest than any other color.

As baby boomers drive the average age of Americans ever upward in the next decades, the power of red will only increase. That's because the cornea yellows as humans grow older, making it harder to perceive small details, whether differences in stair height—it's why seniors often trip— or certain colors, especially blue and green. The aging eye sees the entire world through a gauzy, yellowish lens, so that color, too, loses its power of distinction. This leaves black, white, and red to become ever more important and common to attract the boomer shoppers' attention.

The fifth and final trick that price consultants employ every day is number theory. Think back to the prices themselves on that trip to the mall—that $110 dress at Nordstrom, those $7.77 romper suits at The Children's Place, and Target's $12.99 sunglasses. Retailers know that prices ending in 9 indicate a value product (such as throwaway sunglasses), while a 0 ending shorthands premium and prestige (designer clothing), and 7 or 8 endings signal items priced to move and closeouts (those onesies, the Heinz ketchup, and the paper towels). Divining why we ascribe such irrational meaning to numbers is neuroeconomics' most delicious conundrum.*

Countless experiments have charted the effectiveness of these theories around certain digits. Take the study undertaken by a joint team from two universities in which volunteers were offered the chance to buy two similar pens. In the first round, one pen was priced at $2 and the

---

* Price formulas like these are so ingrained that one waggish British political manifesto a few years ago promised to introduce a 99-pence coin to save on change.

other at $3.99; while the second time, they were priced at $1.99 and $4. A single cent difference caused a 26 percent drop in sales in pen number two. While the price difference was negligible, the sales figures contrasted sharply: 44 percent of the volunteers bought the $3.99 pen, while only 18 percent of them chose the $4 pen. A clique of French academics undertook a similar test, commandeering the grocery department closest to every Gallic heart: cheese. Some of the *fromage* by-the-pound was priced with sharp endings, or 9, and others with whole numbers, ending in 0. The researchers tallied the purchases of 250 shoppers and found that—voilà—the amount of Camembert and co with prices ending in 9 sold an average of €6.53 (around $8.50), while those ending with 0 sold on average just €5.08 (or $6.60). A bargain price juiced the final tally by almost two bucks.

One price consultant even estimates that a $9.99 price tag can, on average, sell 10 to 20 percent more product than a $10 one. Rutgers marketing professor Robert Schindler has spent his entire career studying such dopamine-sparking values, especially retailers' reliance on that .99 ending. One of his most famous experiments involved a fashion company's semiannual clearance catalog. Schindler worked with the firm to divide its usual 90,000 print run into thirds. In the first set of catalogs the prices would end in .00, the standard markdown that would act as a control group. The second set offered identical merchandise with prices ending in .99. And the third set advertised those items with prices ending in .00. Schindler found that sales were 8 percent higher on the .99 catalogs than the .00, despite the price (and profit) difference being just three hundredths of 1 percent. He doesn't believe that it's always strategic to goose sales with that bargain trick, though. "Any products with physical risk, stay away from nine endings," he says. "A dentist? Eye surgery? It suggests it'll hurt."

Prices ending in 7 or 8 are most common in clearance racks or at retailers whose reputation rests entirely on good value, such as Costo or Walmart; they're intended to imply a constant spigot of bargains. Prices such as $36.17, $19.08, or $7.77 also seem deliberately exact, a tacit suggestion of a return to the pre-consultant practice of cost-plus pricing. With that $36.17 tag, it's as if Walmart is saying, *Honest, ma'am, I'm just passing on a standard markup, based precisely on the exact per-unit cost.* If only that were true.

Retailers like Walmart aren't alone in massaging prices, combining sharp and whole numbers to communicate contrasting ideas of premium or good value. The most common example is across the shoe sector, where cheaper styles might often start at $29.95 or $49.99, continuing through to $69.99 or $89.99. As soon as a particular brand wants to switch its customer base from bargain hunters to status seekers, it adjusts its pricing: to $130 or $150, for instance. (See how Johnston and Murphy's cheapest pair of shoes costs $98, while the prices of the rest end in 0.) Value-driven shoppers can feel smart, while shoe fetishists will feel indulged. Fast fashion retailer Uniqlo, the Japanese answer to Gap currently mushrooming across America, prices its jeans at $39.90, shirts at $29.90, and T-shirts at $12.90. The chain claims that the practice is a holdover from cultural norms in its home country—etiquette deems 10 yen change more polite than a single penny, apparently—but it's a stroke of pricing genius that any consultant should envy. Those 9s underscore cheapness, but the 0 presages quality.

There's no better master class in price manipulation than the infomercial, though. Take the one for Cami Secret, an unremarkable product akin to a burka for your bosom, a scrap of fabric edged with lace that attaches to a bra, preserving modesty in plunging necklines. Cami Secret's pricing strategy combines number theory with the reference point to drive a double spurt of wallet-opening dopamine. The velvety pitchman first offers three Cami Secrets for $19.99, then doubles that offer to six for the same price. Once he's established that deal, the voiceover slashes the price in half, to $10. It's a 50 percent discount off an arbitrary but much-repeated price, with the final cost reduced to a whole number, telegraphing quality in that markdown. Given that the per-unit cost of producing a lacy square of fabric is probably less than a couple of sticks of gum, it doesn't make it a truly good value, but the tricks engineer an illusion of a great deal.

Why do these irrational pricing tricks work so effectively? Think of the turn of the millennium or a fortieth birthday—both single-year increases that are rationally no different from any other, yet carry emotionally more heft. This is what's called the *left digit effect*, where we focus on the first number we see. When our brains are bombarded with prices, they have a limited capacity for filing away that information. Rounding them down for efficiency is like compressing a file to save on hard drive space. Research has shown that the human brain can hold only one and a half to two seconds of spoken information; the more complex a price, the harder it is for us to remember. We remember $4 as is, but $3.99 is abbreviated to $3 for efficiency (by one study's findings, every extra syllable in a product's price decreased our ability to remember it by 20 percent).

Explaining the appeal of buying on sale, then, is simple. It boils down to the fact that bargains are physiologically desirable, even irresistible to some, combined with a raft of learned tricks that retailers use to trigger a surge of spend-thrifty dopamine. We know, though, that deals have become more effective, and more commonplace, than ever before. To see the reason why, let's take a trip to the local drugstore. Just don't bring your wallet—you're still paying off that $1,000, after all.

Overstocked, Overpriced, and Overwhelmed

Look for the section marked TOOTHPASTE. That should be giveaway enough; there's an entire aisle dedicated to this one product. Now scan the shelves for Crest, one of Procter & Gamble's most beloved and successful brands. It was launched nationally in 1955, in one version: original flavor standard paste. It took an entire decade for a second flavor, mint, to emerge. By 2013, though, there were a staggering 151 different Crest-branded products: ninety-four flavors and sizes of toothpaste, twenty-seven rinses, seven bleaching strips, and twenty-three kids' products (the number of human teeth, however, has remained stable). This viral-like replication of product is very recent; Crest's own brand of mouthwash, the first major brand extension, was launched only in 2005. Since then, Crest's land grab for drugstore shelf space has been imperial and relentless.

Crest isn't unusual, though, in this product replication. The brand offers a simple example of Too Much Stuff syndrome: things for the sake of things. In such a retail landscape, selling stock at full price is harder than ever. Crest's Duggar-like ability to replicate itself seems like a smart idea; more options mean more choices, more chances to sell something to someone every time. This overload in overstock works more to the advantage of shoppers than sellers. Partly it's due to a reversal in the traditional supply-and-demand equation, foregrounding buyers' power. But unfortunately for sellers, that isn't the only reason. If the P & G powers-that-be considered the findings of Columbia Business School professor Sheena Iyengar, they would slash the Crest portfolio back to a dozen items or less.

Iyengar has built her entire career on proving a simple but counterintuitive point: Human beings want less choice, not more. This idea was sparked while she was still a graduate student in California and she noticed a local gourmet grocer stocked a staggering number of jams: 348 flavors, to be exact. Was that really a smart use of shelf space, she wondered? To find out, Iyengar set up two tables at different times, both of them designed as tasting stations for Wilkin and Sons premium jams. One table was a smorgasbord of flavors, with two dozen different varieties available for customers to try. The other offered a scant six options (classics like strawberry and orange marmalade were omitted to minimize built-in bias). Sure enough, more people stopped to try some jam when there was a greater selection—60 percent versus 40 percent of passersby. Strangely, their interest in sampling didn't translate into sales. When Iyengar pored over the transactions during the tasting period, she found that only 3 percent of shoppers in the former experiment (with more choice) actually bought jam, compared with 30 percent in the latter (with fewer tasting options). Less choice was better for both the customer and the store. Since then, other scientists have riffed on the same topic. One study showed that students were far more likely to turn in an extra credit essay if they were offered a choice of six topics rather than thirty.*

According to more lab-based research using fMRI, the reason for this is straightforward: An overload of choice maxes out our ability to say yes

---

* Iyengar has even studied how the stress from too much choice taxes immune systems enough to make harried shoppers more likely to catch a cold or the flu.

or no. Remember the headmaster-like prefrontal cortex (DLPFC), home of decision-making and cost-benefit analyses in our brains? Forcing it to calculate between too many options overloads its circuits, like leaving too many programs running on a laptop at any one time. To avoid this, our instinct is to whittle down choices before engaging the brain. Using that sale sign is a convenient first cull.

A shopper deluged by too much stuff and too many choices will gladly seize any help in determining which items are more interesting or noteworthy. The more products there are on offer, the more important that "50% OFF" sticker becomes. Sales are more commonplace because stores have greater excess in inventory to clear. At the same time, with our brains struggling to process this overload of choice, we will cling to whatever is the fastest way to slim down that selection. The sale sign is a welcomed solution. No wonder a few retailers are finally scaling back their selection: The Midwestern supermarket chain Supervalu recently announced it would cut back 25 percent of its stock, while Kroger is reducing selection by almost a third.*

So our brains are primed hormonally to react to bargains, in thrall to to every squirt of dopamine. Knowing that, marketers and price consultants have invented ways to artificially trigger the surge and pry open our wallets as frequently as possible. They're employed by retailers that are hammered by Wall Street to demonstrate constant growth. The easiest shortcut to juicing profits, as those shops already know, is the steroid shot of a sale. Unfortunately, it's coinciding with an overload of too much stuff. Our stressed-out, bargain-crazy brains cling to such markdowns as the simplest way to sift through that ever-expanding retail landscape. We've become an unquenchable maw demanding more for less, a closed circle that feeds on itself. At least we never need to worry about running out of toothpaste.

---

* After Kroger's trial slimdown in the cereal aisle, only one brand had to be reinstated after customer outcry: Cap'n Crunch.

Back at the Target in Clifton Park, our Thanksgiving Day Spenderellas are unaware of the chemical warfare about to break out in their brains. Their excitement is visibly rising as the temperature plummets—after all, the first-ever Black Midnight, that newly crossed bargain boundary, is nearing. Red-coated staffers come to remind the front of the line to put all chairs and blankets in their cars. The crowd has swelled to at least seven hundred people snaking around the warehouse-like building; streetlights glint off the deely bobbers festooning one especially festive pair of bargain hunters. "You're not getting a laptop, you know, we're too late," mutters one gray-haired man to his wife, jabbing a mittened hand at the front of the line as they trudge to the back.*

One person who will get that $157 laptop, of course, is gravel-voiced, doorbusting vet Peggy Castle—after all, she's first in line. Castle is palpably excited, hopped-up on dopamine and turkey-induced tryptophan. "It's better because it's midnight instead of four a.m. You get to shop more." Rubbing her hands together for glee and warmth, Castle recalls one glorious bargain blowout. "I had free Christmas at Macy's one year. You couldn't see outta my car windows, I couldn't sit in the car." It was all thanks to one Macy's promotion in a local newspaper that spurred Peggy to get up early one Sunday and buy 250 papers. "They had ten-dollar coupons in every copy for just fifty cents a pop." She isn't alone. The greatest boom in this new bargain era has been in a single area: couponing. It's a thrilling buzz for any shopper to see how easily a few clipped coupons can impact the weekly grocery bill. Though, as we'll see, that explosion in 50-cent chits has come at a surprising price, one which can backfire on shoppers as much as sellers.

---

* Doubtless this is why one enterprising but unemployed teacher in Massachusetts even listed herself on Craigslist offering to brave doorbusting lines on others' behalf, waiting in the cold in exchange for a fee equal to 15 percent of whatever was purchased (payment: cash or Walmart gift cards, please).

2

Couponmania

Stockpiling, the Million-Dollar Coupon
Broker, and the Curious Story of
Breen Detergent

S tockpile. It's a coupon cultist's Masonic handshake, the password to
their secret world. He or she will mention it reverentially, like a half-
price Holy Grail. Devotees can rattle off their holdings, tallied with OCD
exactitude: enough Wonder Bread and anchovies to feed an entire parish, say, or hand soap to last through a lifetime of flu seasons. If the total
value of the groceries stashed there is less than six digits, they'll dismiss
the hoarder as an amateur. No space is sacred in their homes; spare bed-
rooms, garages, an empty corner, all will be commandeered to service
the needs of the stockpile, filled with a few cheap Ikea shelves and a
groaning hoard of almost-freebies.

Many enthusiasts will adopt code names, like superheroes with scissors, a nom de coupon that they use to trade tips and suggestions online.
There, they communicate in a bizarre lingo—DND, GDA, WYB—that
resembles generals plotting military maneuvers (see table on page 39). In
their natural environment, the supermarket, it's easy enough to spot a
stockpiler: Look for the shopper who trundles slowly down the aisles,
binder in hand. He or she will leaf through that carefully filed system of

clipped coupons every time an item is considered for the cart. If there's no coupon, the item won't make the cut.

Fortysomething April Blum from Pennsylvania is a typical stockpiler. The Coupon General (her preferred soubriquet) says she's accrued a $40,000 stockpile after hundreds of shopping trips. On a typical trip, she hands a basket to each of her eight children and tells them to fill up with cereal. The family's final recent haul was two hundred boxes. "We used to put our candies in the gun cage, but then couponing got so big, we couldn't fit everything in," she explains. "So we converted a closet we usually used for Christmas into the candy jar." When one of her kids proved to have a sticky fingered sweet tooth—cannily, he'd open the bottom of several boxes to surreptitiously access the candy bars—April put a padlock on the room.

Such frenzied discount chasing, dubbed *extreme couponing*, is retail's answer to the X Games. Suburban Shaun White–alikes, such as April Blum, are pushing the limits of the ad hoc discount system that exists in today's supermarkets. Retailers are passive targets, eyeballed by these discounters with lip-smacking relish and rarely able to fight back. This is bargain shopping as sport: Blum and her fellow devotees aim to stack, pile, and double coupons aggressively enough to pay only 10 percent or less of the face value for groceries. The goal of this game is to slash the weekly spend: $500 should become $50. The Shangri-la of savings, though, is known as overage—when crack coupon stacking is so astute that the supermarket owes money to the shopper in the form of a gift card. In these cases, a trip to the store actually becomes a money*making* operation. True adherents to the extreme couponing credo don't worry whether they actually need four thousand pairs of diapers or two hundred toothbrushes. If the price is right—ideally, free—they'll buy them anyway. That haul becomes an offering at the altar of their stockpile. It's why nothing better embodies the surge in sales right now than couponing, with its physical temple to Too Much Stuff.

As a hobby, extreme couponing has become a media obsession in the last few years. This breathless account from the *Wall Street Journal* is typical: "Couponers trade deal information and the coupons themselves . . .

motivated as much by competitiveness as frugality . . . [online communities] organize contests to see which member can spend the least cash in a month on essentials. Some couponers brag online about stockpiling free groceries, then selling them at yard sales." Cable channel TLC swooped down and turned the phenomenon into a reality show, *Extreme Couponing*. The show, one of whose stars was Blum, proved an unexpected breakout hit, netting more than two million viewers in each airing. In the ultimate pop culture endorsement, Khloe and Kourtney Kardashian co-opted (ko-opted?) the couponing gimmick for an entire episode of their own skein, trawling the aisles of a New York supermarket trying to score mega-discounts in a meta-reality moment.

One of the longtime producers of *Extreme Couponing* admits that his team originally assumed that the concept would take on a darker tone, more akin to the reality hit *Hoarders*. After all, the products that so many people claim as a stockpile make for terrifying towers in their homes. Now, though, that producer freely admits he was wrong: These women (and a few men) embody the joyous empowerment of the new discount landscape. "We do have people who have taken out insurance on their stockpiles, for thousands and thousands of dollars," he says, "but most of the time, they were really nice people—all kooky and crazy in their own right, of course."

April Blum is quick to point out that there's a difference between hoarding and extreme couponing; couponers, she stresses, don't just keep their pile to themselves. Most donate extra items to the needy. (In April's case, freebies and extras often go to the parish food bank.) A relative newcomer to the cult, she succumbed to extreme couponing only two years ago, after quitting working to homeschool her huge family and such savings consciousness became a necessity. The loss of her income was an immense strain on the family's finances, so much so that they found themselves in line at a food bank for the first time. With her then-seven kids in tow, Blum recalls receiving one box of macaroni and cheese and one can of beans; she panicked when she realized that was all they would receive. Fretful of how to feed the entire family this way, she found sales salvation via a friend, who inducted her into the extreme couponing cult.

April claims to have saved over $70,000 in just two years. If any proof of coupons' power were needed, she is the ideal example, having gone, quite literally, from near destitute to Disneyworld. With the money she saved, April was able to take her entire brood on a vacation there just eighteen months after she started chit cutting. She hauled her coupon binder along, too, just in case.

Blum and her ilk may be extremists, but ordinary couponing has also boomed in recent years. The numbers are a dizzying blizzard: In 2010, 332 billion coupons were distributed, the largest number ever. Using them, shoppers saved nearly $2 billion, as redemption rates increased 7.9 percent over the year before. In the United States, 65 percent of people now rely on coupons regularly for purchases, and 42 percent consider themselves passionate clippers. Average face values are rising—up 5.4 percent annually to $1.57 per coupon—and the habit has taken root among the wealthy. Affluent households, defined as those earning $70,000 or more per year, have come to make up 41 percent of coupon enthusiasts.

There are obvious reasons couponing is clipping along at such a pace. In any recession, when pocketbooks are pinched, it's a low-impact strategy to stretch the family budget that requires little effort or know-how, just some patience and a pair of scissors. Indeed, historically, there's been a tight correlation between surges in coupon redemption and economic slumps. Yet there's something different—even extreme—about both the rate and volume of coupon cashing in. It's a joyous triumphalism, a one-in-the-eyemanship that devotees gloatingly trumpet. The revival of couponing to such outlandish levels is a symptom of a cultural change, a price adjustment in the way we shop that ricochets through every mall. Before we can explore that shift, though, it's crucial to understand what has remained stubbornly the same; namely the antiquated process by which a coupon is developed, spent, and redeemed. The system has as many moving (and often malfunctioning) parts as a Rube Goldberg contraption. In the process, it offers savvy (and sometimes crooked) customers surprising leverage.

The Language of Extreme Couponing

Logging on to any coupon obsessive blog is confusing for a newbie as the vets seem to communicate in dot-com semaphore. This is a bluffer's guide to the commonest acronyms.

B1G1: Buy One, Get One. Also known as BOGO, or B1GX for larger quantities.

DND/DNT: Does Not Double, Does Not Triple. Regardless of store promotional policy, these coupons will not double or triple when used.

DND5: As above, but despite restrictions these will double when scanned. The bar code at the bottom of such a coupon begins with 5.

GDA: Good Deal Alert—a couponeer's rallying cry.

MFC: Manufacturer's coupon. This can be used at any store, rather than being specific to one supermarket.

MIR: Mail-in rebate.

OYNO/OYNP: On Your Next Order, On Your Next Purchase—a delayed-action coupon that offers discounts the next time you shop.

Q: Coupon.

RP (Red Plum), SS (SmartSource), V (Valassis): Various coupon inserts in Sunday newspapers. Tip-offs online to exceptional coupons usually include the issue date and one of these three acronyms.

SD: Super-Doubles. This refers to events when retailers loosen restrictions on doubling coupons—for example, if the usual limit for double-redemption is $1 per chit, it might rise to $1.50.

WYB: When You Buy—for example, "Get one packet free when you buy 4."

YMMV: Your Market May Vary. Deals vary widely by city and state.

Sources: consumerist.com, becentsable.net

A One-Way Ticket to El Paso: Coupon, an Autobiography

Imagine a manufacturer is launching a new product in May. Let's say it's the Kardashians' latest endorsement, Hot Kandy chocolate bars. A classic trick to drive trial new products such as this is a hefty coupon; indeed, part of couponing's uptick is due to the accelerated rate of new product launches in the last two decades. Companies have churned through new SKUs to keep customers' attention, creating that closed loop of overproduction that then requires more aggressive markdowns. When a company plans a coupon on a product, it relies on computer modeling to project the cost of production and redemption—which is the only cutting-edge component in the entire process. When deciding how much the discount on a Hot Kandy bar should be, most fast-moving consumer good (FMCG) firms would guesstimate, from trial and error. Fifty cents is a common choice, largely because anything less than that is unlikely to induce clipping these days.

A coupon's face value can vary, though. It depends on the newspaper in which it's distributed: If the chocolate market is saturated in the Northeast, for example, the coupon will be lower there than in the Southwest, where share could be up for grabs. More intriguingly, supermarkets in some states, especially California and Florida, don't follow the now-standard practice of doubling face value automatically—in other words, applying $1 for a 50-cent coupon. When coupons are issued in those non-doubling states, they compensate accordingly by increasing face value. Crucially, though, the location for redemption is not restricted (doubtless, April Blum brought a fistful of chits back from her trip to Orlando). For simplicity's sake, though, we'll imagine the candy firm settles on a 50-cent offer everywhere.

Now it's time to design that coupon. For good reason, most look very similar. It's crucial that unskilled supermarket clerks recognize coupons easily, to avoid embarrassment or, worse, line delays caused by a strange design. Some staffers are even paid on productivity, so they will balk at the time needed to examine odd-looking vouchers. Designers must make sure the scannable code, known as the GSI, isn't too close to the cutting edge as it will be void if damaged (another risk of slowing down the line), and that the coupon always includes a photograph of the item.* The coupon creators always make them either half- or same-size as a dollar bill. A design like this will fit in wallets and cash register drawers, while subtly reminding shoppers that a coupon is like cut-out-and-keep cash. Then there's the expiration date. Until the 1980s, coupons were open-ended, but as computerized models started trying to modernize recordkeeping, it became more crucial for manufacturers to tally final costs quickly. The standard redemption window has been reduced to thirty days (and shrinking).

Even today, though, people largely source coupons the old-fashioned way via the Sunday newspapers, which contain free-standing inserts (FSIs) packed with deals. This market is essentially a duopoly, a battle-ground between two companies, Valassis and News America. They lob accusations of fraud or copyright infringement at each other with the vim and vitriol of a rebate remake of *The War of the Roses*. That's a sure tip-off to how lucrative a business couponing remains. News America is a subsidiary of Rupert Murdoch's News Corp; privately held, its figures are shadowy, but the last time they were reported, it logged a 28-percent profit margin on $1.1 billion in sales. Compare that to how sister firm (and sometime delivery vehicle) the *New York Post* bleeds millions of dollars in red ink each year. Every time you shame-read a story about the Kardashians on Page Six, remember that that headline writer and maker is, quite literally, propped up by the Hot Kandy coupon (or at least its real-world equivalent). News America is the tabloid's less sexy but far more profitable sibling company.

Once our coupons have been designed, issued in a newspaper, and cut by sweet-toothed reality fans, these chits will soon surface at super-market checkouts. This is when the process begins to corkscrew. The coupon-redemption process is a pitched battle: in the red corner, retail-ers who want to redeem as many coupons as possible, clawing back cash

---

* "Sometimes a woman sends her husband to the supermarket," one industry veteran shrugged when I asked why the snapshot was so essential. Like most of the executives in that female-targeted industry, he is a man.

from suppliers. In the black corner, manufacturers eager to void the maximum number of claims to minimize overheads. This tension creates a process of mutual distrust, like a daily rerun of the hanging chad recount that clouded the 2000 presidential election. It's even more astonishing when you realize this is all over a fee of just 8 cents per coupon, which suppliers pay to the store on each redemption.

Allowing these adversaries to tussle directly would be disastrous, so intermediaries have sprung up to ease such chafing—although these middlemen, of course, only muddle the process more. They act as agents whom each side pays separately to track, tally, and void or validate such claims. It would be near impossible for a harried supermarket manager, cashing up at the end of the week, surrounded by thousands of coupons from hundreds of manufacturers, to sort each coupon and send it back so the store can be reimbursed. Kroger and their competitors long ago realized that it wasn't time- or cost-efficient to do it themselves, so they delegated the process. In exchange for a small handling fee, these agents or clearinghouses will process those piles, sorting them by producer and invoicing accordingly. Just three firms dominate this business: Inmar, Prologic, and NCH.* "See the addresses of the clearinghouses? El Paso, Tecate—they're border towns," explains John Morgan, head of the industry's Association of Coupon Professionals (ACP). "They ship the coupons there, through Mexican customs, and process it all on the Mexican side." Cheap labor is crucial for keeping costs down. Out of sight, of course, means oversight is spottier, too.

Let's turn back to our Hot Kandy bars, which have now been on the market for two weeks. A total of ten thousand coupons have been submitted to an agent by Kroger outlets across the country; the value tallies at $5,000. A $5,000 invoice will be issued to the manufacturer—or would be, if there wasn't yet another step in the way. Unilever and other brands that release coupons don't want to deal with hundreds of individual bills from each supermarket chain, or a scratchy write-up from a family-owned corner store. To avoid such *mishegas*, they also hire a middleman.

---

* NCH stands for Nielsen Clearing House—yes, the same firm that provides TV ratings. It spotted an opportunity to transpose its data-crunching know-how when couponing boomed in the 1950s and set up this sister business in 1957.

The redemption process resembles a real estate transaction, where both buyer and seller are represented by agents acting as proxies. Bizarrely, in couponing, those competing agents could sit mere feet from one another. Peculiarly, NCH and Inmar act as agents for supermarkets and manufacturers (Prologic is an exception, acting solely for retailers). To an outsider, it seems illogical at best, prone to cronyism and corruption at worst, yet the practice persists.

The actual process of redemption corkscrews further from here. The supermarket's agency hands over a bundle of coupons to the manufacturer's agent. *These are worth $5,000*, the supermarket barks, *please pay up stat*. The manufacturer's proxy then combs through the coupons that those Mexican workers have sifted so carefully. Are they really worth $5,000? The second clearinghouse will look to see if any Snickers chits have slipped into the Hot Kandy shipment, for example, or if any coupons seem too fresh looking—thus making them unlikely to have sat in a woman's purse and more plausible to have been salted into the shipment by a retailer with an urgent need to improve its bottom line. Once this second clearinghouse certifies the redemption, an invoice is sent to the manufacturer and a check is finally issued.

With so many moving parts and competing players, canny people can profit from couponing in unexpected ways—some of which, as we'll see later, are far from legal. Culture's shift toward couponing in extremis has spawned a slew of new microcompanies, many of them masterminded by stay-at-home moms who relish the power they can exert on corporations via these throwaway chits. Each cottage company makes a healthy profit out of helping ordinary Americans make a saving when they shop, screwing over those faceless corporations with a blithe charm that would best a Disney princess.

Meet the Million-Dollar Coupon Broker

Dade City, a short drive from Tampa, is a typical Florida town: low-slung, sprawling, and filled with rows of nondescript clapboard houses. Just outside of town, up a long driveway in lush green flatlands, is the home of Ken Woodard, pastor of the Temple Baptist Church. Ken's ranch house also discreetly doubles as the headquarters of The Coupon Clippers, a home business run by his wife, Rachael. Busy moms who don't have the time to sift through the Sunday papers can simply log on to her site, search for whatever coupons they need, and order them. In a few days, they'll arrive by USPS. It's couponing convenience food.

Inside Woodard's home, the setup is haphazard. One room of the house is discount HQ, piled high with plastic bins of coupons, each held together with rubber bands. Rachael's daughter sits quietly in the corner answering customer service e-mails, while her mother, a conversational tornado with a nervous laugh and electric energy, bobs up and down from a chaotic desk. A gold and black banner emblazoned with the Ten Commandments hangs discreetly on the wall above it. The only noise, aside from Woodard's voice, is the wheezy death rattle of the printer spitting out orders; its constant hum underscores how lucrative a business she runs. It's staggering when Rachael says proudly that The Coupon Clippers grosses more than seven figures a year.

Like most dedicated couponers, Rachael's bargain mindedness was born of necessity. As a child she trawled for dented 5- and 10-cent cans with her twin sister outside the local grocery store. Her need for thrift continued when she married pastor Ken, and the couple was living on just $80 a week. "I find it humorous now, but one of my mom's presents to me when I got married was an envelope full of coupons for free products," she trills. "It was one of the best gifts I got because I didn't have to redeem them straightaway." Volunteering at a recycling center, Rachael sweet-talked the managers into letting her take home the discarded coupon inserts. Soon, with more chits than she could spend herself, Rachael spotted an opportunity. It was the mid 1990s, and the Internet was beginning to connect communities—such as couponers—who until then had been disparate. Rachael was intrigued by the market possibilities of selling into the couponing community and hired a programmer to create a rudimentary listserv where readers could order coupons by mail. That was the start of her new career as a coupon mogul.

Though Rachael's business isn't illegal, it irks manufactures. The coupons bear legalese that declares them non-transferable, but that's an almost impossible edict to enforce. The fine print also claims them "Void if Sold," but Woodard justifies a fee by claiming that her customers are not paying for the coupons but instead for the the time it takes to cut them out. It's the *Pretty Woman* defense, exactly the same loophole that every high-class call girl exploits—paying for time is legal, even if the service is not. Woodard uses a simple pricing system on her site, charging either 10 cents or 10 percent of the face value for each coupon, whichever is greater. The savings she secures for her customers annualize at more than $10 million. Of course, since Woodard lives in Florida, her business has an unexpected advantage—Florida is one of the states where supermarkets traditionally do not double. Face values here are higher, a fortuitous kink that makes her even better placed to profit from discounting. That customer from a state where doubling is standard and who bulk orders a $1 OFF coupon on a can of Pepsi from Rachael can easily hunt down a local outlet where it will be worth $2.

Nothing is wasted in Woodard's operation. There's a rickety shed behind her house where the papers are delivered and sorted; the news-carrying portion—worthless to her in its initial state—will be recycled to earn $4,000 a year that she donates to her husband's church. Rachael's initial effervescence about her business dims slightly as she admits to recent interruptions in her supply of Sunday papers, including a former bulk deliverer who tried to siphon off business to her own nascent coupon-clipping service. As a result, for the first time, she spent a few months cobbling together the weekly haul of four thousand papers by sending her husband and family out on dawn raids, but now a new supplier trucks up to her house every Sunday at 5 a.m. Woodard sources coupons in many ways and she proudly shows off a thick wad of vintage discounts she was sent when someone found them in her dead mother's attic. One of these coupons offers 20 cents off Scope, with a "Support the Special Olympics" tag in curvy 1980s typeface. It's decades old, but since it was issued long before expiration dates became standard, it remains legally redeemable.

Woodard is a smart businesswoman whose aw-shuckishness can be both distracting and disarming. "I grew up without a TV—we didn't have stuff, so I loved to read, study time and motion efficiency, that kind of thing," she says casually. By early 2012, her staff consisted of around two dozen people, including a team of at-home workers paid by the piece to sort weekly circulars per manufacturer. Once sifted, she and her four children gang-cut coupons using a guillotine at home. The coupons are then driven to a second site, a rented office in a nearby strip mall. This is where the fulfillment team works, including a homeschooled teen earning pocket money in between lessons. Around twelve hundred orders per day are filled here six days a week. Shelves are stuffed with alphabetically filed coupons. There are so many that even the shower cubicle in the bathroom is crammed with boxes.

Rachael's cheerleading view of *Extreme Couponing* isn't surprising. "It doubled my business. Literally. Overnight," she marvels. "Every two weeks, whenever they would run that show, I would get slammed so badly." Woodard wasn't even aware of the show when the pilot was broadcast during the quiet week of Christmas 2010. In fact, she had shut her office for a break and was even mulling shuttering her business entirely to try a new enterprise. One night her webmaster called, worried that the site had been attacked, since her website was seeing a sudden spike in traffic. It was no attack, just curious newbies. Her average traffic of three hundred had surged to more than sixteen hundred viewers. She reinvested in greater bandwidth and has ridden the boom ever since.

Standing in front of the dozens of envelopes, filled and ready to mail, the scale of her business is clear. No wonder her enthusiasm is undimmed even after almost two decades of professional coupon cutting. Her customer service–trained daughter flutters around, making sure everything is stamped properly and the express mail orders are correct; as Rachael notes, a $3 order (her minimum) will save at least $30, so $18.95 on express shipping is still a bargain.

Woodard's thriving business isn't unique. Several other gimlet-eyed discount lovers have set up services expressly designed to exploit the chinks in retail's full-price armor that couponing affords. Take Nancy Kremin for example, more than two thousand miles away from The Coupon Clippers headquarters, in sunny Los Angeles. She has a single mission: Every woman in America should trade her old-fashioned pocketbook for a new-fangled invention, the Coupon Wallet. This is a Frankenpurse that doubles as binder and wallet. It has divided sections for grocery categories, a pocket with a handy pair of scissors, and easily attaches to the handle of a shopping cart. Priced between $12.95 and $19.95, Kremin estimates annual sales of $300,000. Dow Jones, publisher of the *Wall Street Journal*, has bought Coupon Wallets in bulk to use as subscriber giveaways. One was even supplied for Barbra Streisand as a comic prop in *The Guilt Trip*.

Kremin launched the product in the mid 2000s, juggling the side gig with a full-time job in marketing for local mortuaries. Her first significant uptick, though, was contemporary with Woodard's, a byproduct of the popularity of *Extreme Couponing*. Kremins even has physical proof of the fad's boom. When she started the company, the organizer pocket was 3 inches wide; now, thanks to customer feedback, she scaled it up to 4 inches due to an increased volume of coupons kept on hand. Nothing sums up the surge more neatly than that single extra inch.

At much the same time that Kremins was launching her wallet, another Angeleno spotted the potential in couponing. Teri Gault's business, though, was information. Gault is the founder of The Grocery Game, a membership-based aggregator of supermarket deals. After her stuntman husband's work began to evaporate, as tax incentives drove moviemaking to Canada, the family's finances became strained. So Gault dipped into her hardscrabble childhood (a common trope) for a solution and turned her talent for scrimping into a business. On The Grocery Game, subscribers can scan her vast database of coupons and cross-referenced shopping lists by zip code, store name, or product keyword. The Grocery Game name is a tip-off to the cat-and-mouse approach that Teri takes to shopping. She sees the weekly grocery run as a battle in which knowledge is the ultimate weapon. "My motto is: *Please* don't ever pay full price for anything." Who needs to, she explains, since most grocery items are offered on sale once every twelve weeks? She even suggests that wily shoppers should hold coupons until that discount window begins, maximizing their savings.

Gault's relentless deal chasing has proved lucrative. A decade after starting out, she has franchised her business. By 2012, fifty staffers were compiling two hundred grocery lists every week across all fifty states, with more than twenty staffers focused entirely on what she calls "quality control," or ensuring that lists are timely. The Grocery Game has expanded overseas, too, though she acknowledges different challenges. In Italy, for example, much of the weekly shopping still takes place at small butchers and bakers, making mass-market coupon programs less efficient. As for Germany, it wasn't even legal for hausfraus to use coupons until 2001, but we'll come to that strange story a little later.

Some women have gone further becoming evangelists for coupon cutting, appointing themselves recruiters and educators, cut-price riffs on the Avon lady. These proselytizers stage classes or parties where participants (paying, of course) can be clued in to the secret strategies that all but guarantee ample overage. Jill Cataldo is a typical couponeer. In the summer of 2008, facing financial pressure as her youngest child was born and the diaper tally for the family was spiraling upward, Cataldo turned to couponing. Her husband, a local library worker, suggested she stage a workshop there to share the knowledge she'd accrued. The event turned out to be so successful, it was standing room only. Three months later, Jill was approached by a syndication house in Chicago to write a column about couponing, with the promise to continue it if at least fifty markets ran it. She estimates it was picked up by over sixty in the first year. The column's success launched a career as a motivational discount speaker, and Jill has even been hired by the Piggly Wiggly grocery chain to provide coupon workshops to help customers better maximize their deals. The surge in half price created a full-time job for her.

If the bright-eyed and peppy Cataldo is Mary Kay, then Chrissy Pate, a crafty mom of two in St. Louis, is couponing's Amway. Pate set up a smart pyramid business that involved not only coupon strategies but recruiting fresh fans. Called BeCentsable.net, she began it after her second child was born and her family had to survive solely on her husband's income as a teacher. It's a seductive pitch: In just six months, she told me, she reduced her family's expenses by two thirds, simply via savvy couponing. With her high voice and hesitant manner, Pate has become an unlikely bargain mogul, staging workshops in her area for a fee of $10 or so, issuing instructional DVDs by mail, and even certifying rs to stage their own Pate-branded workshops across the country.

At last tally, BeCentsable.net's correspondence couponing educator course had graduated six hundred people across more than forty states.*

These five women—Rachael, Nancy, Teri, Chrissy, and Jill—share more than simply their obsession with cashing in on coupons. They're part of a generation of thirty- and fortysomething parents who were children during the 1970s, in an era of stagflation and crisis. They grew up watching recession-hobbled elders scrimp and wheedle to survive, and they're primed to seek out savings and continue the cycle—especially in times of economic hardship.

It's this psychological profile that is a central driver behind the current superboom in couponing. Palpably aware of poverty, consumers can tip the system in their favor using a few scraps of paper. Eighty percent of *Extreme Couponing*'s stars had gone to food banks at some point or been worried about feeding their family before they turned to coupon clipping. According to Matthew Tilley, who tracks the industry's trends for processing giant Inmar, there's a cast-iron correlation between the unemployment rate and coupon redemption. As the economy slows, such redemptions accelerate in response. He pegs as much as 70 percent of the uptick in coupon use to the economic cycle in this way: The zenith of coupon redemption—when a staggering 7.8 billion coupons were cashed in during a single year   was in 1992, the nadir of the last major economic slowdown.† The Great Recession's tally is reaching similar levels.

Tellingly, though, while couponers might use discounts as a rallying cry against corporations, bargain offerings are one of the most convenient and effective strategies for marketers. Relatively quick and easy to apply, clipping coupons has had a veneer of frugality and thrift ever since ration books were issued during World War II. The biggest appeal

---

* Not all these cottage operations are quite as self-serving. If you can't spend every cent of that haul before it expires, thankfully, there's the Troopons project, run by CouponCabin. com. This siphons old coupons to bases overseas where manufacturers cooperate on an honor system where they are considered valid for up to two months longer than the printed date.
† The uptick in 1992 was also powered by the heyday of the warehouse club, as manufacturers helped supermarkets compete with their new rivals by magically transmuting prices down to the level of Costco and co.

of a coupon-discount program, of course, is that it's an opt-in. Those with time or worry enough to clip such chits will redeem them, while the price for the rest preserves maximum margins. Remember the price consultants' beloved tenet, *willingness to pay*? The goal of any modern business is to maximize that amount. The ten minutes it takes to find and clip a 50-cent coupon affects the value of a coupon to different customers—it costs more in time, quite literally, to a C-level executive than to a minimum wager. It's easy to be cynical and wonder if couponing isn't the ideal way to seem to be discount-friendly, while in effect fighting price pressures downward.

The uptick in uptake, though, hasn't gone unnoticed by lumbering retail giants. Indeed, supermarkets are rapidly tweaking their policies to discourage extreme couponing. Kroger, for example, has now outlawed stacking, a favored tactic where different discounts (say a print-at-home online coupon, a manufacturer's FSI, and one of those peel-off instant discount stickers affixed to the front of a package) are layered on top of one another to drive the price of a given item down to pennies. Californian grocer Ralph's no longer doubles coupons (the dreaded DND) and instead has substituted a new program centered on gas rewards. "These wack-jobs who spend twenty hours a week stacking coupons? That stuff drives us batty. They dance all over the rules," moans John Morgan of the Association of Coupon Professionals. Supermarkets will continue to tighten their policies in response to the couponing fad, especially as some shoppers start bending the rules.

Chrissy Pate, for one, came under fire for some information in the original version of her DVD. In its Coupon Strategies: Reading Coupons section, she deciphered the bar codes on coupons. Explaining this opaque system allowed consumers to more easily misapply deals at the checkout and game the system. Those gobbledygook streams of numbers along the GSI weren't meaningless after all, whispered the DVD. Checkout tills were usually configured to pass a coupon as long as the first five digits on the coupon and the product matched—so unscrupulous penny-pinchers could use a P & G coupon for conditioner on a sister-brand shampoo, for example. In fact, when one of *Extreme Couponing*'s breakout stars, perky blonde J'aime Kirlew, was vilified by the online community for what it deemed her misuse of coupons, she fought back. "I was only following instructions I'd found on a DVD from Pate," Kirlew bleated. Pate's defense was flimsy: The five-digit rule, she said, was to help reassure customers that coupons could be applied to any product in a range rather than the one pictured on the chit, which was commonly the priciest.

Predictably, some couponeers, such as Jill Cataldo, have even emerged as vocal critics of such frenzied behaviors. She has become the de facto face of opposition to the tactics promoted by *Extreme Couponing*, slavishly recapping each episode and pointing out errors or ways in which supermarkets staged situations for the cameras, like doubling coupons when that isn't standard policy. Cataldo warns about "over-redemption," where companies stung by coupon abuse will adjust the value downward next time to a few scoff-worthy cents. "In the last week, I saw one that was fifteen cents! I cannot remember the last time I saw a coupon like that for anything," she carps, placing blame on TLC.

As for megamogul Rachael Woodard, she says that her customers spend an average of $8 on coupons; following her 10 percent pricing rule, that translates into $80 of savings at the supermarket. Such an amount is far from system-baiting extremes, though Woodard did once fulfill an order for $3,000 (which led to $30,000 savings at retail). Even if Octomom and Kate Gosselin combined their enormous broods, it's doubtful that the monthly tally for food would reach such levels. There must have been another explanation. It's one that provides yet another driving factor in today's couponing boom, a dark side to the clout it wields over retailers: coupon crime.

The Newsbox Bandits

It's just a few hours' drive down I-95 from Rachael's ranch-style home to the office of Fort Lauderdale's then-sheriff Al Lamberti. Lamberti has made couponing crime one of his campaigning platforms. The sheriff credits Facebook, which he dubs "Crimewatch on steroids," as the source of this crusade. "A crimewatch meeting, you get thirty to forty people. You can touch thirty to forty thousand this way," he explains.

The mustachioed sheriff combines the thick twang of the Bronx, where he grew up, with the chestnut tan of someone who's logged decades in South Florida. Populist and popular, he's proven a refreshing change from the predecessor, who was sent to jail for financial shenanigans (No wonder he left the new sheriff a plush $1.6 million office that more resembles that of that predecessor's former law firm. At least it means the big leather chairs in the conference room are unexpectedly comfy.)

The sheriff was an early adopter of social networking, maxxing out his friend limit quickly and setting up a fan page for the excess. He often uses Facebook to comment on the weather or ask for feedback from his electorate. A note there piqued Al's curiosity one Sunday morning, when a single mother posted a complaint that someone had stolen the coupons from her newspaper. Curious, Lamberti canvassed his county and unearthed further stories of coupon rustling, many of them from families who relied on coupons to help pay the bills. Such a revelation stirred him to pursue this case, which many may have dismissed as trivial. Investigating further, he was intrigued. This original poster had bought her paper early in the morning—around 6 a.m.—yet the chits had already been pilfered. Deliveries to the box started at 5 a.m., which made it a tight window for the looting.

Lamberti and his team planned a series of early Sunday surveillance operations. Savvy to the media value of what he was doing, he tipped off a local news reporter, who brought a TV crew to follow Lamberti. It wasn't until the third Sunday morning stakeout that the van appeared. Lamberti watched as a man leaped out furtively and darted over to a newspaper box. Dropping some coins in the slot, he grabbed every single copy. As an accomplice drove him a few blocks to the next box, the petty thief was busy in the back of the van removing every coupon insert. Leaping out at the next box, he swiped the pile of copies once more—but this time, he replaced the papers in the box with his freshly gutted stash. This process was repeated throughout the local area until the perp finished his circuit, returning to the first box and refilling it with the final armful of gutted papers.

Once the sheriff's team identified the driver and his accomplice, they secured a search warrant on his house, less than a mile from the crime scene. Inside the house, the cops found thousands upon thousands of coupon inserts. Lamberti and his team arrested Adolfo Rodriguez and his getaway-driver-cum-partner Wilmian Milian and charged the couple with misdemeanor theft. Later, only Rodriguez took the rap, pleading no contest, and paid a fine and court costs. Lamberti logged more than one hundred responses on his Facebook wall to the arrest announcement. Many were from locals who said that they, too, had been ripped off when buying a Sunday paper from a news box. This type of white-collar, inky-fingered crime spree isn't surprising, given that 90 percent of coupons are still sent to shoppers via their Sunday paper (with an average weekly value of just under $100).

The couple wasn't just stealing coupons for their own use, Lamberti explained. Coupon fraud is a favorite money-laundering and -generating device for organized crime. Gangs set up sweatshop-like factories, akin to phone boiler rooms, where people—often illegal immigrants who can be paid far below the minimum wage without complaint—spend hours each day cutting coupons stolen this way. The criminal ring then uses them to generate income in one of several ways: easiest is eBay, whose thousands of pages of deals for sale have turned it into a coupon Napster, and where those stolen $1 coupons will be offloaded at half their face value. Another common option is stacking those coupons to buy a product in bulk at a supermarket, then fencing the merchandise for a profit at a street fair or flea market stand.

Undoubtedly the most tempting route, at least according to Lamberti, is selling the coupons to a dishonest shop. Say a coupon fraudster has one hundred chits for $1 off Heinz ketchup. He or she might visit a neighborhood corner store and offer them to the owner at the bargain price of 25 cents each. When the store fraudulently redeems the coupons, it makes a $75 profit, while the fraudster has pocketed $25 instant cash. Sometimes, the sheriff shrugs, fraudsters will cut out the retail middleman by obtaining a business license, registering it to a PO box, and making the claim directly. Since the redemption process involves so many middlemen and agents, such petty crime is near-impossible to police.

Shoppers might shrug at such seemingly small-scale crime, but it has a direct impact on ordinary Americans' pocketbooks. Each fraudulent coupon that is successfully redeemed is a cost that manufacturers must offset. Most consider such cases an unavoidable overhead, choosing to offset them with higher prices. The honest shopper makes up for those lost margins. The impact on prices can be significant, given the size of some of these rings. Take, for example, a fraud operation busted in Arizona in July 2012, run by a trio of innocuous-looking middle-aged-mom types. They were caught printing ersatz coupons overseas and funneling them to shoppers here via a web store, savvyshoppersite.com. Police estimated the face value of the coupons seized at $40 million.

Coupon rustling isn't limited to organized rings, though. Couponer Sybil Hudson, of Denton, Texas, is typical of the small-time coupon crook that also has emerged in the wake of this boom. The 37-year-old single mom got her start waiting eagerly for the paper every Sunday, teeing up a grocery list based on the bargains she found in the inserts. But Hudson became so consumed by her devotion to coupons that she was driven to break the law. In July 2011, she was spotted by police outside a local Whataburger, snaffling the inserts from every copy in a newspaper box. When she was arrested, Hudson indignantly denied the accusation. Once charged with a class A misdemeanor, though, and facing up to $4,000 in fines, the perp became aggressively unapologetic, barking to the local media that she'd pay any monies owed from whatever she saved via coupon clipping. Another chit filcher from northern Arkansas told cops she belonged to a coupon club and was trying to ramp up supplies by grabbing 185 copies of the local paper left unsold outside her local supermarket. So bad has the coupon theft become in Alabama that one local newspaper has offered a $500 bounty for any successful citation for it.

Indeed, such fraud has become so widespread, by organized rings and opportunistic shoppers, that the couponing industry even convened to discuss it.

The Detergent That Cleans Away Dirt and Crime

Once every year, couponing's poo-bahs come together for a three-day all-discount summit run by the Association of Coupon Professionals

(ACP). For the twenty-fifth anniversary of their power powwow they've chosen Nashville, gathering in a few airless rooms a few yards from the neon-lit downtown strip of Broadway, where every bar boasts a cowboy-hatted crooner strumming on an acoustic guitar.

At the coupon summit, reps from across the industry—from lawsuit-obsessed distributor Valassis to manufacturers like Unilever or the publisher of Walmart's *All You* magazine, a couponing Bible—sit together. Hewlett-Packard has shipped in an entire team of wonks to showcase its newest machine, which has a dedicated coupon-printing button ("It's what our customers told us they wanted," one saleswoman chirps). So many cut-price power players sit together in one room that a lawyer starts the summit by spouting boilerplate warnings about collusion between competitors. If there were a Davos of discounting, it would be here.

Whatever their role in the industry, each attendee shares Al Lamberti's obsession: the rise of coupon fraud, and how to prevent it. One man above all has made it his entire life's mission. Bud Miller, small and owlish with thick glasses and a shaggy beard, is the sheriff of Couponville, USA. As head of the Coupon Information Center (CIC), a nonprofit funded by members like PepsiCo, Kraft, and Pfizer, he has crusaded against counterfeiters and fraudsters for the last twenty-five years, a veritable Javert of the supermarket. Miller says his job was reasonably straightforward until 2001, then as coupons boomed, so did associated crime.

Miller reserves a visceral loathing for *Extreme Couponing*, visibly bristling at the mention of the show. He blames it for much of the widespread misbehavior, and gloats about proving that one of the stars, a teenage boy in California, had used counterfeits on camera. Miller says it's impossible to quantify the annual cost of coupon fraud, especially since the industry is keen to downplay it in public. In fact, the last study of coupon fraud was thirty years ago, when Arthur Anderson pegged the annual cost to the American economy at $500 million. No one has gone on record with a firm number since then, but one industry veteran hazarded it had doubled, or even tripled, by 2012 (to over $1 billion).

Miller preens over the ongoing litigation against collapsed clearinghouse IOS, a pile of dragged-out lawsuits worthy of "Bleak House." In

2007, IOS CEO Chris Balsiger and ten of his colleagues were handed a twenty-seven-count indictment; prosecutors claimed the high-level execs had run a decade-long organized fraud. As a clearinghouse for retailers, IOS focused on tallying redeemed coupons, so the government charged that Balsiger and his cohorts padded invoices for Kleenex, SC Johnson, Unilever, and others to a total of $250 million. The indictments centered on eleven staffers, responsible for what the industry calls "salting"—in essence, adding extra coupons to the deliveries. These stunt stand-ins had been doctored to seem as if they'd passed through shoppers' hands—in this case, investigators suspected some of coupons were tumbled in a dry cement mixer. IOS then allegedly recruited a cadre of small retailers who would claim the submissions as theirs in return for kickbacks. Though four of the defendants have taken guilty plea deals at the time of writing, the belligerent Balsiger maintains his total innocence and has even sued Miller several times, though always unsuccessfully.*

Another recent highlight for Miller was the arrest of an elusive Internet fraudster dubbed The Coupon Guy. The feds believe his true identity is 23-year-old Lucas Townsend Henderson, a pasty-faced Rochester Institute of Technology computer security student with a straggly goatee. Miller estimates Henderson would spend as much as nineteen hours manipulating a coupon template pixel by pixel, until he had forged a perfect fake. The Coupon Guy produced Tide coupons that were so plausible that Procter & Gamble and its retailers had to absorb $200,000 in fake redemptions. He also churned out counterfeits for Magic Hat beer, Campbell's soup, PowerBars, and even Sony PlayStations.

More than anything, though, it was the fifty-one-page manual that The Coupon Guy compiled and posted on 4Chan and Zoklet that Miller calls "a game changer." This is a step-by-step counterfeiting Bible aimed at helping everyone custom design a coupon or two. The Coupon Guy's

---

* Another of Miller's vanquished bêtes noires is Glenn Rodgers, a sixtysomething smooth-talker who crisscrossed the country for years in a car that he'd turned into a mobile coupon-printing station. He passed hundreds of homemade coupons for Gillette, Olay, and Norelco—Target alone said it lost $25,000 to $30,000 this way. Rodgers then sold his swag on eBay for a profit, making enough to live in a lavish manse in Las Vegas. He was apprehended by an especially diligent security guard at Target, who, Miller assures me, got a very nice plaque for his efforts.

primary motive wasn't money, either; a section of his manual is dedicated to his railings against the evils of American capitalism and his desire to upend the system. When the FBI finally tracked Henderson down via an IP address, they sent in a SWAT team at 5 a.m. to apprehend this economic Osama bin Laden. At the time of writing, Henderson had pled guilty to two charges—one of wire fraud, the other for trafficking in counterfeit goods. His sentence included three years of supervised probation and a restitution fine of $900,000. Had he risked a trial, he could have received sentences of twenty and ten years respectively on conviction. Of course, it's too late: the manual has gone viral and reappears regularly online, despite Miller's constant trawling.

These problems spotlight how important technology has been to couponing's rebirth; it's been as much a boon as a burden. Technology allows trading services like eBay and The Coupon Clippers to thrive as well as criminals like The Coupon Guy; and it has been a B12 shot for the sluggish grocery sector. Grocery discounts are a natural fit for social media. Picture a sample status update on Twitter—*I can't believe I saved $1 on mustard this week! Click here for the same coupon*—accompanied by a proud snap of a stockpiler showcasing the haul. Retailers have responded by turning their attention to limiting sharing via Facebook, Twitter, and other social media platforms. Everyone at the ACP remembers the Vryl Mkt debacle from 2008, when a handful of know-it-all tech nerds, aiming to showcase a commercial add-on that the firm had developed as a marketing tool for Facebook, produced a few deals that could be shared via the network. Vryl Mkt budgeted $10,000 to spend on twelve different products, like Cheez-Its. Naïvely, they failed to limit duplication. The social networking power of coupons turned so explosive that the firm was bankrupted by costs that finally leveled off at around $1 million.

Vryl Mkt's flameout hasn't derailed the couponing industry's efforts to expand into digital discounting, though; see how Supervalu, which owns branches of Jewel-Osco and Albertsons supermarkets, has a full-time social media coordinator to liaise with bloggers and give them freebies. Paperless discounting has proved less than seamless: Rupert Murdoch's own News America launched SmartSource Xpress, an app that digitally clips and saves coupons for redemption in person, only to see it stumble due to problems with scanners failing to read the coupons unless the phones were held a particular way. Another problem surfaced after Coupons.com demonstrated a proprietary redemption-limiting software. It prevented digital duplication, Vryl Mkt–style, but couldn't stop people from photocopying a printout.

Those detailed bar codes on each coupon have made it easier than ever for P & G or Kraft to plan an effective couponing campaign, automating and streamlining how tailor-made a discount can be, perhaps to a single item. But again, technology is shortcircuited by humans. There's little incentive for a retailer to program its registers to be too exact: the nightmare scenario would be a customer trying to use a Pantene conditioner coupon on a shampoo and hearing a beep, then facing reprimand from the checkout clerk, red faced. It's the same issue as rejecting a potentially photocopied printout; no staffer wants to accuse a customer of fraud. Supermarkets would rather fudge that code and accept a misredeemed coupon to keep the customer happy—and then just tussle with manufacturers later. It was this very quandary that Chrissy Pate's DVD helped unscrupulous shoppers to exploit so profitably.

In the new couponing landscape, it might be better for large retailers to team up with manufacturers rather than argue with them. They could do worse than draw inspiration from a legendary sting in late 1977, another era when the stagnating economy boosted coupons' use and profile. That year, not long after manufacturers had launched the then-novel Sunday FSIs, manufacturers started sniffing out widespread abuse for the first time. Tempted by the "free money" lurking in the newspapers by the checkout, some retailers had started padding weekly receipts, grabbing spares to bulk up weak takings, say, or help cover the cost of breakages by customers.

Manufacturers' response was ingenious: Create a coupon for a nonexistent product and tally how many retailers tried to redeem it. Tasked with executing this sting, the US Postal Service turned to Procter & Gamble, which volunteered a trademarked name it had never used: Breen. A 25-cent coupon was designed for Breen, marketed as "The Detergent That Cleans Away Dirt and Grime" ("We wanted to say *crime*," one old-timer told me, laughing). This body double for Tide was distributed alongside standard coupons in the New York metro area (one of the markets where the most misredemption was suspected). The operation launched in the December 11 issues of the *New York Daily News, Newark Star-Ledger,* and *Newsday.*

The results were astonishing: 2.5 percent of the fake coupons were redeemed by retailers, across 2100 stores in forty states. This translated to seventy thousand supposed first-time trials of this magic liquid. Investigators moved quickly, and twenty-six retailers were indicted by the Brooklyn DA on charges of grand larceny and scheming to defraud. Seventy-five-year-old Earl Ellsworth, a coupon-industry veteran, was deeply involved in the sting, tagging along with federal agents on raids. He would wait in the car while the coast was cleared, then enter after the agents. More than once, he would be confronted with the same scene: a seemingly innocuous bodega with a room behind it dedicated entirely to cutting and redeeming fraudulent deals. "We were getting those Breen coupons back from some of the Midtown cigar stands in Manhattan," Ellsworth marvels, then shudders. "But it was mostly organized crime [redeeming the fake coupons]. We even got threats of death and dismemberment."

It's staggering to realize that those garish circulars, so often discarded for bulking out every Sunday newspaper, might be worth so much, whether to a woman who can turn a few 50-cent coupons into a million-dollar business, or to organized crime co-opting them as a money-laundering tactic on Main Street. The power of coupons in the American economy is the clearest signal of how discounts have come to dominate the way we shop in the twenty-first century.

How, though, did we reach this point, one in which shoppers wield such sway and discounts are so tempting that they'll drive ordinary Americans to crime? Such markdown mania started just over two hundred years ago, when a Victorian-era accountant employed by a drug-addicted pharmacist came up with the idea of a coupon. That accountant would be astonished at how widespread its use has become, since all he wanted was to sell a few extra glasses of soda.

3

Purchase History

*The Strange Stories Behind the Blue Light
Special, the World's First Coupon and
the Outlet Mall*

The World of Coca-Cola is a mecca of pop culture. It sits on the edge
of a public park in downtown Atlanta, part of the reclaimed land left
over after the city's Olympics-driven makeover in 1996. A gleaming,
spaceship-like hulk, with a giant bottle levitating above it forms part of
the local skyline. Staffers' name tags proudly trumpet their favorite
product: Vanessa in the gift shop loves Vanilla Coke, "But I'd be just as
happy with a glass of water," she whispers. Upstairs, there's a Willy
Wonka–inspired soda fountain that dispenses Coca-Cola's products
from across the world. The room is filled with columnlike machines,
each of them flagged as representing a different continent and dispens-
ing sodas that are sold there. Most children hover around Europe, daring
or tricking one another into trying a blast of Beverly, the Italian soda.
Too bitter for most, there's a titter every time a child is sweet-talked into
sipping it and spits out the mouthful, disgusted. In the atrium, the newest attraction is a Donald Sutherland–voiced multimedia adventure that
theatrically climaxes with a look-but-don't-touch glimpse of the bank
vault in which Coca-Cola's top-secret formula is stored.

Yet close by, overlooked entirely by most visitors, is a treasure that matters arguably far more to the world than that much-cloned recipe. It's hidden inside the exhibit that details Coca-Cola's history: Among the faux soda fountains, sponsorship memorabilia, and ads in every language possible sits a dark vitrine. Few people stop to linger and examine the faded papers inside; after all, there are glossier and more appealing trinkets on show. But in one corner, next to a dozen or so scraps of paper, is a small sign. "In 1887, the Coca-Cola company pioneered the use of sampling coupons," it reads, "enticing people to try the new drink—for free." In fact, these were the world's very first coupons, so we have more to thank Coca-Cola for than cavities and "I'd Like to Teach the World to Sing."

As Coca-Cola's century-old chits demonstrate, the idea of bargains isn't new. The English word for *discount* was coined by the Jacobeans, a corruption of medieval Latin *discomputare*, meaning "to reduce." Centuries before that, Roman matrons were doubtless haggling for a price break at the local forum whenever they bulk-bought a new batch of house slaves. The system of sales that dominates how we shop today, however, is relatively recent. This familiar retail landscape of coupons, annual markdowns, and off-price outlets dates back just two centuries, when the modern world was smelted in the crucible of the Industrial Revolution. That's when shopping habits underwent a radical shift that kickstarted the momentum still driving discounting today. The ploys that define shopping 3.0 were seeded in the preceding two phases, eras dominated first by manufacturers and then by retailers.

Many might imagine that such markdown mania began in America— after all, this is a nation founded on the penny-saving thriftiness of Benjamin Franklin. They'd be wrong.* It's actually in Paris where the story of discounting as we know it really begins, thanks to a canny French shopkeeper with a unique je ne sais quoi.

---

* During World War II, though, there was a brief period when the federal government's Office of Civilian Requirements issued an edict asking storeowners to nix the word *sale* to help funnel energy away from shopping and toward the war effort.

Retail's Own Robespierre

Until the French Revolution, merchant guilds held a retail stranglehold in Paris: Unionlike, they protected each vendor by mandating that no one could sell diverse goods in a single store. A milliner, for example, couldn't cobble together a few pairs of high heels and offer a matching set of accessories; if he could do that, fretted the guilds, what would happen to the shoemaker next door? But once the ancien régime was toppled, its retail rules were abandoned, too. A new soon-to-be institution emerged: dry goods stores offering diverse stock. Dubbed *grands magasins* or *magasins de nouveautés* in French, we know them better as department stores.

Aristide Boucicaut, a furrow-browed would-be ladies' man, opened his own such *grand magasin* on the Rive Gauche in the 1850s. He called that retail palace Le Bon Marché—loosely, the Good Deal—and within sixteen years had done well enough to hire soon-to-be Eiffel Tower architect Gustave Eiffel to build an even bigger store that still stands today.*

As part of Le Bon Marché's reopening in 1869, Boucicaut instituted the price tag, a new promotional gimmick that was intended to be an implicit promise of trust. It turned retail from a haggling business, where each shopkeeper or assistant was primed to bargain and barter with customers, to a reliable, consistent setup. Customers no longer had to brave a conversation with snooty sales girls to ask the cost or worry that they might be overcharged. It's no coincidence that the middle class as we know it was created by the Industrial Revolution at much the same time. This arriviste group of the white-collar wealthy, so concerned with keeping up appearances, found negotiation distasteful and déclassé. The price tag cleverly elided such grubbiness.

Boucicaut's little trick, so seductive and democratic a move, was one

---

* Fittingly, given how much he owed to the Revolution, Boucicaut was born on Bastille Day in 1810, and gained fame enough within his lifetime that potboiling French novelist Émile Zola based an entire book on Aristide and his shopping emporium. *Au Bonheur des Dames* (*The Ladies' Paradise*) features protagonist Octave Mouret, a hamfisted but charming Casanova manqué, who ricochets between potential conquests. Since Boucicaut himself was stout, with a receding hairline and a pitchfork beard, the novel truly is a tribute to the impressive power of Zola's imagination.

of the key reasons that the department store became a backbone of nineteenth-century living. The shopper friendly price tag spread quickly across Europe, and from there it hopped the Atlantic. Two men have a viable claim to introducing it stateside: either serial failed entrepreneur Rowland Macy in New York, whose one-price policy meant bargaining was forbidden in his stores, or Philadelphia's John Wanamaker, an evangelical teetotaling Protestant who treated fair business practices as both a moral and a financial obligation.*

Of course, once prices were fixed, the natural next step was to cut them. Even Victorian-era retailers had guessed the dopamine-boosting power of a reference point decades before science even coined the phrase. At Le Bon Marché, Boucicaut introduced the first-known annual sale, using price cuts as a way to clear last season's sluggish stock while attracting extra footfall. White sales also originated with him—dubbed the *blanc*—and during this event each year in late January or early February, the entire store was festooned in white: sheets, towels, curtains, bed linen, and flowers, all at a cut price. The first day of that sale usually tripled standard daily grosses, and the total week boosted Boucicaut's bottom line more than any other promotion, with sales of 1 million francs or higher (roughly equivalent to $6 million today).

By the 1870s, the basic rules of retailing as we know it had been established and accepted: Fixed prices were shown on a tag, which could then be marked down in various ways to help move stock. But the discount circus was only just beginning, and one man above all was about to appoint himself ringmaster. He was an irrepressible shopkeeper with a fondness for lifts in his shoes and a flair for making a scene out of making a sale.

Introducing "Mr. Selfridge"

The scene is a carpet warehouse in the west of London. Outside the hulk-like building it's 2012, a landmark year of celebrations: the queen's

---

* In 1927, five years after his death, Wanamaker's namesake store still refused to sell playing cards, as he'd promised his late mother never to profit from gambling.

Jubilee and the Olympics both paralyzed and energized the city. Inside the building, though, it's 1909—an Edwardian-era shop that's been built for a new TV show set in that year. The set is a painstaking replica of one of London's grandest department stores, all faux marble, grand columns, and vitrines full of furbelows and fripperies. Actresses playing bored shop girls stand around looking like, well, bored shop girls: not a hair out of place (in their case, a pincushion-like brunette bun—no peroxide, of course), carefully dressed in black (but the skirt to the floor), and gossiping about the rest of the room (no change there). The star of this series has been shipped in from Hollywood: Jeremy Piven, best known as the erstwhile Ari Gold in *Entourage*. He's dapper in period costume: a tight waistcoat, jet-black beard, and shiny shoes with a slight heel. Piven struggles with a scene, constantly sputtering a character's name. "Fuck me, dammit, dammit," he spits, jarring the genteel surroundings.

The actor's foul mouth would horrify the man he's playing, Harry Gordon Selfridge, whose dirtiest exclamation was "My stars!" Selfridge was one of discounting's true pioneers, but more than that he was the man who invented almost every trick and gimmick familiar in a department store today. Though more of a household name in the United Kingdom than the United States, Harry was actually born in Wisconsin in 1864. He grew up to be a Victorian combination of Steve Jobs and Richard Branson, an ambitious, controlling genius with a flair for headline grabbing. The sparkpluggish Piven, other than his incongruous language, is well cast. He's dynamic, fast-talking, and not that tall: the five-foot-eight Selfridge always wore lifts in his shoes. He also shaved more years off his age than even the steeliest Hollywood starlet would dare (straight-facedly, he claimed to be fifteen years younger than he was).

Harry started as a stockboy in Chicago's tony Marshall Field's department store at just fifteen. Thanks to both his flair and his ego, just eight years later he'd risen to become the ornery owner's right-hand man. Dapper and irrepressible, Harry grasped the joyous power of shopping in a way that money-minded Marshall Field, a standoffish New Englander, never quite did. Admittedly, Field was a wily businessman, who moved into retailing after he spotted the opportunities in Chicago. Then the country's boomtown, the city was filled with newly minted nouveaux-riches types building Victorian McMansions and peacock-ishly keen to show off their newfound wealth at every opportunity. Field took over one of the early department stores in Chicago, and was all too glad to cater to the whims of the spend-happy shoppers. Field's maxim was "Give the lady what she wants"—or rather, let Harry Gordon Self-ridge do it (his willingness to please has more than a whiff of shopping 3.0). Since Field left a fortune of $118 million (around $2 billion today) when he died in 1906, it was a smart decision.*

"Marshall Field had a knack of employing good people and letting them have their head," explains Lindy Woodhead, whose biography of Selfridge was the basis for Piven's new show. "Harry Gordon wasn't by any means as financially astute as Field, but he was far more savvy about what customers wanted. He was a very unusual retailer: part merchan-diser, part promoter and part imagination." Mile-a-minute Harry's favor-ite book was by P. T. Barnum, and his showmanship is evident in the shopping tropes that he invented. It's entirely his fault, for instance, that there's now an annual nagging countdown of shopping days until Christ-mas. Harry introduced time-sensitive offers, discounts of usually 10 to 20 percent, designed to drive customers into his shop during quiet times, like Monday mornings. Yes, even the Victorians had doorbusters.

Harry had one innovation that his boss refused to authorize, though. He fretted that the Chicago store was perceived as too pricey. How better to shatter that assumption, he reasoned, than to find a new use for the hot and stuffy basement floor, one which would siphon shoppers down to what was certainly the least conducive part of the retail palace in a pre-air-conditioning era? He wanted to create a cut-price department. Field disagreed, worried about the impact on the store's image. With characteristic self-belief, Harry just waited until his boss was traveling to Europe and did it anyway. In 1885 he unveiled the world's first bar-gain basement. Before then, retailers had small sections devoted to

---

* Intriguingly, it's to Chicago that we owe the 99 pricing policy, too. Though often claimed to have been a loss-prevention tactic, forcing clerks to open a cash register to make change and so record the sale, this is an urban myth. Rather, it's likely that it began for the same reason that it's used now: cheapness, at the Fair, the bargain-priced alternative department store downtown near Marshall Field's.

discounted merchandise, but no one had dedicated an entire floor to a selection of goods where every price tag was marked down. It was Harry who saw how to turn discounts into an advantage rather than an embarrassment.

To ensure that shoppers weren't shamefaced to trawl the bargain floor, Selfridge didn't focus on grubby, soiled merchandise banished from upstairs. Rather, he introduced specially bought, lower-grade goods aimed at the thriving working classes. As the nouveaux riches had mushroomed, the staff who catered to them had been buoyed up, too; household maids, for example, had seen their wages more than double in the wake of the Civil War.

This entry-level floor was retail's gateway drug. Once shoppers had sampled the experience at Marshall Field's this way, they would yearn to move upstairs. "He gave them glamour at a price they could afford to pay," says Woodhead. There were cascading displays of bath salts, mountains of soap, and piles of hosiery. Notoriously finicky about language, Harry didn't use the words *cheap* or *discount*, but promoted his new annex, artfully dubbed the Budget Floor, as "Offering even better value." It was such an instant success that old man Field had rather counted the profits than carp at the insolence of his protégé: By 1900, annual sales at the bargain basement were $3 million, or almost a quarter of the store's total. Two years later, when Field opened a new and expanded store, the bargain basement was the single largest salesroom, topping out at almost 140,000-square feet. For comparison, most Walmart-style megastores today occupy less than 100,000-square feet.

After years of making money for Field, Harry yearned for free rein, specifically the chance to create a store from scratch without such meddlesome bosses. He got that opportunity by moving to Great Britain, where he commandeered a site at the western end of Oxford Street, London's version of State Street in Chicago. Thanks to an especially advantageous exchange rate between the pound and the dollar, Selfridge arrived a wealthy man and sunk his entire fortune into a namesake store: Selfridges, which opened in 1909. (Its opening is the starting point of Piven's TV show.) Three years after the opening, Harry Gordon—who had tellingly switched his name to H Gordon on crossing the Atlantic, giving himself a more patrician mien—introduced his signature detail, the bargain basement, to the curious Brits.

Selfridges as a store was a booming success, but the bargain basement didn't thrive as it had in Chicago, despite being advertised as the perfect destination for "thrifty housewives." One challenge was that wages for blue-collar workers in London had remained flat in the preceding decades. Rather than catering to a newly cashed-up working class, Selfridge's discount floor had to appeal across social boundaries. Such miscegenation could prove all-around awkward, Lindy Woodhead explains. One grande dame of London society was spotted on the escalator descending into the basement while her maid was coming up on the other escalator. In that *Upstairs, Downstairs* era, each looked at the other, transfixed, unsure whether to smile and wave or ignore what they saw.

Social niceties aside, the bargain basement did often prove the highlight of a shopper's trip to the store, as one particular letter in the Selfridges archive attests. A Mrs. Valerie Ranzetta reminisces about shopping there in the 1920s, saving up enough money to buy a special Easter hat in the bargain basement. "We ignored the other floors and the enticing displays there for our delight. Down there it was hot, noisy and colourful. [My friend] said it reminded her of what the French Revolution must have been like," she writes. Indeed, Valerie sees her ideal hat, made of leaf-green straw, on a haphazard pile. "I wanted that hat more than I had ever wanted anything in my life. Then, as if in answer to my silent prayer, it emerged close to my elbow in all its tantalising glory. I made a frantic grab, and got hold of the thin elastic which would hold the hat to the wearers head in windy weather. Strangely, it would not spring free, and I soon saw why—the girl next to me clung to the other end of the elastic." But Valerie has a determination that any modern Black Friday bargaineer might recognize. "I dig my spare elbow into her ribs while at the same time treading down, hard, on what I hoped was her foot. It worked . . . Like a miracle, the green hat sprang into the air, striking me on the cheek so hard that the tears came into my eyes." Doubtless, her bested bargain rival was weeping, too, albeit for different reasons.

Back in America, the bargain basement was spreading across the country, notably to Boston, where Edward Filene opened his twist on the concept. Jealous competitors at first dubbed his new discount plan Filene's Folly. In 1909, the same year Selfridges debuted in London, Filene announced the Automatic Bargain Basement. His floor used dated price tags where discounts increased the longer merchandise lingered unsold—10 percent off at first climbed to 25 percent after twelve days, 25 percent more six days later, and a final fire sale 25 percent six days after that. Anything left unsold went to charity. Experts estimate that only 3 percent of stock was off-loaded in this way, clear evidence that the system was near foolproof. Filene's Basement was successful enough to be spun off as a standalone store; one economist calculated that it was only this profit center that had kept the company from bankruptcy during the Great Depression of the 1930s. Sadly, it didn't weather the downturn after 2008 quite as heartily—but we'll come to that story, later.

The Piven-helmed *Mr. Selfridge*—essentially, *Downton Abbey* in a shop, complete with Harry and family upstairs, and the working classes downstairs—fudges the bargain basement by moving goods on sale to the main floor (extra sets can be pricey, after all). One episode does revolve around Harry's obsession with bargains, and his idea to introduce them to stiff upper-lipped Brits.* Selfridge's own story ends in ignominy—he squandered his fortune after his wife died in the Spanish flu epidemic of 1918 and he was forced to sell the store to rivals. Ostracized by the glitterati he'd once serviced, he died a near pauper, half blind in a tiny apartment in West London. Thankfully, though, Selfridges still stands on Oxford Street, a testament to one of retail's most colorful pioneers. The basement, however, is now just another selling floor.

Single-handedly, Harry took bargains from an ad hoc annual stunt to a crucial booster of a store's daily bottom line, spreading the idea from the United States to Europe (Walmart's beloved rollback sale owes a royalty to the retail pioneer). At the same time that Selfridge was teaching Britons the value of a bargain, though, something else was popping up

---

* "This sale has come from your eyes and your initiative," Piven-as-Harry beamingly and inaccurately tells his staff as bright red "50% OFF" signs surround them. "The point about this sale isn't just to sell goods cheaply. I want hard-working everyday people to come in." Ironically, while the series' first episode was being screened in January 2013, the actor was shopping at the store and asked to use his affiliate discount. The staff didn't recognize the star and demanded proof.

back home, an idea that would become as iconic a discount gimmick as that cut-price basement. By this time, America had a new favorite soft drink, Coca-Cola, which had spread through the country's soda fountains like a sweet, fizzy weed. Its startling success was down to a promotional mechanic that others would soon race to ape: the coupon.

I'd Like to Buy the World a (Half-Price) Coke

When Coca-Cola was invented by pharmacist John Pemberton in 1886 in Georgia, it was one of many new life-affirming cordials touted as "Delicious!" "Refreshing!" "Exhilarating!" "Invigorating!" Most pharmacies had a soda jerk who doled out one of two dozen or so flavored syrups and added carbonated water to the order; the rows of marble taps along the back bar offered chocolate, cherry, lemon, or perhaps the oddly named Coca-Cola. Coca-Cola could have been any other unremarkable tincture on that bar, were it not for Pemberton's bookkeeper. That money-minded accountant, whose name has been lost to history, decided to create a deal for Coca-Cola in order to spark sales. He scribbled out a few handwritten chits that offered the bearer a free glass of Coca-Cola from any soda fountain. He passed out the coupons much like a flyer on a street today. These were the world's first coupons.

Called Coupon Cards or Free Tickets, they were an instant success. None of the coupons from this first batch survived in any archive, as they were both too fragile and too eagerly redeemed. Nevertheless, thanks to such promotions, Coca-Cola's business boomed. Pemberton, though, was ailing. A couple of years after launching the firm, he'd slumped irretrievably into a morphine addiction, spurred by injuries incurred during the Civil War. To feed it, he off-loaded the secret formula for $2,300 to Asa Candler. It was Candler who masterminded the syrup's rise, taking Pemberton's couponing gimmick as his central marketing strategy.

"[Candler] was a strict, teetotaling Methodist, as Christian as the day is long," explains Ted Ryan, the bookish and genial archivist at Coke's Atlanta headquarters and one of the masterminds of the exhibitions at the World of Coca-Cola. "If you'd called him a showboat, he'd be very,

very upset."* The uptight would-be soda magnate recognized the power of Pemberton's couponing gimmick, but reconfigured its purpose. He wasn't going to hand out chits casually to passersby, but rather offer the coupon to his commercial customers so that they would expand sales exponentially. It wasn't about driving casual trial, Candler reasoned, but driving bulk consumption. He was willing to take a short-term dent in profits to maximize word of mouth. When a fountain owner ordered one gallon of syrup, Asa would send two gallons for the same price, plus a fistful of coupons. *Use these ONE FREE GLASS tokens until the first gallon is finished*, he suggested, *and watch as the second gallon sells briskly.*

It was marketing alchemy. Between 1886 and 1920, 10 percent of all Coca-Cola in the world was given away for free via a sample coupon. The cost was carried on company advertising budgets as a separate line item. By some estimates, one in nine Americans had sampled Coca-Cola this way by World War I—8.5 million glasses drunk gratis. Under Candler's stewardship, Coca-Cola's spread across America was unstoppable: Ten years after he bought the recipe, this Georgia tonic was for sale in every state in the country.

Ryan estimates that there are between four hundred and five hundred Coca-Cola coupons in his archive, each of them trilling, "This card entitles you to one glass of free Coca-Cola at the fountain dispenser of genuine Coca-Cola." Most of these coupons are now worth $200 to $300, and can easily be picked up on eBay. Rarities, like the Spanish-language versions possibly produced for the Cuban market, are prized, as are earlier coupons that were printed only in black and white with the curlicue logo.

By the time Coca-Cola finally outgrew such need for sampling via giveaways, other manufacturers had Xeroxed the couponing concept. Post cereals was typical, and the firm's 1895 riff on couponing seems familiar even today: It offered 1 cent off the purchase of a box of its new healthy cereal, Grape Nuts. Couponing was boosted during the Depression (sound familiar?), but four years after 1929, as US retail sales halved

---

* Notably, Harry Gordon Selfridge installed a soda fountain in his store in 1924 to help market Coca-Cola to thirsty Londoners. Imagine how squirmy a meeting between Candler and the razzle-dazzle Selfridge must have been.

from $48.5 billion, this discount mechanic was both normalized and turbocharged. Companies started printing coupons on the wrappers of their products, such as Colgate's coupon on its lye-based Octagon soap, so that each item came with a built-in discount on the next purchase.

By the 1940s, chain supermarkets started offering coupons as a way to lure customers from mom-and-pop neighborhood stores. Indeed, in this same era Nielsen started NCH, the clearinghouse business spun off from its TV firm. As the atomic age ended, one in every two Americans used coupons regularly, likely clipping them at the kitchen table every Sunday with a glass of Coca-Cola at hand. Soon, though, they'd be spending those coupons at an entirely new kind of store.

Greenlighting the Blue Light Special

The year 1962 was the year of beehives and the Beatles, overdoses (Marilyn Monroe) and overreactions (the Cuban Missile Crisis). What no one knew then was that it was also a landmark year for shopping. Three stores that would go on to dominate America's discount landscape for decades to come appeared almost simultaneously: Walmart, Target, and Kmart. The last of the three, a Filene's Basement–esque budget offshoot of the middle-brow Kresge department stores, was the first to thrive, all thanks to an accidental innovation cobbled together by a frustrated store manager.

Prompted by the emergence of America's sprawling postwar suburbs and the malls that served them, Kresge opened a Kmart in Garden City, Michigan, in March 1962. It planted some of its brightest staffers into the new division to help boost growth. One of them was Earl Bartell, born in Toledo, Ohio, who'd joined the firm after college as a graduate trainee. By the time he was twenty-four, Bartell was the assistant store manager in Fort Wayne, Indiana.

Three weeks before Christmas 1965, Earl faced a problem. The store had accumulated a pile of low-quality wrapping paper that didn't sell, even after it was aggressively marked down. He decided to try a different tactic: a fifteen-minute flash sale. Now, how could he tout the bargains to customers? Bartell needed some kind of attention-grabbing gimmick. He considered balloons, before realizing that they'd look like a kid's birthday party. Then came the brain wave. He darted into the sporting goods aisle and found a little light that would flash. He stuck the light on to the end of a two-by-four and wrapped the whole thing in crepe paper. "It was kinda tacky," he recalls, "but it worked. You could still see the light." He then attached the flashing contraption to a stock cart and parked it next to the paper; on the store's loudspeaker system, he announced that for the next fifteen minutes, the wrapping paper would be a special deal. The price was the same—still on sale, reduced from 86 cents to 56 cents a roll—but the difference was how he promoted it.

Earl's jury-rigged gizmo feted the first Blue Light Special—though the bulb he initially used was red. "Old ladies would call in and say the revolving red light was too suggestive," he says. Bartell kept tinkering, swapping out the bulb for a blue police light on top of a long pipe, powered by a 12-volt battery. He hauled it out to shift any sluggish overstock, and started tracking its impact on sales. On average, he spotted a 10-percent increase in sales of any Blue Light Special item. After spending nine months beta testing his new discount tactic, he took his idea to the head office. The reaction was rapturous. By Christmas the following year, Earl's Blue Light Specials were mandatory in every Kmart store. His bonus for inventing one of retail's most enduring gimmicks? "I got a twenty-five-dollar reward," he says, shrugging.

For the next twenty-five years, Blue Light Specials were a staple of the American retail landscape. In stores, out of the, well, blue, a voice would boom, "Attention, Kmart shoppers, the blue light is rolling . . . ," for a sale that lasted anywhere between five and fifteen minutes. Soon Kmart introduced competing specials on rival brands like Coke and Pepsi, dubbed a *shoot-out*. Bartell recalls how customers would tip each other off by phone and rush to the store, or come and ask whether a special would run today. Every Kmart store was mandated to run such promotions, but the cost to buy one of those blue lights was off-loaded onto managers. "You could make your own, but they wanted you to buy these ones that were set up with a nice battery and lasted quite a while," he told me. For that very reason, Bartell, the inventor of this iconic gimmick, doesn't even have one to keep on his desk at home—just a photo in which he's holding his invention.

Bartell left Kmart in 1975 and eventually started an insurance firm, but his lights kept blaring there until 1991. That's when a new regime at Kmart deemed the sharp-elbowed atmosphere of manic discounting undignified. In an attempt to upscale the brand, Kmart extinguished Bartell's idea. Ten years of falling sales later, the bulbs were back. A new CEO made Blue Light Specials the centerpiece of reviving Kmart in the Internet era, going so far as to acquire bluelight.com. Bartell was spotlit at a splashy PR launch in New York City when the company announced the reintroduction of the Blue Light Special. The outlook seemed ominous from the start, especially when the fast-talking marketing exec tasked with updating the program raved about a rap that employees had been asked to write in celebration of Blue Light 2.0. Unsurprisingly, the Blue Light update lasted less than a year.

The Outlet MO-Ment

Most of today's discount gimmicks—coupons, flash sales, bargain basements—were already retail staples by the early 1960s, lurking quietly like shopping sleeper agents until the moment when they could come together to help buyers wrest away control from the sellers. It wasn't until a decade later that another now-familiar discount trick surfaced, though, one that would grow into a multibillion-dollar industry in less than thirty years: the outlet mall.

The outlet mall was born in a small town in semirural Pennsylvania. Since industrialization spread across the country after the Civil War, this state had been one of the textile hubs of America, filled with factories churning out hosiery and underwear proudly made in the USA. The town of Reading, home to firms like the Reading Glove and Mitten Manufacturing Company, was typical of the new Pennsylvanian retail landscape. Reading Glove was founded in 1899 and became one of the town's successes, a niche manufacturer that broadened across almost every rag trade sector. In the process, it shifted from a regional factory to a countrywide behemoth. Via that quest to expand, the company snaffled up a slew of household names like Wrangler, Lee, Vans, Eastpak, and Nautica. It was this exponential growth, and the resultant oversupply, that was behind the creation of the first-ever outlet mall.

In 1969, longtime CEO Manfred O. Lee (known as M.O.) renamed the rag trade conglomerate VF Corporation. A farsighted and entrepreneurial garmento, M.O. had taken the firm far beyond mitten making. The companies he bought, though, all had the same problem: Their balance sheets were hobbled by unmovable merchandise. The excess inventory of the namesake jean company moved M.O. to try a strange new kind of shopping one Saturday morning in 1970: the discount mall.* Eventually, the discount mall would turn the nondescript town of Reading into an outlet Disneyland.

M.O. ordered his machinists to move the knitting engines to one side and clean up a small corner of the factory. Side tables and racks were brought in and loaded up with merchandise; a tarp was strung between this proto pop-up shop and the machines, pistons blasting as usual. Word-of-mouth promotion proved powerful enough that the merchandise sold out completely in a single morning. M.O., bagging goodies and manning the register himself amid the frenzy, saw the profit potential immediately. He still wanted to make sure that that morning was no fluke; after a sellout second run two weeks later, he was convinced. M.O. set up a formal multibrand outlet, selling overruns and distressed merchandise from VF's family of brands. Crucially, he wasn't selling defective merchandise (seconds or irregulars), merely excess. Just as today, his discount program was triggered by a surfeit of too much stuff.

---

* Certainly, factory-direct stores had existed since the late 1940s, when Anderson Little, of Fall River, Massachusetts, created the first such outlet. The end of World War II transfused millions of freshly demobbed GIs back into the work force, birthing the baby boom and the arrival of the Atomic Age. At the same time, the government resupplied clothing manufacturers with material to restart their businesses since most had switched over to uniform manufacturing during the war. Unfortunately, the Fed overestimated demand for suits from those GIs, leaving wholesalers such as Anderson Little with a surplus of materials. It was this firm that first started selling that excess from the factory—after all, cutting out the middleman made those suits cheaper, too. But these were standalone single stores, rather than an outlet enclave like that which would emerge in Reading and act as the template for contemporary cut-price malls.

Reading was perfectly placed for a discount megastore operation: not too close to full-price accounts that would object to such markdowns, but near enough to urban centers like Philadelphia or New York to entice daytripping bargain hunters. It wasn't long before three hundred buses full of deal-hungry tourists clogged the local streets on Saturday afternoons. VF's success lured other lookalike malls to open nearby, and the effect snowballed.

Real estate investor Fred Maloof founded one of those rival malls. Maloof's story was typical for the time. As manufacturing migrated toward cheaper sites in the American southeast, opportunities to lease factory real estate in the rust belt grew scarcer. But wily Maloof didn't worry, or try to find industrial tenants. Eyeballing VF's success, he reconfigured his business for the 1970s by offering space to companies who wanted to off-load excess merchandise rather than manufacture new product. This was far more lucrative, too; rents for factories hovered around 50 or 60 cents per square foot, while retail rates hit $2.

Rich Maloof, Fred's nephew, started working for his uncle while still a teenager (he's now the real estate czar for onetime-rival VF Corp). Rich recalls scrubbing the grease off the floors and cleaning the gulleys (the grooves that once housed knitting machines) to prep for uncle Fred's new tenants. The four-story setup had no elevator, and the decor was basic. The bargains, though, were irresistible. "In the beginning, things were just in cardboard boxes on the tables, and cost twenty percent of the regular retail price, if that," he marvels. Maloof offered a tweak on VF's formula: He allowed tenants to sell seconds and irregulars, at even cheaper prices. "I remember going shopping at Izod and Lacoste, and things were maybe missing a button or had the wrong-colored button and you'd get them for five dollars a piece. It was ridiculous." This mall was home to the first-ever Polo outlet. Almost forty years later, one Ralph Lauren exec estimated that Polo's off-price operation contributes $1 billion to the firm's bottom line.

Within four years, at least five extra mini discount malls had joined this cluster in Reading, and the town's reputation for deals was spreading. Competition for those busloads of shoppers was growing fierce, drawing bargaineers from beyond New York or Philadelphia. Eager shoppers were hiking down from as far away as Richmond, Virginia, and New England. Every outlet wanted to be the first mall on their itinerary, when neither wallets nor energy were exhausted. "There's no question there were bribes to the bus drivers—food, coupons, money," Maloof admits now. The outlet owners set up VIP lounges for the drivers, for instance, and group leaders often received a cash thank-you. Never was the mania for shopping at these malls clearer to Maloof than the day he witnessed police flag down a bus that had pitstopped at each of them in turn. Somebody had taken some merchandise from a purse store, and unless the stolen bag was surrendered immediately, the police warned, they would board the bus and conduct a search. "That was a time when the bus windows still opened, and instantly about thirty purses came flying out the window." Sadly, all that tale proves is that even slashing prices doesn't deter the occasional sticky-fingered visitor.

Shoplifting aside, Reading enjoyed a decade-long heyday, with one hundred fifty or so different outlet centers in the area by the 1980s. The town was an outlet outlier among retailers, until the shopping landscape began to shift and Reading's fame dimmed, as its idea was cloned across the country. This was all thanks to a rise in real estate investment trusts (REITs). Such shell setups emerged as real estate's answer to mutual funds, which allowed investors to sink money into a trust that then owned and operated income-producing commercial property. Of course, the margins on product sold at these cut-price malls made them especially attractive to speculators.

VF wasn't left lingering in Pennsylvania, though. More people formed REITs, pumping extra financing into the industry that led to conglomerates building five or ten outlets simultaneously. During the 1980s, outlets became a true retail strategy rather than an incidental offshoot; VF Corp could mark a 50-mile radius from its wholesale customers and plan an outlet mall wherever there was a viable site that didn't overlap with any of those circles. It was during that REIT-crazed time that Steve Tanger, a garmento-turned-real-estate-czar, started opening his namesake centers, arguably now America's best known malls.

Outlet malls and off-price stores continued to boom through the 1980s and 1990s, becoming a fixture in, and a draw at, vacation destinations such as Orlando and Las Vegas. By 2012, there were almost one hundred eighty outlet malls in America, each ruthlessly picked clean every year by fifty-five million visitors. VF, chief among the outlets, retains a proud point of difference: Unlike many manufacturers who fill their store with specially produced product that was never offered at full price (more on that later), VF still focuses on selling excess and overruns, items that were intended for regular retail but never needed.*

The next major shift in shopping occurred in the 1990s. It was the bellwether of a shift into shopping 3.0, when buyers would seize control from sellers, whether retailers or manufacturers. VF and its fellow outlet mallers were thriving, but the decades-old scattershot strategy on which they relied—lure some shoppers with deep discounts and heavy advertising, then hope that they splurge—was proving more and more inefficient. Retail was yearning for a way to target individuals with precision, for a fail-safe way to find the free-spending needle in a discount haystack. Surprisingly, the solution came not from a large corporation but from an unassuming middle-class British couple with an affinity for numbers.

Discounts, Data Warehousing, and Dirt-Cheap Diapers

The townhouse in which Clive Dunn and Edwina Humby live and work in London's tony Notting Hill is hidden behind a high hedge, more apologetic than grandiose. The setting is fitting for such a reclusive couple, rare to grant interviews and shellacked with modest reserve. In person, though, they're disarmingly charming. Clive, jolly and with a hearty paunch, is the computer whizz. Edwina, hair expensively chopped and always half-smiling, is the number whisperer. She is also single-handedly

* Ninety percent of the stock at North Face's small clutch of off-price stores, for example, is simply last season's—and a bargain at that. Vans opens one outlet for every five full-price stores, a standard ratio; any firm with a greater number is almost guaranteed to need to produce outlet-only stock to keep the shelves full.

responsible for fast-forwarding discounts into the twenty-first century with a laserlike focus on shoppers.

By the 1980s, grocery retailers in America and the United Kingdom were using computers to track their sales. The challenge was data storage. With data warehousing in its infancy, it was too expensive to keep such information for longer than a year, so retailers could do little with that information. Enter Clive Dunn, who created a special program that used mathematical sleights of hand to compress that data so that it required far less storage space on a floppy disk. Dunn also changed the way the data was stored, so that sales figures could be more flexibly assessed. In 1994 he offered to road test his programming with supermarket Tesco, a perennial also-ran in British retail that was struggling to catch up with market leader Sainsbury's. Tesco was the ideal new client for Dunn and Humby—hungry, determined, and a little desperate. In exchange for a project fee of £750,000 (around $1.35 million), the pair promised Tesco they could transform its fortunes.

Their real innovation wasn't Clive's clever programming but rather recognizing how to leverage such data once it was stored. To do so, the couple created an entirely new kind of loyalty scheme. Such programs weren't new—S&H Green Stamps, for instance, had been issued in the United Sates starting in 1896, and later overseas, allowing customers to receive tokens at supermarkets and department stores that could be redeemed for goodies in the S&H catalog. The twenty-first-century model of loyalty programs, however, offered a two-way dialogue. Customers would be rewarded for their purchases, but supermarkets could also cull intel on what and when those same shoppers bought. In response, the grocer could mine a customer's shopping habits in order to tailor-make deals; these customized coupons would give the supermarket, puppeteer-like, immense control over its stock. Clive wrote the algorithms and Edwina transmuted the data into useful insights. Fortunately, she had a savantlike ability to see patterns that others had missed.

Theirs was a mammoth task: The average person goes to the supermarket ninety times in twelve months and buys thirty items on each visit, which means that stores are tracking 2,700 transactions per customer each year. Multiply that by the number of shoppers—the UK population has hovered around sixty million for several years—and the data sets were staggering. Nonetheless, Dunn-Humby managed to process and analyze it all on schedule, and the Tesco Clubcard was launched in 1995. That innocuous program, which made loyalty cards the most important discounting gimmick of the last decade, is the single reason Tesco is now a world-beating operation. Profits skyrocketed from $860 million in 1994 to $5 billion in 2010. By then, Tesco was the second-biggest retailer *in the world* by profit.

Once a Tesco customer signed up for the Clubcard, he or she would receive coupons in the mail, much like the Valpak envelopes so familiar to Americans. But there was a crucial difference: customization. Initially, the envelope-opening rate hovered at junk mail industry standard, around 10 to 12 percent, but soon it started to climb. Eventually it leveled off at about 70 percent or more. "People thought *This is not junk mail, this is money,*" Edwina remembers. "And as soon as the coupons were opened, we saw it crossed over from *I'm a poor person shopping with coupons,* to *I'm a very savvy shopper.*" Customers were happy. They felt like VIPs because their bundles of bargains were personalized. This was a decisive shift in discounting that suggested the shopper was in pole position—and it ushered in a change in mindset that helped birth the new mania for discounts that's dominated the last decade.

On Tesco's side, the impact of the loyalty programs was twofold: The company learned more about its customers, certainly, but Clubcard also safeguarded Tesco's margins. The program allowed for prices to not be slashed for everyone. Those who were less budget-minded could ignore the chits, while the more price-sensitive could be steered to swap brands or try a new item by custom coupons, hacked up by Tesco's computers like discount hairballs. The supermarket, guided by Edwina's savvy hand, could then Braille how promotions impacted behavior.

Tesco and Dunn-Humby soon learned that coffee and hair care, for example, were two categories rarely driven by deals; shoppers are ferociously brand loyal in these cases, and a price cut will simply encourage fans of a certain brand to stock up. In other words, selling Nescafé or Herbal Essences at a discount just erodes margins for no reason. Beer, on the other hand, is price sensitive. Dunn-Humby found that most people bought a variety of beers to experiment with tastes. So in that category the strategy became simple: Promote it to sell it. Proteins like chicken or fish are similar; most shoppers are looking for variety in a weekly dinner menu, so they can be coaxed into trying something new by a coupon.

Diapers are Clive's favorite example of how discounting can manipulate shopping habits. "When you have your first child, you think of Pampers. It's a trusted brand, and you want to buy the best," he says. "By the time the baby is six months old, you realize half the nappies fall off anyway so why waste money on an expensive brand? And the data bears this out." Sidestepping such a revelation is simple: Using the Clubcard personalized discount program, Pampers can generate a coupon about five months after diapers first appear in a shopper's basket. That price promotion immunizes against a brand swap.

Clive often jokes about the idiosyncracies of his business and data, remarking on how often chardonnay and condoms appear together in a single basket, and marveling how, "Old ladies will scrimp and save, eat absolute rubbish for themselves, but they'll still buy the most expensive pet food for their cat. And cats much more than dogs." His wife, though, is more serious. "We've been tutored for fifteen years on never, never finding any of it funny, because all this data is about real people," she says. There's no risk of Google-style privacy intrusions, though, as Dunn-Humby's processed data is aggressively anonymized, making it impossible for staffers to manually link shopping habits with a particular customer.*

As the discounting landscape shifted, Edwina and Clive continued to refine their strategies. Take the rise of sale-only shoppers in the early 2000s; known as cherry pickers, they buy only a product that is marked down. Dunn-Humby told Tesco to largely ignore their needs and focus on its best customers, offering deals to the most free spending as a thank-you gesture. That strategy ran counter to the advice offered by MBA-equipped number crunchers at Bain Capital–like consultancies, who

---

* There are some intriguing inequalities. A group of students at the London School of Economics tested how influential the Clubcard might prove on the discounts a given customer is offered by applying for car insurance, one of the supermarket's many subsidiary divisions. Tellingly, applicants who provided a heavily trafficked Clubcard number with high annual purchases saw discounts vary, with the highest a staggering 18 percent off standard rate. For a virgin Clubcard number, with zero data, the discount was just 1 percent.

advised their clients to protect their margins at all costs; sell fewer items, retailers were ordered, but keep the prices high. In retail, Edwina stresses, this is a fundamental misstep: Foot traffic is the most important consideration. Drive people with open wallets into the store, whatever it takes, as they form a hungry, captive audience once they're inside. "Stimulating sales through offers is about increasing footfall, the opportunities to sell," Clive adds. "Managing margin is about making sure you make money on the products you're selling. But what if there's no lever to pull to get the customers in the door?" Discounts are that trigger.*

After Tesco swallowed its subsidiary in 2011, Dunn and Humby became multimillionaires (estimates place their wealth around $80 million). That fortune springs solely from figuring out how and when to offer people the right deal. In the United States, grocery chain Kroger was the first to headhunt Dunn-Humby's expertise and is now the firm's official partner. Most industry experts were cynical that the pair could translate its program from a small country like Britain to the sprawling United States. Americans received so much more junk mail, ten or twenty times the amount that clogged the Brits' mailboxes, they warned, that envelopes would be discarded unopened. The doubters were proven right at the outset, with an envelope-opening rate on Dunn-Humby's mailers of just 3 percent; by 2012, though, the rate had steadily risen to 30 percent and climbing. During one of their first meetings at Kroger's headquarters in Cincinnati, Dunn-Humby showed firsthand how universal their expertise might prove.

Humby, analyzing the supermarket's customer shopping baskets for the first time, was surprised to find detergent purchased less frequently than she expected. After a visit to a local store, she was staggered to see that the laundry soap aisle was almost entirely orange. In other words, there was little on offer but Tide in all its forms. Humby suggested a tweak. Ditch some of this brand, she said, and offer some cheaper promotional

---

* But even then, it's possible to make mistakes. In 2012 a smaller British supermarket chain, Morrisons, was pilloried in the media when news leaked that it was reneging on its longtime stand against the loyalty card. But it wasn't rewarding its most loyal customers; rather, it teased a 10 percent discount card to heavy buyers at rivals like Tesco. Loyal Morrisons shoppers got nothing.

alternatives. Kroger was terrified of upsetting local partner P & G, but trialed her advice in some stores, swapping out a few SKUs and introducing a discount product alongside the premium detergent. After a few weeks, Edwina's number whispering paid off: Total laundry soap sales climbed 16 percent, while Tide increased 4 percent. Kroger was able to please price-conscious customers, while buffing the pride of those who opted for a more premium product. Americans, it seems, are just as susceptible to Dunn-Humby's retail voodoo.

The discountmania that dominates shopping in the twenty-first century didn't emerge overnight. It's the culmination of two centuries' worth of retail tricks that have been reinvigorated thanks in part to both the warp speed of technology and the slowdown of the economy. There's DNA from Harry Gordon Selfridge, or a shot of Coca-Cola's coupon culture, in everything from Groupon to flash sales sites to sample sales for luxury brands. Next, we're headed to Manhattan's Upper East Side, to explore the secretive world of high fashion at low prices. Enough of the history lessons—let's go shopping for shoes.

4

How the Other Half Saves

The Secretive World of Sample Sales, VIP Discounts, and Why Some Designer Bags End Up in a Document Shredder

No shoe brand gets Mollie Fitzgerald more pumped than Roger Vivier. "It's a classic look that's not going out of style. I travel a lot and I like the fact the heels aren't sky high—they work just as well with a suit for a client dinner as with blue jeans," says the Pittsburgh-based owner of a travel agency, a WASPish blonde with a weakness for pearls and an earthy laugh. "I must have eighteen or twenty pairs." French cobbler Vivier invented the stiletto in the 1950s, long before Louboutin and his ilk stepped up to start selling shoes. Today, the Roger Vivier brand is aimed squarely at the well heeled, charging between $500 and $1,000 per exquisitely designed pair. Stateside, the brand's distribution is exclusive, far from oversupplied—restricted to only half a dozen outlets, including its own jewel box–like store on New York's Upper East Side.

Even Vivier, however, makes an occasional misstep, with a few pairs left unsold at the end of each season. Maybe one style was too outré for a practical American woman, or Fitzgerald and her fellow regulars just didn't shop enough. With fresh styles looming, there's pressure on Vivier to quickly liquidate whatever dawdling stock remains. It would never hold a clearance event, though; like many ultra-luxury brands, the cobbler is wary of reminding shoppers too blatantly that it's blowing a discount dog whistle, one that only certain customers can hear. Rather, Vivier hosts an invisible sale, hidden in plain sight.

Fitzgerald is one of the elite few made privy to this retail speakeasy. "I get a gorgeous engraved card, an invitation to the private sale, about two days before it's happening," she explains. The invitation contains *Mission: Impossible*–style instructions. For a short time, it notes, small dotted stickers (blue for 30 percent off, red for 40 percent) will appear on the soles of certain shoes; otherwise, but for a tiny tented "SALE" card in the window (a legal mandate), there will be no mark of markdowns. It's the silver lining for longtime loyalists like Fitzgerald. Walk-ins from the street who inspect a shoe and spot the same dot will be told it's stock-taking (dismissive and deceptive, sure, but technically true). Calling the subterfuge "a huge pain in the ass," one former sales assistant explains that he was asked to demur when casual passersby would dawdle or ask what the dots meant. It was easy, given the minimal evidence. "This tiny, *tiny*-ass little [sale sign] in the front window. You literally could walk by and never notice it." Hopefully at least in some killer shoes.

Cash for Calvins

Vivier isn't alone. Luxury brands like this face a quandary: the new lure of mass-market appeal (and profits) versus the ease of operating the old-fashioned way, as a contained, almost cottage industry. Inevitably almost everyone, from Chanel to Dior via Prada and Armani, has opted for the former. The price for such expansion, for reaching women from Manhattan, Kansas, to Manhattan, New York, has been steep. Larger volumes carry bigger risks: Mistakes are magnified, overruns greater.

Imagine a pap snap of Paris Hilton toting a certain bag turns sales of it toxic overnight. Suddenly, no one wants to buy that purse. In such a case, where demand drops almost instantly, the increase in production volume is lethal. It means that dozens, perhaps hundreds, of the style are now doomed never to sell, or at least sell at full price. Opting to avoid the public humiliation of a mass-market markdown, such brands hold sales in secret, discreetly liquidating their upscale merchandise without damaging their PLU cachet. These events are positioned as a thank-you to existing customers rather than a desperate attempt to clear the warehouse shelves. "I suppose it makes me feel like it's a loyalty thing. Any way to say thank you, we appreciate you," Mollie Fitzgerald admits, glowing about the 45 percent off she nabbed during a recent Vivier blowout. "You have the feeling you're being rewarded—the store is open to the public during those days, but you're getting the first dibs. It's just like elite frequent flyers are upgraded to first class all the time."

The luxury world has even developed its own euphemism for that approach, of putting shoppers at the center of the sale: *clienteling*. Such glad-handed flattery is intended to prize banknotes from the notable, whether by remembering their birthdays or offering them VIP-only bargains. Many other brands have adopted a similar sale-on-the-down-low strategy to Vivier's. For most, a simultaneous and invisible sale like that is too logistically complex, but there are other ways to limit the best deals to the best customers. Ralph Lauren, for example, hosts biannual events where markdowns begin long before the traditional, flashy signage appears. Regular customers are notified that it's starting, so they can shop the inventory at a secret discount of up to 40 percent before the markdown becomes public—and the hoi polloi arrive to pick the inventory clean. Unlike chez Vivier, though, if an uninvited shopper wanders off the street and buys something, the sale still applies. The drop-in shopper doesn't know he'll get a discount, and will be surprised at the register to receive 40 percent off an item that he was already prepped to buy at full price. This makes the sale gratifyingly insiderish for regulars, and a pleasant bonus for walk-ins. After that forty-eight-hour or so window, the shop launches a conventional, heavily promoted sale.

Ralph Lauren doesn't stop there. In a touch that might be dubbed *clienteleing-plus*, VIPs receive a card for an extra 15 percent discount. Those prices are 55 percent less than standard retail, or more than half off, before there's even a nod to the sale to the casual passerby. Such cherry-picking is known as presale or pre-shop, and has become commonplace.

Presale started in department stores, long before luxury became a mass-market product. It was used as a practical tactic for certain lines:

Space-hogging commodity items like bedding or kitchenware could be pre-sold as a markdown to avoid taking up too much space on the floor during a sale's busy first few days. Inevitably, of course, the lure of financial front-ending was too great. As luxury clothes and accessories took up more and more selling space, presale spread to that section. Once department stores were offering it on brand names, the marquees' own boutiques quickly adopted the same tactic.

Now personalized pre-shopping has become standard—at least for lucrative loyal customers. "Of course we did private sales," confesses a former personal shopper at Saks Fifth Avenue, who worked at the store's New York flagship for seven years but would speak only anonymously. He would call his regulars, who could shop in secret for the seven days before the sale began, and purchases would be set aside and rung through as soon as the signs went up. Insiders admit that Gucci offers a similar, unstated service, as does Hermès. An ordinary shopper can join this elite quite simply: Target a staffer at any given store, chat with them, and visit regularly. Buy their affection with a couple of pieces at full price (sales commission is their *raison d'être*) and exchange business cards. A phone call or e-mail invite should follow by the end of that season—and if it doesn't, it's time to try another sales assistant.

If a big spender doesn't nab a must-have item before the official sale, it's unlikely that it will linger long enough to be marked down, at least in department stores like Bergdorf Goodman. One former floorwalker confides that employees snap up the best pieces before customers can even see them. "They hide them—they're not allowed, of course, and it could get them fired. The security room is like the FBI, hundreds and hundreds of cameras." He pauses, then continues, "But the people policing this are doing the same things."*

Some stores go even further. They don't use discounts as a discreet tactic at season's end, but rather as a shadowy strategy to keep the right people shopping there year-round. Clothing boutique Intermix, which resembles the inside of Kate Moss's closet, full of girly must-haves from

---

* Such restrictions aside, Bergdorf treats its staff especially well, deeding a courtesy lifetime discount to staffers who log at least a decade's service at the store.

the likes of Rag & Bone, Vanessa Bruno, and Thakoon, quietly sends a 15 percent discount card to its one thousand most free-spending regulars, offering them a year-round thank-you (and, of course, motivating them to spend even more).*

One freelance personal shopper reports that both Barneys and Bergdorf Goodman offer a professional courtesy discount of 10 percent—a margin she can choose to pass on to clients, or simply pocket the difference. And Bloomingdale's has a bargain program, too. It's restricted to its four flagship cities: Chicago, Miami, San Francisco, and its two stores in New York City. Any visitor browsing racks in those stores can receive an instant 10 percent off at the register. The definition of such a visitor—out of the country, state, town, maybe just someone who walked farther than normal from the parking space—rests entirely on the sales assistant's mood.

Some discounts aren't codified but casual, and almost always involve cash. One fashionisto reported browsing a $5,000 coat at the Calvin Klein store in New York and lowballed an offer of half price in greenbacks. He walked out minutes later with the coat, having carved out his own 50 percent discount. Another wrangled a spontaneous deal at Prada in Venice, Italy. Drawn to a pair of classic loafers, he hemmed and hawed over the impulse purchase. "I asked the sales assistant if there was a cash discount. I mean, I was joking," he recalls. He was stunned when the girl nodded instantly. "She said, 'Oh yes, I could do twenty percent.'"

Whether clienteling with a chance for pre-shopping, mailing a discount card to cherry-picked VIPs, or letting cashed-up customers name their own price, it's a stunning shift in the way upscale goods are marked down. Both furtive and lucrative, these deals mean that two shoppers simultaneously browsing the racks in a luxury boutique or a department store might pay dramatically different prices for the exact same item. Sneaking into this secretive world to find that It Bag for half price or less is much easier than it might sound—as long as you know the right people. They are known by just their first names, Shelly and Renée, and

---

* Or at least it did until it was swallowed whole by Gap Inc. in 2012, with plans to roll out the brand worldwide. Expect elite programs like this to morph into more conventional markdown programs.

they are the elusive czarinas of fashion's favorite way to slum it: the sample sale.

Fashion's Cut-Price "Fight Club"

Meeting Shelly and Renée in person, the need for discretion was obvious from the outset. They prefer to meet away from their office, in a coffee shop opposite Bergdorf Goodman—their choice, a cheeky thumb to the department store with which they share so many customers.

Despite their success, these women are easily overlooked, almost unassuming. Shelly Antebi is dark haired, with a broad Jersey twang and a warm familiarity; Renée Salem, her business partner, is carefully coiffed, more watchful, and armed with a flirty wit. They're like a glamorous pair of Roald Dahl aunts. Exhausted shoppers around them, laden down with brand name bags, fill the tables nearby. If those women knew what these two could do—provide the same items at 60 percent off—they'd mob them for autographs (and access to their next sale). Yet the duo prefers to remain in the background for those in the know. Shelly and Renée Productions masterminds Manhattan's most exclusive cut-price events; ultra-luxe brand designers turn to them whenever they want to discreetly and efficiently offload excess at a sample sale. In 2012, Shelly and Renée had never been busier.

Sample sales were a staple of New York's Garment District for decades. As mass-market brands began to launch splashy outlets at Reading and beyond, sample sales were low-key events where Seventh Avenue designers would offload leftover clothes for a pittance. Long a garmento secret, the sales were held in the grubby offices near the swanky showrooms, mostly on weekends when nine-to-fivers wouldn't interrupt or chance on the stash. These ad hoc shindigs were discreet ways to liquidate samples, produced for review or wholesale but never put into production; leftovers of a previous season's styles, known as deadstock, were often included, too. By the 1990s, though, the luxury fashion business had grown enough that showroom staffers no longer had the time or inclination to stage such events. They needed someone trustworthy and efficient to organize and execute them, while ensuring that they were filled with the right kind of customer. Enter Shelly and Renée.

Antebi started out as a consignment dealer, helping wealthy women sell unwanted clothes, while Salem worked as a personal shopper. Their shared clientele brought them together when a friend asked the pair to team up to stage a sale of some stock remnants at the Marc Jacobs showroom. That was fifteen years ago, and they've helmed hundreds of sample sales since then. Their competitive advantage lies in bringing clienteling to the cut-price world. They make even bargain-hunting shoppers feel cherished and valued, the center of the experience. "The key to our success is that we're hands on. We know our clients and we work the floor— we're there, we're part of the sale," says Renée. "I'm not going to say we know 100 percent of the clientele," Shelly adds, "but we could have a thousand people and we'll know one hundred fifty of them very intimately."

Despite that ultra-exclusive approach, there's no snobbery to their sales—little wonder, given the hammy flair that slips easily out of Renée. During a sluggish La Perla-Frette combination sale, she wrapped a towel around her hair, slipped into a bathrobe, and began parading through the aisles. She winkingly claimed to be a woman whose humdrum-housewife life was transformed by napping on luxury sheets and wearing a few scraps of fancy lingerie. Then she made announcements to the room: "We have a disclosure. Please, ladies and gentlemen, as you buy your Frette sheets, choose your partner carefully. They'll never want to leave." Or she'd grab a rack of slow-moving robes and walk around. "This is the mother-in-law gift robe, ladies," she'd say. Or, "Okay, this is. 'I'm not in the mood tonight.'" At another midsummer sale, there was a four-hour wait to enter, and the building's owners had forgotten to turn on the air-conditioning. "But once people get in the room, they don't care how hot it is, or how long the wait was," Renée says. New York women will endure almost anything for a luxury bargain.

The pair is as picky about its clients as it is about its shoppers. All brands must agree to mark down prices at least 60 percent off retail and stage the sale in whatever venue Shelly and Renée decree is right; a downtown label should be close to its target clientele, rather than surrounded by starchy matrons, for instance. They won't sell jeans or swimwear (too low end and too much work respectively). As for customers, the rules are simple: no shopping bags, no coats, no dressing rooms. "We know exactly when they've had their breasts done, too," Shelly says, laughing. "Because they are oh-so-happy to strip down and walk around the room nude."

While S&R Productions may be the most insiderish option for brands keen to quietly cash out on cut-price merch, it's no longer the only one. Soiffer Haskin is a similar setup. It has a more discreet showroom in the Garment District with a VIP invitation list of 85,000 names that brands salivate to reach. Hiring Soiffer Haskin is recognized as a turnkey option, famed for its flawless execution and strict rules (no children under twelve, thank you very much). Another rival venture is Misorena, run by reformed fashion PR man Yochai Azani. It rarely advertises to consumers but is an all-access operation, with a permanent sample sale venue at street level. His 6,500-square-foot store in Manhattan's Flatiron district is where brands like DVF host their sales. Open year-round, it offers a rotating stock of off-price upscale goodies, sometimes at up to 90 percent discount.

The most exclusive operation is undeniably the one run by socialites Kim Kassel and Lizzie Tisch. The pair created Shop Secret to act like a sample sale fight club, having corralled friends and other flashbulb-prone red carpeters onto a tight-lipped list where the only rule for participation is promising not to talk about the sale. One member, Marjorie Gubelman, was brave or foolish enough to break rank. "Shop Secret is like the Black Card of sample sales. You have to be on the list and you don't know when they are happening . . . or who the next designer will be. It is all very mysterious. Then an e-mail appears in your inbox and the excitement begins," gushed Gubelman in an interview. "Sometimes you go into the actual store and shop and when you pay, your name is on a list for a discount. And other times, the sale is at an offsite venue. Needless to say, you shop from current collections at a great discount for one day only." When Gubelman's recommendation went viral, Kassel went ballistic. Poor Marjorie was only doing what everyone else would do these days: sharing an irresistible discount with her friends.

Invitations to such discreet discount shindigs are a thank-you to season-long supporters, a prudish and prudent way to avoid promiscuously discounting in department stores. A sample sale offers a crucial chance for clienteling, too, which is why a few brands, like entrance-making-gown guru Carmen Marc Valvo, have resisted subcontracting, even to the likes of S&R. His gowns are still sold from the showroom, many of them one-offs sewn for runway shows but never mass produced. What Carmen Marc Valvo and S&R Productions have in common, though, is the price: at least 40 percent off retail. The guest list for his VIP shopping event is elite but eclectic; think brides-to-be and lip-synching drag queens, tussling over the same showstoppers. The only hiccup is the designer himself. "We have to do the sale when Carmen is out of town," says the label's Frank Pulice, "or he has a habit of coming through and saying 'This is my baby,' and we can't sell anything."

Hermès today might coyly suggest it never discounts—as famous fan Kanye West raps in "Otis," rapt, "Couture level flow, it's never going on sale." Yet the brand is far more flexible about price than it might suggest.* In the early 2000s, the onetime saddle-maker rented a warehouse space in Tribeca for a one-week sale with 50- to 60-percent discounts on almost its entire line: home wares, scarves, ready to wear, shoes, and towels for $50 (no Birkins, of course—but we'll come to the sidestepping ways to source them soon). A decade later, Hermès still stages stock sales, with a smaller selection, lower discounts (around 30 percent), and a limit on how many scarves a single person might purchase. However the product may vary, though, there's been one constant since that blowout bargain warehouse: Martha Stewart. She is one of the boutique's top full-price customers who nevertheless won't miss a sample sale. Stewart usually sends a staffer to stand in line in her stead until he or she is close to the front, at which point Martha will glide into place and go straight for the bargains.

What happens to the merchandise that won't sell even at a sample sale? Such pieces are usually dubbed, somewhat squeamishly, as *editorial*—outré, impractical, and downright unflattering. Their final destination

---

* One longtime visitor to St. Barts was staggered when the boutique there told her that she could now receive a 10-percent discount on its goods after buying property on the island. Franchised Hermès stores, such as the one at the King of Prussia Mall, will often be a little keener to shift sluggish merch however they can.

proves a murky story, as shadowy and secretive as the sales themselves. Sitting on retail's death row, this stock might be sold to the fashion world's bottom feeders known as jobbers.* According to industry insiders, jobbers typically pay 5 to 10 cents on the dollar to luxury brands for those pieces that sample sale mavens disdain. The jobbers will also sign contracts that restrict where and how they can be sold. In the past, the merchandise was often shipped overseas, perhaps to sub-Saharan Africa in bales.† Otherwise, the haul might be split up between vintage shops. Increasingly, what has replaced these two options is for the jobber to host a sample sale of his own with even deeper discounts off retail (hardly an outcome to thrill many upscale labels). These are the strange, multi-brand stores with no names that increasingly pop up, temporarily plastered with gaudy "80% OFF" stickers and a selection of clothes that is worth little more.

The one option that most labels resist, though, is donation. They want to avoid that awkward moment when a panhandler compliments a passerby on his jacket—only to discover that it's identical to the one he or she is wearing (yes, even senior executives at such brands roll their eyes knowingly, admitting it's a pathetic excuse). The only solution to avoid it, they reason, is to destroy such precious yet unwanted merch. One world-famous brand initially subcontracted the task to outsiders—at least until it noticed that the burly men were arriving to collect the bales clad in the very same items that they'd been hired to destroy. Now the label calls in document specialist Shred-it, and the bags, shoes, and whatever else are pulverized without ever leaving the warehouse. Some brands go even further. "For years, I heard Chanel burned their clothing by taking it out to sea," says raspy veteran Alysa Lazar. "As a way of reclaiming the duty they paid bringing the clothing in."

If anyone would know the truth behind that rumor, it's Lazar. Sample sales, once hush-hush events where firms could discreetly offload their

---

* *Real Housewife* Ramona Singer amassed her fortune this way, though she rarely manages to reference it on the show in between glugs of Pinot Grigio. The largest and best known jobbing op is Schottensteins, which has stakes in Value City, American Eagle, and DSW.
† The arrival of secondhand clothes from the developed world is such a familiar sight there that the word in a local African dialect for *secondhand* is *salaula*, which literally means "to select from a pile in the manner of rummaging."

overstock (whatever was left would be debranded and either sold or destroyed), are now part of pop culture, thanks to Lazar and her ilk. It was she who first broke the industry's code of silence, pioneering the outing of these down-low discounts to the public at large. For thirty years, the ex-banker has specialized in a niche form of fashion espionage.

Headlines and Hemlines

Alysa Lazar was out in the Hamptons one day, sitting on a friend's deck, when she first wondered if she could earn a living out of sample sales in some way. Since that friend was erstwhile *Vogue* editor and future designer Vera Wang, Lazar certainly had the right connections. She was a lifelong clotheshorse herself, having spent many childhood Saturdays (the Garment District's day of rest) driving into Manhattan from Long Island with her family to attend the earliest ad hoc sales. Racks of beautiful clothing at bargain prices were a little girl's dream dress-up box, after all. As an adult, she'd accumulated influential fashion friends like Wang who tipped her off to these exclusive uptown markdowns. What did the women do, she wondered, who didn't have Vera on speed dial?

That was in 1985, and Lazar had just turned thirty; a former Citibank VP and recent divorcée, she had a yen to make over her life as much as her look. Lazar was convinced there were enough other women in New York who'd pay up front for the chance to save money. Back then, of course, sample sales were the *Brigadoon* of fashion, shimmering fleetingly into view and disappearing before word could spread. A regular roundup of these events, she reasoned, would be priceless. Funding the business with $10,000 of her own savings, Lazar compiled a small pamphlet of sample sales and named it the S&B Report (for sales and bargains). The publication of her pamphlet was the first time someone dared publicize such insiderish events to ordinary shoppers, and it changed the industry forever.

Distribution relied on what she calls the "old Chinese menu method"—slipping brochures under acquaintances' mats by sweet-talking the doormen. Lazar's instincts around that first mailing, limited to just two thousand copies, proved astute. The world outside New York's Garment District was captivated by these secretive luxury Shangri-lows. Lazar's success was such that she was hired as the onscreen sales guru for Regis and Kathie Lee within four years of starting her report. At that time, her annual turnover was $400,000 and S&B needed a full-time staff of seven. That was a heady time, an era when a Ralph Lauren warehouse sale in New Jersey would involve garbage bags in place of shopping baskets and the chance to bulk buy $25 cashmere jackets.

Lazar soon moved from reporting on sales to staging them herself, a friendly rival to Shelly & Renée. Her Giorgio Armani bash brought in over $1 million in sales in two or three days in the early 1990s. She similarly sold 100,000 Stella McCartney x LeSportsac bags in one week. Lazar's signature move was to staff her events with a phalanx of off duty New York police, a smart precaution given that sales were cash-only.

Lazar still compiles her own list, but others have followed and expanded on her template of spilling sample sale secrets to the world. Foremost among them today is Izzy Grinspan, who has taken news of the deals from back office to front row. Tiny and birdlike, with her long hair, vintage clothes, and giant glasses, she resembles a hipster librarian and bubbles with a breathless enthusiasm. As editor of shopping blog Racked.com, she's one of the most powerful women in fashion—at least for New Yorkers. Grinspan spends much of her time compiling and sharing the sample sales (which, of course, allows the more brazen to gatecrash, as she freely admits). She says such reports are the site's biggest page-view boosters: Sample sale posts are always heavily trafficked, up to 40 percent higher than a standard blog entry about a hot new trend or a store opening, for example. Many fashion brands have issued a virtual, viral omertà to stop anyone from tipping her off about top-tier sales.

Grinspan has learned to be resourceful in response to such secrecy. For one, she obsessively monitors fashion editors' Twitter accounts during the sample sale season, usually May and mid-October to mid-November. Though few will be foolish enough to boast of #samplesale purchases, most can't resist bragging about bargain buys with photos. As soon as

Grinspan spots a cluster of three or four editors tweeting about the same brands that way, her bargain antennae start twitching.* She feels there's disingenuousness to such rag trade cloak-and-daggery, especially when brands claim that the event is a hush-hush operation but then buy banner ads on her site. "My theory is that there's a certain cachet to having a sample sale now, or calling it that at least," she notes. "It brings people in because it feels a little insidery and secret."

A few sales truly remain half price Holy Grails. Carrie Bradshaw's beloved Manolo Blahnik, for one, is still truly exclusive. It's always held at the Warwick Hotel on West Fifty-fourth Street and is presided over by *Voguette* André Leon Talley, who pronounces opinions—solicited or otherwise—to the women scrambling at his feet to find a pair. "It's tables in all sizes, lots of Russians and a big bunch of black drag queens," says one veteran. Likewise, crowds jostle to sneak into Christian Louboutin's sale, which has replaced 1990s favorite Prada as the top-tier bash.† That luxury cobbler's sale is run like a movie premiere party, with an RSVP list and clipboard-toting guards at the entrance. The brand tries to keep it secret, but it's become so mainstream a marquee that ordinary New Yorkers' interest is piqued. "Last time, they actually invited me—but the deal was that if I RSVP'd, I wasn't allowed to write about it," the ever reader-loyal Grinspan said, who declined.

Even at sample sales, boldfacers and loyal customers are given preferential treatment. Celebrities, fashion editors, and the occasional top shopper will usually be invited twenty-four hours earlier than everyone else so they can snap up the best bargains. Louboutin's sale officially starts on Wednesday, but high-ranking fashion editors are invited to

---

* The simplest way to Braille for unlisted sales is to create a dummy Twitter account following only the fashion world's thin-waisted and -skinned. When a designer's name starts trending, in hashtags or photos, it's a tip-off that someone, somewhere, is holding a secret sale.
† Prada was the first to treat the operation more like a nightclub than a sale, complete with velvet ropes and guest list; it was what one veteran wittily dubs "social media before social media." Weeks beforehand, the chatterati would be grilling one another for tips on where and when it was held; once the sale was over, those fortunate enough to have finagled entry would wear head-to-toe Prada with pride, a tip-off to their social shopping status. No wonder bargain hunters staged infuriated sit-ins when the sale coincided with New York's blackout in 2004, stymieing any chance of their checking out with a bargain haul.

peruse the racks a day early. "And on Monday, Blake Lively is always spotted walking out of the building with millions of shopping bags." Grinspan sums up the new rules succinctly: "Before the sample sale is the VIP sample sale and before that, the secret VIP sample sale." In other words, by the time a regular New Yorker can shop, stock on the racks is thinner than a supermodel at the start of Fashion Week.

One savvy trick, Grinspan suggests, is just to turn up early. Many brands start their public sales in the afternoon or evening to catch the after-work rush, downtown darling Alexander Wang among them. Editors will have been invited that same morning for a shopping preview, so an enthusiastic bargain hunter who turns up an hour early will likely not only be allowed to shop but do so in peace before the frenzied crowds start arguing over the final size 0 dress. No wonder fashmag staffers fret when they don't receive a preview invitation to a must-shop sale; they know it's likely a punishment for having failed to feature a given brand with enough prominence over the previous season.

Such is the frenzy around sample sales that when Ferragamo held one recently in New Jersey, it was open for only an hour or so before a brawl broke out and the police shuttered the event. The risk of fisticuffs explains the strategy employed recently by French candlemaker Diptyque to announce its upcoming sale; its staff personally telephoned valued customers, one by one, with an invitation and the address (since then, it's run heavily promoted, more mass-market sales). An additional benefit to this approach was that no details were e-mailed that could be forwarded to Grinspan and her fellow bloggers.

In the past, slashing the price of a $500 pair of shoes on Madison Avenue was a thank-you to loyal customers, a way to offer them an off-price treat at season's end. Private sales happened in plain sight. The rise of breathless blogs and newsletters like Racked.com, however, which chronicle every imminent markdown, has birthed a new category of shopper. All it takes to have this season's It bag is a laptop, patience, and sharp elbows. Indeed, one dot-com company has made mass-marketing across America of these once-secret sales in New York its entire business strategy. That's turning out to have been a brilliant, but risky, idea.

Setting a Good E-Sample?

Two ubiquitous divas duel over the loudspeakers, rival summer anthems hogging airtime: the Euro disco of Nicki Minaj's chirpy, rappy "Starships" segues into a blast of Carly Rae Jepsen's "Call Me Maybe." It's a warm Friday night in Manhattan's Chelsea, and the room is heaving with people. Black-clad bartenders dole out drinks frantically in one corner, while men modishly dressed like a cross between Pee-wee Herman and JFK—rolled up trouser legs, plaid bow ties, crisp pressed shirts—mill around. It could be happy hour at one of the area's glut of gay bars but for the women marauding through a table piled high with purses and dozens of racks of clothes. This is a night out, but it isn't a bar: It's the Gilt Groupe sample sale. The room looks like the inside of Anna Wintour's mind, rack after rack of clothes haphazardly organized from the likes of Nanette Lepore, Acne, and Helmut Lang. Flouncy gowns by Marchesa and Reem Acra are slung on the end of each row, tags marked $499 dangling languidly.

The men's section is less frenzied—most of it seems to be Paul Smith, anyway—but a pair of Ferragamo brogues studded with thousands of Swarovski crystals sits like a twinkling trophy on one table. By 10:45 p.m., the women's fitting room is full, and a line of more than thirty patient shoppers waits for the semiprivate chance to try on a few finds. "I'm so dumb. I should just try it on in the bathroom," one woman carps. The brave strip down in public, like 26-year-old fashion designer Alex Robinson. Lean and freckle-faced, she's hauling on a J. Mendel lemon chiffon ballgown over her sneakers. "I bought a wedding dress last year. It was two hundred dollars and it fit like a glove. I tried it on as a joke but it fit so perfectly I said, I gotta get this." Sadly, she's unlikely to find a groom among the assembled fashionistos.

Since 2007, Gilt Groupe has transformed the idea of sample sales in ways that even Alysa Lazar might not have imagined. Gilt was built on a simple calculation: Traditional sample sales could reach only a handful of Americans, mostly one percenters, who either lived in or could afford to fly to New York City. But Lazar and co had helpfully prepped the 99 percent of the population outside New York about sample sales, sparking a latent envy in them about such access. So Gilt hitched itself to the trend and decided to issue some invitations.

Gilt Groupe* was one of the first flash sale websites, where for a limited window—in this case, a 36-hour period starting at twelve noon Eastern time—exclusive merchandise would be available at a 60 percent discount on its website. (That's not a new idea, of course, just a dot-commed riff on Earl Bartell's Blue Light Special.) To amp up the cachet, only members could browse those sales, though rooting out an invitation was usually easy enough with a little judicious Googling. Whatever wasn't sold would be stockpiled and off-loaded at events around the country like the one in Chelsea. From Miami to Chicago, this was another way of making luxury accessible to all.

The hoary story of Gilt's founding has been much repeated. Two hot, smart BFF blondes were hanging out in their Harvard dorm room when a eureka moment struck and turned them into multimillionaires. In fact, Alexis Maybank and Alexandra Wilkis Wilson ended up running Gilt only thanks to a fashion fairy godfather. The pair knew each other peripherally as Harvard undergrads but truly bonded during their stint at Harvard Business School. After getting their MBAs, both ended up in dissatisfying jobs. Maybank worked to help launch eBay motors but then left for a failed startup, while the luxury-mad Wilkis Wilson joined LVMH, the luxury conglomerate that owns Louis Vuitton, Moët Hennessy, and a slew of other brands, only to find herself stepping in as an interim store manager uptown.

Internet multimillionaire Kevin Ryan rescued them both from their respective drudgeries. Cleft-chinned and bespectacled, Ryan was best known as the CEO of Doubleclick, an online ad company, when it was sold for $1 billion in 2005. Wallowing in his fortune and wondering what to do next, Ryan was walking around Manhattan one day when he saw a long line of women patiently waiting for access to a Marc Jacobs sample sale. "All I could think was, if there are two hundred people who are willing to stand in this line, that means in the United States there are

* The *e* was added to convey a French *je ne sais quoi* but rather has a whiff of *eau de poseur*.

probably hundreds of thousands," he explained in one interview. "But they don't live in New York, they're busy right now, they just can't do that. And I can bring this sample sale to them."

Indeed, once he started researching, Ryan found that the business model had already been tested in his wife's home country, France, where a company called Vente Privée (Private Sale) helped European labels discreetly liquidate overstock. His original plan was to call the American operation FirstLook; he invited Alexis, an Internet veteran, for a meeting to discuss the new venture. She lacked a background in fashion, so she roped in her pal Alexandra, whom she knew best understood that market. Ryan cannily installed the two as the day-to-day managers and, crucially, figureheads of the operation. Cool and elegant, the icy blondes were the ideals to which the Gilt Groupe shoppers could aspire.

Their company was an instant success. In part it was due to its strategy of homing in on smaller designers like Zac Posen and Alvin Valley, offering to stage a cheaper, digital alternative to their usual brick-and-mortar sample sales. Fashion labels were also lured to work with the site since it offered some crucial pluses over a conventional channel: Data capture helped designers learn more about their actual customers, details which department stores had been loath to pass on and which warehouse sample sales also couldn't offer. Gilt's password-protected member mechanic also stopped search engines from scraping the site for information and posting high-end designers' low prices in public.

For shoppers its lure was immediate: the chance to snap up crave-worthy clothes, at 60 percent off, without leaving your desk (and even on your employer's clock, given the timing of those sales' start) was invigorating. The membership mechanic was also a flattering blandishment, in keeping with the tone of shopping 3.0. Gilt's promos became so frenzied that one woman clicked on an item one thousand times hoping that it might drop out of another shopper's basket because of time limitations.

After conquering fashion, Gilt Groupe swiftly branched out into other discount offers to include vacations (Jetsetter.com), experiences (Gilt City), furniture (Gilt Home), food (Gilt Taste), and even a VIP tier (Gilt Noir, where big spenders are clienteled with private dinners). The firm made Alexis Maybank and Alexandra Wilkis Wilson—or A&A, as they became known—pinups for Internet moguldom. The pair was so crucial to the company's success that packers at the warehouse were tasked with dropping a card with gold cursive lettering into each beautifully wrapped box, which said, "Thank you for your purchase. Alexis + Alexandra, the founders."

At the time of writing, the firm is private so statistics are hard to verify, but by its own account, around 200,000 of its 5 million members now log on every day to browse one of the 150 or so sales held weekly across its various categories. Gilt is circling an IPO, having slimmed down its workforce to reduce overhead and divested itself of peripheral units like passport-required Jetsetter.com. But there are concrete reasons most observers are doubtful about the success of an initial public offering for this onetime tech darling.

The problem is that the Gilt story is more one of good timing than uniqueness. Like fellow discount wunderkind Groupon, the company's model can easily be replicated and, indeed, has been—see RueLaLa.com or Ideeli.com, both similar virtual sample sales. Another fortunate hiccup was the fact that September, the most important month for retailers to sell goods at full price, was torpedoed twice in the same decade as Gilt's founding. The first time, the tragic events of September 11, 2001, put few Americans in the mood to shop. It created a frenzied markdown season. Incredibly, Saks, having lost five selling days shuttering its Manhattan store, which represents 25 percent of the chain's business, started slashing prices by 80 percent in response to that shutdown and 9/11's consequent shopping torpor. The 9/11 sales set a new precedent that was repeated a second time in the same decade, in September—after the Wall Street meltdown of 2008. Luxury brands and retailers were again caught with vast inventories that, almost overnight, stopped selling.

Hobbled once more and wincing to remember the red ink that flowed the first time, high-end vendors had an alternative. Rather than slashing prices in stores, as they had in 2001, big-name brands could discreetly offload that unwanted product via Gilt. Gilt had a yearlong heyday, as the twelve months following the collapse of Lehmann Brothers was a nuclear winter for luxury: Bain Capital estimated that just 25 percent of high-end goods sold at full price during this period. Much of the rest was probably liquidated through Gilt Groupe, creating a boon time for A&A and overlord Kevin Ryan.

Yet just three years after its founding, fresh shifts in retail began to threaten Gilt Groupe's long-term prospects. The spigot of supply was slowly turning off. Greedily eyeballing the revenues of the operation, full-price retailers moved into off-price online. It's entirely illegal for a store to demand that one of its suppliers not sell to another customer. But what if the buyer at, for example, Neiman Marcus were to tell a struggling label something like: *We value our partnership so much and we love selling your clothes full price. I know we're a crucial account for you. It would make us so sad to feel that affection wasn't reciprocated—say, by off-loading whatever excess you have at an online sample sale through Gilt.* Indeed, Neiman has already launched its own Gilt-like site, Lastcall.com, where such merchandise can be discreetly liquidated. Rival HauteLook.com was smart to accept a $180 million buyout offer from Nordstrom, which swallowed the startup as an online counterpart to its thriving Rack chain.

There may be an excess of supply, but it's being rerouted from the stand-alone online discounters to the half-price subsidiaries of mainstream stores. "It's not that hard to sell things when you put them at fifty or seventy percent off. The challenge is to get merchandise at this sale level," warns Sucharita Mulpuru, a Forrester analyst who follows Gilt Groupe closely. She sees Gilt as already tarnished. "To me, there is a big possibility that there is a house of cards here." Gilt is vulnerable because it doesn't have a full-price sibling company; its attempt to create a men's channel where every item is offered at full price, the dapper and urbane Park & Bond, sputtered for just over twelve months before finally being euthanized in the fall of 2012.

Much like the brick-and-mortar outlets we visited earlier and that Gilt set out to displace, it has turned to a grubby secret: specially made product. In 2010 it was estimated that 35 to 40 percent of its women's stock was supplied this way. As at an outlet, such stock isn't just lower priced but lower quality. The savvy luxury shopper whom Gilt has cultivated is unlikely to be satisfied.* The flash seller has also been slap-dash about pricing. In one instance, Aden and Anais muslin blankets in the baby section usually priced at $49.95 were offered for the "Special Gilt Price" of $49.95. Gilt has been fortunate that such snafus haven't yet earned a volley of Internet brickbats.

It didn't help that Gilt was valued at a staggering $1 billion during a funding round in spring 2011. It's had to scramble to expand its business to justify that level of projected revenue. While its revenue that same year hit $500 million, a 90 percent leap from 2010, Gilt still bleeds money. Estimates put yearly losses around $45 million. Mulpuru worries, too, that Gilt's premise for the brands it sells is wobbly. The company claims brands can reach younger customers on the web, and lure them in with a discount on their first piece. The theory, it explains, is that a customer will then trade up to shopping at full price next season. It's the same theory that Harry Gordon Selfridge used to justify the first bargain base-ment a century earlier. However, as we've seen, dopamine in the brain has the power to simultaneously code a shopper's habits as well as make her favor deals. It's therefore likely that Mulpuru's concerns are well founded. "It's such a flawed analysis," she told me. "All you know about that person is that they're cheap."

Still, none of this seems to bother the crowds at Gilt's offline sample sale in Chelsea. The tags at the sale, interestingly, do not show Gilt's pre-vious markdown price, just the original one, driving the reference point higher. The meta moment that its Chelsea event is a flash sale of a flash sale is less bizarre than how willingly the four hundred shoppers here ponied up a $20 entry fee for the privilege of shopping. Most seem thrilled, though, scrambling to try on precious clothing as midnight closes in. The line to pay is growing, with at least eighty people waiting patiently. One woman is buying so many shoes that she has to kick the boxes along in front of her because she can't carry them all. Another is haggling over a beaded ballgown, hemming and hawing, bobbing in and out from the street until she finally haggles the price low enough. Norma Cordero, an

---

* Frankly, it's better to sign up for a service like ShopItToMe, which scrapes the web for mark-downs on merch at full-price stores and avoids such gimmickry entirely.

HIV counselor with hair as bouncy as her personality, leaves the pop-up beaming; she has two shopping bags full of cut-price shoes. "You find stuff you don't see on other people. And it's not embarrassing to say you got it on Gilt. You're getting a good price, not dirt cheap." Advertising exec Corinne Srisilpanand agrees. Petite and sharply dressed in expensive white pants and a blazer, she's come for picture frames and is thrilled when she finds exactly the right pieces. "Gilt is associated with luxury and you know you're going to get good quality at a very low price," she says. "As women, you're the hunter of the bargains, and it's always good not to pay retail. I shop Gilt every day."

Sadly for Corinne, Gilt Groupe's closeout sales happen only sporadically. There is one place, though, where luxury leftovers have long been available to the ordinary shoppers whenever they wished: the outlet mall. When VF Corp launched the first one in Reading in the 1970s, outlet malls were an exception in a seamy business, free of any sense of coy furtiveness. They were egalitarian places, where ordinary Americans could nab a bargain slice of Seventh Avenue from a clutch of top brands. Of course, that was before specially produced merchandise started seeping onto shelves, diluting the quality but upping the firms' profits. Such discreet salting of stock is now widespread, but that isn't the only dirty little secret that makes outlet malls so lucrative today.

"Everyone Needs an Outlet"

It's the Friday before Labor Day, and by 10 a.m., it's already almost impossible to find a parking space at Woodbury Common Premium Outlets, about an hour north of Manhattan. Tight-faced staffers prowl around the lot, deftly jigsawing cars into place, some doubtlessly mindful of Midnight Madness on Thanksgiving night in 2007, when cars were backed up for ten miles on the New York State Thruway. Every vehicle belongs to a bargain hunter, lured here like a moth to a cut-price flame. Among the thousands of off-price retail meccas in America, this is the ultimate destination, where almost every Madison Avenue brand has a sale outlet year-round.

Woodbury Common opened in 1985 and has expanded twice since then. Less than thirty years later, it has 850,000 square feet of retail space spread among more than two hundred discount shops; the low-rise white buildings resemble a Disneyfied New England town. At this open-air mall, cheery, manicured flower beds rim the walkways. On one avenue there's a row with Dior, Chloé, and YSL, while on another there's Balenciaga, Oscar de la Renta, and DVF. There are already stanchions staking out lines for the most popular stores: A dozen or so men and women wait patiently at Prada and Burberry, while the Coach crowd is at least fifty deep and building fast. Almost everyone carries a few bags, and several people tote Rollaboard suitcases. The shopping center is popular among tourists; Woodbury estimates between 40 to 50 percent of its income is from Japanese visitors alone. Certainly, though, there's also an ample number of Manhattanites, grimly determined to make the most of a day-long discount orgy.

There's a clear distinction between the locals and the visitors. While the former barrel through the crowds with purpose, checking off a mental map of their favored stores, the latter clutch crumpled pieces of white paper, torn from pads at every cash register, a map-cum-onslaught of bargain stores. Some shops are bashful about their purpose, as if the very word *outlet* would offend—it's Salvatore Ferragamo Company Store, thank you very much—while others celebrate it (with trademark insouciance, the Kenneth Cole bags proclaim: "Everyone needs an outlet"). Crabtree and Evelyn, the froufrou beauty brand, is festooned with sale signs. "All gift sets are buy two, get one free—and they're already fifty percent off, too," says one staffer, an older lady with a warm smile. Rock-starrish menswear brand John Varvatos has its own outlet—sorry, Company Store—tucked away in a corner, its only off-price venue in the world. Walking in, a bright-eyed sales clerk, another middle-aged lady with a curly perm and a wicked grin, chirps a greeting. "Hello, you know we have an extra twenty percent off? It's our Labor Day sale," she says, then turns to a pile of shirts on a table nearby, jabbing the clothes accusingly. "You know, these polos are actually in the regular store *right now!*"

Though the shoppers are frenzied and the discounts seemingly irresistible, don't be fooled. High-end brands at Woodbury Common

Premium Outlets use several clever tricks that undercut the true value of these bargains. Bottega Veneta, the logoless marque known for its woven leathers or *intrecciato*, offers that signature style at its outlet but only in bright colors like egg yolk yellow, rather than the more crave-worthy (and perennial) black or brown. Its sister company, Gucci, is similarly sly. Merchandise at the outlet may be authentic but it's unlikely to be last season's, and it certainly won't be a style that anyone lusted after on the runway. That purple sequined flapper dress that sits unflatteringly at mid thigh? Fifty percent off but still $7,500. Ditto the slightly too flashy leather jacket, also half price at $2,379. Some discounts are nominal—CK One underwear, officially $20 a pair, is $16, the same price as it would be at Macy's on any given Saturday. Most shoppers clutch a coupon book that they've been lured to retrieve from a kiosk at the center of the mall in exchange for a little personal data; it's filled with discount deals, offering an extra 10, 20, or even 30 percent off. The only problem is the small print caveat: The coupons can't be used on any merchandise already on sale. Of course, that excludes nearly everything in a given store.

The trickiest gimmick is that much of the merchandise sold, even here, has never been on racks anywhere else. As with up to 40 percent of Gilt Groupe's current inventory, it's produced specially for the outlet. Just look at the labels on shirts and blouses at Banana Republic or J.Crew: Where once the word *Outlet* was added at the nape of the neck, now there are just three dots discreetly beneath the standard logo, a tip-off for any sales clerk facing dishonest returns at a mall store. It's far less ego-denting than the original way of marking remaindered merchandise, with a big red X through the label that guaranteed red-facedness on every trip to the dry cleaner. Disney's $15 toddler dolls, each a chubby-cheeked riff on one of its stable of princesses, are cannily flagged "Outlet Exclusive." That's just another way of saying that they were never sold at higher prices in a standard shop. Chico's stock includes product labeled "Additions," which is its euphemism for outlet-only dresses. Then there are the department stores' outlets: Saks Off-Fifth, Barneys New York Outlet, and Neiman Marcus Last Call.

Staggeringly, insiders say that 60 to 70 percent of whatever is on view there was bought specially to be sold at off price. At Last Call, one expert believes, up to 80 percent of product is specially produced. Similarly, at Off-Fifth, a former Saks buyer explains that in many categories—shoes, handbags, and sunglasses, for example—almost the entire holding is specially bought.

Next time you're at one such outlet, just examine the labels: This is the reason that much of the clothing and accessories is own brand, rather than third party like Chanel or Hermès. It's also why a price tag at Last Call doesn't mention a discount from retail price, but says simply "Compared to" and lists an arbitrary higher amount. This is a common trick: Rather than claiming a discount, which would require that merchandise was sold at the higher price for a certain period, tags at outlet malls will use euphemisms like "Original Value" or "Retail Value" then "Today's Price."

Of course, most department stores are wily enough to realize that regulars will notice a lack of familiar branded merchandise. So they respond much like a bartender offering a free round to keep his regulars bingeing or a dealer offering the first hit gratis. To maintain its veneer of deep discounting, an outlet will sprinkle in the occasional loss leader. "They bring out residue for grand openings, and four or five times a year. I found a Chanel sequined jacket that way, for example," explains one consultant who worked closely with the firm. "It sets expectations: You can always find a good deal here." (It's also a classic trick of reference pricing.) That may be true, but for much of the year, such a deal won't be a Lagerfeld-endorsed original.

Even then, stock can vary wildly between locations, especially if you're looking for those elusive loss leaders. To see whether a department store's outlet offshoot might be better stocked than average, think logistics. The best Last Call operations will always be near a major Neiman Marcus. The Sawgrass Mills site in Fort Lauderdale is a satellite of the heavily trafficked full-price outpost in Miami's Bal Harbour, for instance, while the Austin outlet benefits from its adjacency to the corporation's retail distribution hub.

None of these sleights of hand seem to faze the hordes of shoppers at Woodbury Common. The real estate company that owns Woodbury Common, along with fifty or so other outlets nationwide, is Simon

Property Group. Frenzied bargain hunters helped the company tally revenues of $4.3 billion in 2011, 11 percent over the previous year. Since 1995, the amount of square footage available at outlet malls in America has increased from 51 million to 71 million, another sign of the more-is-more impulse that underpins the entire shift toward bargains in our culture. When *Consumer Reports* conducted an outlet investigation in 2006, the average saving was 38 percent; five years later, it had risen to 60 percent. The stratospheric rise of outlet malls, along with the explosion in sample and flash sales in the luxury sector, hasn't happened by chance. The shift from shadowy secrecy in the showrooms of New York's Seventh Avenue to multibillion-dollar businesses comes down to two people: Carrie Bradshaw and Mr. Big.

Carrie'd Away by "Big" Deals

The erstwhile hero of *Sex and the City*, Mr. Big (played by Chris Noth) was a wealthy Wall Street financier, a flattering portrait of an archetype that loomed large in New York at the end of the twentieth century. These loads-o'-money bankers first had a window onto fashion in the 1980s; a well stocked wardrobe was a must-have marker that greed was, indeed, good.

Ten years later, those same moneymen had fallen far more in love with fashion than just wanting a sharply cut suit. They now wanted to take such companies public. Brands, keen to shore up the always-shaky balance sheet that dogs the rag trade, were happy to acquiesce. In short succession, a series of household names went from catwalks to bull markets: Tommy Hilfiger in 1991, Gucci in 1994, Ralph Lauren in 1997, and even Donna Karan's hiccupy debut in 1996. Unfortunately, as those would-be Mr. Bigs quickly found out, in high-end fashion, green isn't always in season.

Fashion has always been a cyclical, unpredictable business. Traditionally, if a style proved slow selling, the policy was simple: Hide it in a warehouse and forget about it. Of course, this didn't matter in the era before the prying eyes of the investing public could comb through a company's books. Unfortunately, post-IPO, that dead stock appeared as a drag on the balance sheet, and fashion firms were firmly encouraged to be more efficient in the way they disposed of merchandise. Bigger sample sales were a quick option, while outlets offered a longer-term solution. Those cut-price stores became reliable bright spots on annual reports, providing steady income and high margins. Sometimes, of course, those stats were a little misleading, as a former number cruncher for one such brand explained. Imagine a full-price division has ten thousand dresses sitting unsold, each a $100 blight on the balance sheet. Sales otherwise have been solid, so there's enough of a profit margin to take a write-down on that style without causing panic. Slashed to a cost of 1 cent per item, they will then be "sold" to the off-price division. Its raw costs, then, are minimal: When each dress sells for $50, it shows as a $49.99 profit per item. It's robbing Peter to pay Paul Smith, as it were.

When Mr. Big and his ilk started meddling in fashion, they imported a new way of assessing success. Wall Street relies on a simple metric to gauge a company's health: rapid, constant, and consistent growth. Retail has been all too happy to acquiesce—remember, store space has grown steadily in America by 4 percent each year since 1980. In the late 1990s, Gap even boasted it was opening a new shop *every day*. But the population wasn't growing at such a rattle. No wonder each American now has 46 square feet of retail space to call his or her own. Unfortunately, that chugging growth, so beloved by Wall Street, is unsustainable in retail. The world of too much, whether stock, stuff, or shops, emerged to help pacify Mr. Big.

Wall Street's demand for growth has seen luxury labels place larger and larger orders for product, too. In response, factories have expanded. China, now the crucible of creation in the world, operates monolithic factories far larger than traditional operations—a smart decision, since it allows producers to leverage economies of scale. The problem is that running a factory at half capacity is no cheaper than running it at maximum, which means that output is excessive. Picture a buyer from an American brand who needs to order ten thousand T-shirts but is told that the minimum is fifteen thousand shirts. She's reassured by the production manager that lower unit costs on the larger volume will mean the total cost is the same. What happens to those spare five thousand shirts she never wanted and that have no impact on the firm's profit and loss statement (P&L)? They are allocated to the outlet from the outset, and can be bulked up with whatever fails to sell from the main line.

If real-world Mr. Bigs provided the push to expand these off-price upscale malls, his fictional girlfriend Carrie Bradshaw provided the pull— or rather, her fans did. During *Sex and the City*'s initial run between 1998 and 2004, Bradshaw and her trio of designer handbag–toting handmaidens were such cultural touchstones that they could transmute the ordinary into an overnight trend with a single episode (blame or thank them for the global girly menace of Fendi baguettes, nameplate necklaces, and the inexplicably enduring cupcake phenomenon).

In *Sex and the City*, designer fashion was as much plot point as set dressing. When Carrie needs her boyfriend to promise to keep a secret, she insists he swear it on Chanel. Dragging another plus one to a nerve-racking summit, her voiceover is typically arch. "In every relationship, there comes a time when you have to take that important next step. . . . For some couples that step is meeting the parents. For me, it's meeting the Prada." (Unfortunately, Prada also forms the fulcrum of the couple's screaming match by the end of the same episode.) A jobbing journalist, Carrie constantly splashes out couture—unrealistic, maybe, but an example that others craved to follow. The more responsible way to live like Carrie would be to browse the bargain racks at Prada or Chanel in Woodbury Common. Anyway, if your own Mr. Big held stock in Donna and Ralph, wasn't it only supportive to shell out for a few pieces from the current season?

One scene, more than any other, proves *Sex and the City*'s power to educate almost anyone about high fashion. Strolling in an alleyway downtown one afternoon, brooding over her latest romantic misstep, Bradshaw is accosted by an armed thug. "Gimme your bag," he barks. "It's a Baguette," she squeals, meaning the Fendi design that was the first-ever It bag. After he grabs her purse, watch, and ring, the burly assailant pauses to look at her shoes. "And your Blahniks. Gimme your fucking Blahniks." It's a modern world indeed when a gruff, gun-toting ruffian namechecks a pricey stiletto on sight. Carrie is crestfallen as she removes them.

"Please, sir, they're my favorite pair," she bleats. "I got them half price at a sample sale." Together, *Sex and the City* and sample sales made luxury labels common parlance for the American public.

Re-Sale of the Century

The secret is out: A system that was once akin to the Masons of markdowns is now a mass-market mainstay, more Taylor Swift than tailor-made. Such a shift has meant that finding a true deal on this season's It bag has become almost impossible. Little wonder, then, given the financial potential of satisfying that yen for YSL, that a subculture has emerged in response to this shortfall. Over the last decade, the business of resale has boomed. It is dedicated entirely to providing pricey treats at affordable rates and is undoubtedly luxury's dirtiest discount secret.

Think back to that gimmick of presale, when staffers are authorized to call regular customers and offer them the privilege of VIP browsing. At Bergdorf Goodman, nowhere is that more important than in the shoe department. Earning 4 percent commission, colleagues report that staffers there regularly earn $200,000 or more each year. A large chunk of those monies is earned in the presale period, as one former floorwalker explains. In the days before a big sale, a shoe seller would call a repeat customer to tell them, perhaps, that eighty pairs of Manolo Blahniks would be offered for 60 percent off at the sale next week. *How many pairs would you like?* the staffer would ask the regular. And the response was usually consistent: all of them.

That shopper, of course, wasn't planning on wearing eighty pairs of stilettos. Rather, those Manolos were destined for resale on eBay or Craigslist or at a consignment store. Technically secondhand, but unworn, with a Bergdorf Goodman label to buttress authenticity, such items offer ordinary shoppers the chance of a discount on top-tier merchandise. The department store turns a blind eye to this practice, since it simultaneously liquidates passé inventory and logs a chunky commission as a sop to the sales staff.

Such reselling can cause conniptions among sniffier designer marques, of course. At one time, the Neiman Marcus Last Call at Sawgrass Mills in Florida regularly received end-of-season Chanel purses. Many started showing up on eBay marked "NWT" (New with Tags), the outlet logo's visibility another reassurance of condition and authenticity. After Chanel found one too many such listings, it carped about the problem to Neiman Marcus headquarters, specifically citing the south Florida outpost's tags as a high-profile problem. Neiman Marcus adjusted its distribution practices accordingly, as one seasoned Last Call shopper found out firsthand. Her regular sales assistant had tipped her off to a new delivery (classic clienteling), and as she was rifling through the cardboard boxes at a presale, she received a nasty shock. For the first time, there were no Chanel bags in the pile. "Apparently, they've taken away the ability for Sawgrass to receive any Chanel merchandise—it will all go to Orlando and we can drive up there if we want to," moaned the crestfallen luxury maven. If only she'd called up Fashionphile, a multimillion-dollar swap meet for the rich.

Housed in a small but gleaming showroom just off Rodeo Drive, Fashionphile is a new kind of business, one built entirely on luxury resale; in this case, handbags. Women who no longer want or need that fancy tote can come to Fashionphile and turn it into cash. It's a purse pawnbroker. Were the showroom an orphanage for unwanted luxury purses, Ben Hemminger would be Miss Hannigan, his charges largely restricted to Chanel, Hermès, and Louis Vuitton.

A business-savvy Mormon who's more financier than fashionisto, Hemminger stepped up to help his sister-in-law when she found success dabbling in resale on eBay. That was in 2002. After ten years under his stewardship, Fashionphile logged its first million-dollar month in March 2012; annual revenues were projected to top $10 million for the first time the same year. The firm sells around one thousand secondhand purses per month, with each purse selling for an average of $869. Most transactions are online, either through fashionphile.com or eBay, although Hemminger does have a few Hollywood types who stop in at his all-white Aladdin's cave to browse in person.

The Beverly Hills boutique, which lurks in a discreet alley just off Rodeo Drive, sits right behind the local Louis Vuitton store—the rivals even share a garbage can. The location is deliberate, since Hemminger says that many of the LV sales assistants understand what he calls "the long game." Defying corporate edicts, they will discreetly tip off clients to Fashionphile's existence. A woman who has overspent on LV but still wants to keep shopping will be quietly steered his way. *Ssshhh, just over there,* the staffer might stage-whisper, *you can bring an old bag, sell it, and then spend the money you make with us on a new treat.* When a customer arrives and drops a certain sales assistant's name, Hemminger is glad to give that floorwalker a spiff, ranging from $20 to $100, depending on the deal he strikes. "I love to do that," he gloats.

According to Hemminger, Vuitton makes up almost half of the branded bags on the resale market, and over 40 percent of eBay's offerings. Its secondhand popularity is down to the brand's refusal to offer sales of any kind, to anyone—a true rarity today, as we'll see a little bit later.* What doesn't drive its resale value is craftsmanship. "It plays to people's need to be recognized as someone who has luxury taste. It's not about the quality, to be honest," he says and shrugs. "Look, it's fine, not horrible quality, but other stuff like Bottega Veneta uses higher grades of leather. But it all boils down to the fact that other people recognize what you're carrying."

Hemminger sees his business as symbiotic with the Rodeo Drive mainstays a few yards away. Indeed, one of Fashionphile's key suppliers was first steered to them by her personal shopper at Neiman Marcus after she griped about the $5,000-a-month cap on her fashion addiction placed by her bill-paying spouse. That savvy stylist saw an opportunity. Calling it a "revolving door," Hemminger would pay cash for the wealthy woman's barely used bags, which she could then spend at Neiman, doubling her budget without riling her husband. "It's a backdoor way for her to get fifty percent back," he says. Not to mention for the sales assistant to keep creaming off commission on every full-price sale.

---

* Hemminger is pragmatic about the label that powers his business. When an LV bag arrives, Hemminger will inspect it, and before offering a price, he'll cross-reference it with their decade-long catalog of previous sales—monograms will reliably sell for 75 to 85 percent of their original retail price, while the men's Taiga line will struggle to reach 50 percent.

The first time another Neiman referral walked into the tiny Fashion-phile showroom, she exclaimed, "Oh! This looks like my closet. I could stock the whole thing!" Cannily, Hemminger offered to make a house call; she consigned two hundred bags in a single trip. At another house call, he loaded up four entire SUVs with purses, an ample hoard of famed Birkins included. That haul took six months to sell, and earned its con-signer a staggering $400,000 profit. Thirty percent of his suppliers pro-vide 70 percent of the inventory, and the best will even moonlight as secret shopping agents on his behalf like fashion fifth columnists.*

One story sums up the business better than any other. When Celine discontinued the blue version of its $1,800 Mini Luggage bag long before demand had subsided, Fashionphile was deluged with requests for the item. Hemminger called one of his top consigners and asked for her help. Mrs. X was a valued customer at Neiman Marcus so he offered her a deal: If she could persuade her personal shopper there to produce one of those elusive bags, Hemminger would make it worth her while. No personal shopper wants to disappoint a free-spending regular, and that secret shopping agent produced a pristine bag soon after. Mrs. X received a tax-free finder's fee of $1,300 from Hemminger. Hours later, Fashionphile sold the Celine bag for another $700 profit.

Operations like these, whether selling pre-loved purses or shilling scoop on the latest sample sales, have changed luxury's value, in all its senses. Paying for a round-trip ticket to Orlando simply to go rooting through the cut-price stock at Last Call might still prove cheaper than sav-ing up for a double-C Chanel tote through conventional channels. More than any other sector, luxury has suffered through the multiple bargasms of the last decade, tarnished by the very offshoots, such as Gilt, that claim to buttress its status. Too tempted by the lure of mass-market profits, lux-ury has been the highest-profile victim of oversupply. In no other sector is the buyer in a more powerful position.

---

* Given the huge numbers involved, Hemminger was amazed at the success of layaway when he introduced it; now 40 percent of his online purchases are on sixty-day terms. "These are high-priced items, so it's not that they're poor and can't afford it." Talking to clients, though, he realized it was another subterfuge—breaking up payment into $500 increments stopped high-ticket items from being flagged when the credit card bill arrived at the end of the month, and was another way to bypass a husband's financial ire.

Wait long enough, search hard enough, dig deep enough, and the price of every treat will be cut in half, as every shopper now knows. Indeed, one company took that new premise and built an entire operation around it. In less than five years, this firm has become a pop culture touchstone—or perhaps a punch line.

5

"Let's Make a Deal" or You'll Never Pay Retail Again

Groupon Anxiety, Why Airlines Never Print the Price on Your Ticket, and How a Milk Carton Might Mean Your House Sells for 10 Percent Less Than You Hoped

The Magic Markdown Wand should prove a classic among late-night TV infomercials. The pitchman's voiceover is cartoonish but compelling, the satisfied customers cheerily scripted. "I couldn't believe the money I saved," coos one. "It took fifty percent off the check when I went for dinner at my local bistro." Another raves about the skiing lessons she planned. "It was, like, shazam! They were half price." But wait . . . there's more! The Magic Markdown Wand can be used to reduce the price of haircuts, massages, or even cupcakes. "The only thing it can't do," smarms the pitchman, "is cut the calories in half." Who wouldn't dial the number instantly after that irresistible shill? Of course, the infomercial is fiction, but that Magic Markdown Wand exists. It's called Groupon.

Groupon is a business whose premise is timely, a natural byproduct in an era of oversupply. It offers a turnkey solution to liquidate unsold inventory that requires far less capital investment than opening an outlet mall or even printing a coupon. Every day merchants, including shops and cafés, gyms and spas, lose money on unsold inventory—food spoils, appointment slots go empty, and tables are set but never served. Until Groupon appeared in 2008—tellingly, as a decade of overstocking collided with the sharp economic slump—it was difficult for smaller operations to stage crucial discounting programs. Groupon though, was an instant, all-digital discounting option that even mom-and-pop shingles could adopt.

Groupon promises to help small businesses convert sluggish stock into cash, or fill half-empty classes—a sterling silver wedding ring for $19.99 instead of $99.99, or 71 percent off a lie-detecting seminar (both, sadly, real examples). The catch for the businesses whom Groupon persuaded to partner with the start-up lay in the revenue-splitting deal, whereby Groupon took 50 percent of the already-reduced price. In other words, that jeweler would see only $10 for each $19.99 ring sold. To reassure vendors, the firm devised a failsafe. Deals would "tip" or activate only if a large enough number of customers signed up. In this way, Groupon could offset the steep price cuts with a radical uptick in volume; hence the name, a mashup of *group* and *coupon*.* Guaranteeing much the same as Gilt, Groupon swore that once a newbie sampled a product or service for the first time at 50 percent off, they would be converted to regular customers—racing back for countless repeat visits and paying full price—for those businesses opting in to their programs. It's a seductive theory, at least.

Such Groupthink-style shopping grew out of founder Andrew Mason's original project, a Kickstarter-like site for do-gooderish initiatives called The Point. Groupon's unconventional origins still manifest in the quirky corporate culture that Mason cultivated at its Chicago headquarters. Mason was determined to carve out a unique personality for his company as more than just another whizzy dot-com. Nothing embodies this better than the bizarre office at Groupon Central known as Michael's Room. It was dedicated to a fictitious teenager who "lived" there, complete with an unplumbed toilet whose basin was filled with mini candy bars, some half-eaten cereal boxes, and an exercise bike that

---

* Groupon's name is misleading, though—legally, it's more a gift certificate than a coupon, retaining its face value even once the promotional period expires. In other words, it's always redeemable for $5 of cupcakes, even after the $5 Groupon bonus period ends.

powered a record player loaded with a 45 rpm of Sade's "Smooth Operator." Clearly, Michael was still stuck in 1985.

Goofy corporate culture aside, Groupon became a serious player in e-commerce almost instantly for two reasons. First, it spiked customer demand during a deep recession, helping sectors from restaurants to stores unload excess inventory relatively quickly. Second, that 50 percent revenue split filled Groupon's coffers overnight. The firm could make $15.6 million on a single deal, as it did in November 2010 after offering a $50 voucher to Nordstrom Rack for $25. Predicted to be the fastest company ever to bank $1 billion in revenue, Groupon was valued at a staggering $16 billion during its IPO in fall 2011. Clearly, that was an overoptimistic valuation, but the scale of the firm's operation was undeniably impressive. Less than five years after its founding, the Chicago start-up had seventy million subscribers across forty-seven countries, and managed to attract, then spurn, a $6 billion takeover offer from Google.

Perhaps the clearest mark of its success is the passel of zeitgeist-surfing offshoots it spawned. A slangy term, *Grouponomics*, was coined to describe such flash-mob-style discount shopping. More neologisms followed suite, then even a mental illness emerged. According to Urban Dictionary, Groupon Anxiety is, "That feeling of anxiousness and not being able to sleep knowing that a new Groupon will be released after 1 a.m." CBS developed (then shelved) a sitcom, *Friend Me*, in which two brothers from Indiana move to Groupon's LA office and hilarity.com ensues. For the chattering classes—a crucial market, as 54 percent of households with incomes of $150,000 or higher now subscribe to at least one daily deal site—the ultimate endorsement came with Groupon's very own *New Yorker* cartoon. A scratchy homage appeared in the April 11, 2011, issue, barely six months before Groupon's $16 billion valuation. Two moms walk down the street, chatting, while a pigtailed tyke trots in front. "It wasn't our first choice of schools," one mother explains to the other, "but we had a Groupon for it, so what the hell." One behavioral economist even conducted a study that ascribed a Stockholm syndrome–like power on our psyches to the Groupon phenomenon. Until Groupon appeared, he noted, shoppers would disdain as cheap or poor not just coupon users but those caught standing near them. Thanks to Groupon, though, such shame had transmuted into pride; discount chasing is a mark of intelligence rather than indigence.

More than any other innovation, Groupon and its ilk have, quite literally, made deals an everyday thing. Such sites are a prescient glimpse into retail's future, timewarping forward to an era when sales have become the norm rather than the exception. It won't take long to reach that point; after all, 40 to 45 percent of inventory in America in 2011 was sold at some kind of promotion, and the proportion is rising year after year as the shoppers' power grows. Indeed, nothing embodies that shift better than Groupon, which relies entirely on buyers clubbing together to strong-arm a deal from sellers. Soon, every business and service will have to answer the same tricky question that Groupon and its vendors face every day: How do you make money when a full price isn't guaranteed? How do you satisfy a shopper's demand for discounts while protecting the bottom line? Even more crucial, how does a business change over time when prices become entirely flexible?

Were Groupon more functional and fiscally responsible, the firm might offer a playbook, but the company has spent the last few years torpedoing the concept of paying full price along with its own long-term prospects (as we shall see later). It's best to look elsewhere for hints of how the future might look, since shoppers already hold such sway that fixed- or full-price is an alien notion. Some industries have already weathered such changes, adjusting their business models to address this cut-price cultural tsunami and soothe a discount-demanding market. Each company in its own way is a pioneering patient zero. As retail transforms, the strategies and tactics sellers employ can offer solace and inspiration for other businesses (not to mention some tips for shoppers). Enough of that for now, though—it's time for a vacation.

Have Discount, Will Travel

It's been a grueling few months in the office, and you deserve a short break in the sun—Costa Rica sounds nice. You found a bargain last-minute ticket to a beach on the Pacific, packing little more than flip-flops, shorts, and plenty of sun lotion. The Out of Office bounceback is already on your e-mail and your cellphone is switched off; for once, you aren't even taking your laptop. Suddenly, there's a startling announcement from a soothing voice on the loudspeaker. "Thanks to tail winds, this flight is expected to land forty-five minutes early," coos the flight attendant. Could it get any better? you ask yourself, smugly.

Then she continues, purring, "This flight has been randomly selected for a customer survey, and the captain has asked everyone to kindly participate. Starting with seat 1A, please stand up and announce how much you paid for your seat. Please include fare, taxes, and baggage charges. I will be bringing a handheld microphone around the cabin so that every passenger can clearly hear the answer. Many thanks." It would be less impertinent and uncomfortable to ask passengers to flash their underwear (thank goodness you remembered to wear a clean pair, though).

Few of the passengers don't squirm as they disclose how little—or how much—they paid for the exact same seat. You ready yourself to proudly explain the deal you hunted down, just $299 round-trip, when 18C—a woman whose purse alone costs more than your monthly mortgage—announces that she paid just $229. It wouldn't be so bad if you weren't suffering from upgradeitis. How was that gloating CEO-type in a flashy suit bumped up to business class when he paid the same price as you did, and you're stuck back in coach? It's a no-fair fare, you think to yourself.

Such midair confessionals may be a fantasy, but the yo-yoing fares are fact: On average, 92 percent of passengers on any flight have paid some kind of discounted price. Rarely, though, did they pay the same one. A plane's rate chart is almost algebraic: The same seat has usually been sold for around twenty different prices, each determined by various factors. For example, Saturday-night stays traditionally shaved off around 13 percent of the full fare. Think back to the last time you bought a plane ticket or booked a hotel room. Didn't you click around a few sites to see if there was a better rate or price anywhere else? In travel, it's instinctive: With a little effort, shoppers know all too well there are always deals lurking online. Both airlines and hotels have long been operating in the all-sale model that others will soon have to adopt to address customers' expectations. How each has, well, fared is telling.

Even the travel industry once enjoyed a full-price heyday. The 1960s were truly jet-setting's golden age. Back then, there were just four rates: economy, first class, night economy, and night first class, each denoted by letters Y, F, YN, and YF respectively. Prices were as genteel as the service on board: white-gloved and feminine, except on Northwest, whose smoky downstairs drinking dens were deemed unseemly for girls and so staffed by male barkeeps. The government set ticket prices; if airlines were struggling, it simply hiked the rates. That's the real reason the 1960s were a halcyon era for high fliers: Airlines were freed from any worries about competing on price since they were centrally assigned their own regional territories. This distinctly uncapitalist approach, where supply was centrally controlled and restricted, allowed PanAm et al to focus on the in-flight experience, such as improving seats, rather than profit margins.*

Then came the economic malaise of the 1970s, spurring the government to reexamine the retro monopoly such carriers enjoyed. The federal government mulled a then-revolutionary step: deregulation, unfettering the restrictions that had maintained decorum and prices in equal measure. Senior airline executives were divided on this plan. The government agonized over one question: How risky would it be to offer discounts on plane tickets? United CEO Richard Ferris wasn't worried. "Deregulation will be the greatest thing to happen to the airlines since the jet engine," he crowed. But American Airlines CEO Robert Crandall was less enthusiastic. "You fucking academic eggheads! You don't know shit," he barked at a senate committee considering the change. "You can't deregulate this industry. You're going to wreck it. You don't know a goddamn thing!"

Most contemporary economists agreed with United's Ferris, predicting that the vigor of competition would spark a slew of new shingles and expand the airline industry's reach. But given that just three of the eleven legacy carriers survived past the first decade of the twenty-first century,

---

* Regulations abounded over more than just fares, but canny staffers always found ways to get around them. Alcohol restrictions were typical. "When we started serving drinks it was a two-drink limit [on board]," recalls Joyce Avriette, who was one of American Airlines's earliest cabin crew in the 1950s. "We had a sixteen-ounce low ball for the first, and a little carafe as big as a glass for the second—so it was two glasses, but about eight drinks."

and the industry's collective losses over the three decades since deregulation topped out at $60 billion, perhaps Crandall had a point.

Crandall didn't sulk after losing that argument, though. In fact, he was the company leader who embraced the all-discount model most aggressively (and American Airlines was one of that remaining trio). His innovations helped transform the industry into one that is now so familiar; he invented and named the concept of *yield management*—aviation's answer to demand-based pricing. This was the ultimate admission that customers control their own costs. *Plan ahead, and we'll give you a bargain; if you wait until the last minute, it's only fair we charge a little more.* The equation must have seemed like a smart trade-off: price versus convenience. This is when the four letter codes denoting seat and price were joined by an alphabet soup of similar shorthands (K, L, U, C, B, I, and so on), a practice that still persists today. There's another reason that practice has endured on boarding passes. Printing fare categories rather than hard numbers is deliberately evasive, a way to avoid reminding passengers of those different prices paid for the same seat. Strangely, though, rather than allowing the airlines to inflate their fares, such yield management kept pushing prices downward, for reasons almost entirely within the airlines' control.

Hotel room rates now vary as wildly as the price for seat 18A. Although it took longer for this half of the travel business to surrender to similar pricing pressure, once the shift started, it was rapid. Traditionally, every hotel room had a so-called rack rate, the standard or full price that could be charged per night. That price was usually posted on the back of the door. But in the 1990s, a new kind of broker appeared that transformed hotel booking: the online travel agent, or OTA. Orbitz, Expedia, and Travelocity weakened the rack rate's clout, which hotels had long been able to levy unchecked. Until then, comparing prices on rooms was a time-consuming process, an afternoon of calling different agents with a copy of classified ads from *The New York Times* spread on the living room floor. Now, with the click of a mouse, travelers could log on and see every four-star room in a certain city, complete with competing prices. The Internet enabled price comparison and transparency at a granular level, yet another power shift in favor of the shopper.

The industry's response was aggressive: It adopted that same yield management–based pricing structure as airlines, but with added complexity. One senior executive at Hampshire Hotels, a Mumbai- and New York–based chain with 2,500 rooms in Manhattan and properties from the United Kingdom to Thailand, told me that the firm can tweak room rates up to twelve times a day. That's 4,380 potential (discounted) price variations for just one room in one year. It makes the rack rate effectively meaningless. Travel agents moan how Thompson Hotels, a snazzy boutique chain with nine properties across America and expanding worldwide, is notorious for its zigzagging rates within a twenty-four-hour period. "There must be fights in the lobbies. 'I booked it at ten o'clock!' 'I booked it at two o'clock!'" says one agent. The Hoxton Hotel in East London is known for its annual promotion, where a clutch of rooms is sold for £1 per night (around $1.60). Typically, the sale is over in less than sixty seconds. Iconic hotelier Ian Schrager mimicked this gimmick when he wanted to drive awareness of his newest hotel, Public, in Chicago. In forty-eight-hour bursts, he offered a limited number of rooms for $1 per night—60 cents less than even the Hoxton, or a discount of almost 40 percent.

Airlines and hotels can execute such Rubik's Cube–like pricing thanks to automation. Computer modeling determines just how variable (or, sometimes, not) a price should be. The algorithms independently determine a compromise cost that will both satisfy a discount-driven clientele while still preserving the company's margins. Two firms dominate this industry: SABRE and fierce rival Micros Fidelio. They manage inventory with the steely dispassion of a trauma surgeon, relentlessly commodifying rooms or seats. Airline fares, for example, change three times a day for domestic rates and five times a day for international routes (though that's likely to change soon to a totally dynamic, constantly updating model).*

---

* The industry is evasive about how it uses cookies to track fare searches, but insiders suggest that you launch a new browser program each time you return to check a price to make sure the price doesn't rise. It's a similar principle as haggling in the bazaar: If you return more than once to inspect that antique, the stallholder knows your interest is piqued, however poker faced your expression. Launching a new browser to recheck that LAX-SFO fare is a smart idea, the equivalent of wearing a fake nose and glasses when you go back to reexamine a hand-tufted rug.

Indeed, two or three dozen staff at each airline spend their working day solely monitoring competitors' prices and inputting such data to feed their own systems' algorithms to try to beat those of their rivals.*

As a result, a new role has emerged in hospitality that's more IT than VIP: revenue manager. These staffers oversee their pricing models, working a year or so in advance to set hotel rates. He or she tasks algorithms with calculating rates that will squeeze the greatest profit from customers while offering enough of a discount to keep travelers happy. It's the hotel world's answer to stock control, a crucial move when an industry exists in a permanent state of excess. New lingo has emerged to replace traditional buzzwords like *rack rates*. Under the computer-modeled system, the lowest possible price is known as the Best Available Rate (BAR); it exists to safeguard basic margins. It is the lowest price for which a given room can be sold at any time. Savvy travelers should always call a hotel after making an online booking to ensure that the BAR was charged. If not, it's easy enough to request a price match.

A mark of how important revenue management has become to hoteling is the rise of execs to upper management with a background in such boffinry. Hilton president Paul Brown has a number-heavy résumé via a stint at Expedia, as do several of the senior figures in the Marriott group. Used correctly, such automation can please picky bargain hunters while still keeping the company profitable. One senior staffer at Starwood, the conglomerate behind St. Regis, Le Meridien, Sheraton, and others, told me that profits are 8 percent higher using such algorithms than if discounts are decided more deliberately, infrequently, and manually. No wonder that the company declared very healthy recession-era revenues of $5.62 billion with a net income of $489 million.

Although most hoteliers have seized on the new discounting model

---

* Sometimes, though, such automation can backfire, as in the case of so-called Fat Finger Fares. When a human has to manually input the fares that supercomputers have devised, they sometimes make mistakes. That is how in 2012, United offered frequent fliers the chance to book a first-class round-trip from New York to Hong Kong for just four miles, plus taxes and fees. Grand total: $33, or a saving of $10,217 on the regular fare. The airline refused to honor the tickets, but that isn't standard practice. If you're ever browsing an airline's own site and see an inexplicably low fare, book it and cross your fingers; sometimes, for goodwill and good PR, the ticket will be issued anyway.

and leveraged it profitably, that isn't true across the hospitality industry. Airlines, especially, have been far less savvy. American Airlines declared bankruptcy in 2012, the last of the surviving legacy carriers to hold out; Continental had gone bust not once but twice (in 1984 and 1990); US Airways and United had succumbed in 2002; and both Delta and Northwest filed within four minutes of each other in 2005. But at least those firms survived the transition. Other companies such as PanAm and TWA, icons before deregulation, just collapsed.

Both airlines and hotels are using cutting-edge computing to set discount prices. Yet one industry is thriving in an all-sale environment, while the other clearly stumbles. One reason is the different ways that each has handled their additional revenue streams over and above core charges (a seat, a room). Hotels have a greater number of secondary sources and have also been savvier at leveraging them. Few locations debut these days that don't include a wedding or banquet hall, a handy extra-profit center. Lobby piano bars are a license to print money from the martini-chugging salesmen propping them up most Monday through Friday nights. Hotels have long billed for every extra, whether a meal on a tray, a massage, or even WiFi.

Compare their practices to the flight industry. Other than cargo, admittedly a hugely important but hidden revenue stream, airlines were slow to monetize extras until driven (flown?) to by the aviation crisis after September 11, 2001. Until then, in-flight meals had been free, rather than the now familiar buy-on-board programs. It's the equivalent of a hotel offering free room service to every guest—madness for its margins. In the bargain-driven era, it's especially hard to instigate new charges on items that customers have been conditioned to expect gratis. Pushback will be ferocious and risky. Spirit Airlines was pilloried for introducing a levy for carry-on bags, which steadily climbed to reach a maximum $100 per satchel by the end of 2012. Tellingly, such nickel and diming makes up a staggering 40 percent of the carrier's current revenue. The lesson for business is clear: The only way to survive deep discounting on a core business is to create additional revenue streams to replace that lost income, no matter the snippiness that it might generate. The lesson for travelers is simpler: Pack light.

The difference in how airlines and hotels operate their loyalty programs also contributes to their varying financial health. Such setups are a pricing shell game, intended to steer travelers to focus on more than just the deal, to feel cherished and welcomed (a smart strategy in shopping 3.0). In Starwood's case, the Preferred Guest Program is a crucial part of the marketing plan, with 50 percent of Le Meridien's guests and a staggering 69 percent of W overnighters being members of the program. Starwood's program allows travelers to earn points toward free night stays, so that weekday loyalists will be as focused on accruing freebies for a weekend getaway on the company dime as on checking quite how cheaply they could have booked a room elsewhere.

Airlines also rely on frequent-flyer programs, though these loyalty shingles are iffier. The problem with their premise is that after years of such programs, the weight of unspent miles on airlines' balance sheets is hefty. The nerviness among investors that this system engenders is well founded. Airlines fret that if there's a rush to redeem those billions of frequent-flyer points all at once, perhaps after poor financial results makes travelers race to spend them, the airline might go bust. Thankfully, according to one longtime airline executive, such programs are buttressed by the fact that most male customers never want to cash in those miles. Their tallies are noted with preening pride, a manhood-enhancing status symbol that they're unwilling to deplete (women, apparently, are far less insecure and more free-spending). These programs certainly shore up shaky periods: No doubt, American Airlines helped stave off bankruptcy by selling AAdvantage points to Citibank as part of its co-branded credit card program, generating crucial stopgap revenue. Nonetheless it still eventually slipped into the red in 2012.

Airlines' overheads also make them more vulnerable to downward pricing pressure than established hotel chains. Jittery oil prices make their already wafer-thin margins even more fragile, while throwback employment contracts with hefty pensions are a leaden drag on the bottom line. Both hotels and airlines have time-sensitive inventory, but one suffers a far greater financial hit when that inventory spoils. An unsold seat that flies empty still burns off precious fuel, a debit on the company's balance sheet. Unsold rooms, on the other hand, are almost revenue neutral, as it costs barely a few bucks to pay the maid when she fluffs the pillows before a guest next checks in.

Revenue streams, loyalty programs, and varying overheads go some way to explain how hotels have weathered the all-sale era so well, while airlines have imploded with worrisome regularity. None of those reasons, however, is the most significant for such incessant stumbling. Aviation's Achilles' heel is pure ego.

The hotel world operates on a basis of friendly rivalry. As any hospitality veteran will admit, hotels engage in a tacit rate-parity premise, so the prices for a room at most four-star hotels in any given town will be within a few bucks of one another almost every night. Operators understand that undercutting competitors too fiercely will only damage everyone's business in the long term. Wounds are painful on all sides after a price war. During the 2008 recession, for example, Starwood didn't want to slash prices at its luxury chains, as this would dent equity. It still focused on travelers, though, cognizant that a near-empty hotel is a melancholy experience for the few guests unlucky enough to be staying there. To stave off this decline, Starwood increased the number of nights its corporate staff could stay gratis worldwide, using them to bulk up thinned-out guest numbers. Good business sense generated goodwill.

Airlines, on the other hand, treat one another with a petty ruthlessness and persist in waging discount battles. They have shown a suicidal squabblesomeness over the past four decades since deregulation, chipping away at one another's rates, death spiral–style. To lure cost-conscious shoppers who planned ahead, the airlines, once the government unshackled them, launched so-called Super Saver fares. The idea (much like Groupon's) was that bulk would offset lower margins. It was a boon for the customer, but a bust for the airlines. In 1992, American offered a JFK–LAX round-trip fare of $199 for a short period, as part of its effort to streamline pricing. This was an attempt to use a headline-grabbing deal to promote an overall simplification by American; it reduced the 500,000 different prices in its systems down to just 70,000, with the average coach fare dropping 38 percent. Unfortunately, the stunt backfired. For one thing, it set an unrealistic reference point, a price that customers still cite as a near-mythical deal for that same route. More important for its financial health, though, rival Northwest (notoriously aggressive on pricing until it was subsumed by Delta in 2008) saw American's move as a chance to launch its own half-price sale. Others followed, which pushed fare prices even lower. That six-month slugout eventually sliced a staggering 30 percent off airline share values when a truce was concluded. It was Waterloo at 30,000 feet.

Any attempt since then to roll back discount-driven pricing has pratfalled, too. Airlines' finances grew even more fragile after 9/11, when wariness among travelers about flying collided with the airlines' need to up revenues in a recession. The companies resorted to even more desperate discounting in response. In 2005, then-Delta CEO Gerald Grinstein announced the spiffy Simplifares program. "Let it be clear. This is not a fare sale," he crowed. "This is a fundamental change to our pricing structure." He might as well have been an American Airlines executive in 1992. Grinstein unveiled caps on single-leg fares at $499 (economy) and $599 (first). Within eighteen months, under pressure from shareholders, oil prices, and falling revenues, the program was quietly retired.

Now it's a fact for airlines that pricing is forever in flux. "While you're sitting here talking, someone is fucking you," former Continental CEO Gordon Bethune told *Fortune*. "Changing a fare, changing a flight, moving something." (Like AA's Bob Crandall, Bethune puts the crew in crude.) No one sums up the problem better than iconic marketing expert Al Ries. "They're saying 'We have two kinds of seats for you: cheap seats and stupid seats. What do you want?' That's some choice," he says. "It's a dual class system, but here's your choice: Sit in first class and feel stupid for paying all that money, or sit in coach and feel cheap."

The travel industry is a pioneer of the Grouponifying world, providing handy examples of both how to thrive and how to stumble. Airlines have treated deals like weapons, wielded with a territorial, testosterone-fueled aggressiveness, that were lobbed at customers like cheap grenades in an attempt to lock up their business. No wonder travel has long been an industry where CEOs were unembarrassed by four-letter tirades, a macho culture built on a cliché of swaggering pilots and simpering stewardesses. Hotels, on the other hand, were subtler and smarter, using deals to strike partnerships with their customers, treating price cuts as a persuasion tactic that builds loyalty over the long term. Hotels didn't lurk behind letter codes that fudge real prices, but allowed comparison and even set a rock-bottom rate as reassurance.

Nothing sums up the disparate attitude to shoppers better, though, than the automated kiosks that have come to litter every airport terminal. Although they're nominally there for speed and convenience, the airlines crow, they are quietly grateful for the slimmer staffing levels that they allow. Notably, no well-known hotel, though, has copied that move. Such automation elides the chance for clienteling, after all, and a human being can establish a rapport with a customer (or even sniff out a problem) with far more speed and convenience than a computer. That attitude cascades down into how well, or poorly, each sector has juggled the discount juggernaut.

Soon, travel will no longer be an outlier in the discount racket, as every industry faces these same challenges: bargain-conditioned shoppers demanding constant deals, confident in their powerful positions. Such a transformation may be worrisome for Wall Street, but ordinary Americans should be winners. Envisioning a world where haggling, or hacking at prices, is an everyday occurrence might seem intimidating, especially given the speed at which it is happening. After all, how does someone pick up the skills to game that system? Perhaps, unwittingly, every American already possesses them.

The Real Deal

Once a grubby East Village crossroads in downtown Manhattan, Astor Place has been gussied up in the twenty-first century, largely through the addition of a gleaming, undulating modernist skyscraper. On the second floor of that Tron-like building sits TOWN Residential. It's another of those offices where the staffers are too thin and too gorgeous to ever touch the huge jars of day-glo candy in the lobby (one canister is propped up rather forlornly on an unthumbed book, *500 Buildings of New York*). On a summer Friday, gauzy and hot, the offices are near silent at 10 a.m., save for the few agents who have signed up to attend a special training session, Bidding Wars and Negotiation Strategies. Tussling over price, clearly, is such a constant in real estate that staffers need special training to tackle it. This lesson is Haggling 101, aimed at schooling newbie agents to handle the nuances of negotiation, arming them to triumph on their client's behalf in that battle. "But don't call it price wars," cautions the professor, real estate industry veteran Jeff Appel. He is a Californian with a hammy flair and great teeth. "It's ongoing interests from multiple parties," he says, stressing every sentence with one of his gleaming smiles.

Americans have long had to practice haggling. In fact, they used to have to negotiate over the two highest-ticket items they owned: a home and a car. Car dealers underwent a transformation in the early 2000s when their sales model changed from haggle-heavy negotations to a clean, fixed-price transaction.* Real estate, though, remains an area where rarely, if ever, does anyone pay the exact initial price asked. The best way for shoppers to practice the art of negotiation, a skill soon to be central to every purchase, is in buying a home. Their agent can coach them at every step, which is why Appel is here to share a few expert ploys.

For two hours, he is a mesmerizing mentor, handing out advice on how to win that price war (*Pax, Mr. Appel*) with a Barnum-esque charm. Were airlines less hotheaded, they could sidestep the pitched price negotiation, but real estate transactions are inevitably hard-fought. When repping a buyer, Appel counsels, think coquettishly, and never pressure. Avoid the "It's only good until 12 p.m. on Tuesday" gambit, an offer that expires. After all, he shrugs, does that mean your client is no longer interested at 12:01 p.m.? Brinkmanship will only backfire. Rather, try to meet the seller's agent for a drink, and waterboard them with charm

* The change dates to 2005, when struggling automakers resorted to what seemed like a smart employee tactic: discounts for all. GM launched the program in June and saw sales surge 41 percent; when Chrysler followed a month later with its Employee Pricing Plus, it sold the most cars ever. (One study found that most cars were pricier during the first fortnight of the promotion than they had been before that period, a clear case of the "SALE" sign mattering more than the price per se.) The next year, of course, to keep the illusion of value, the manufacturers had to slash list prices, including reducing rebates. The result left dealers empty-handed as brands such as BMW and Mercedes now mark up around 7 percent, while Japanese brands hover at 12 percent. By cutting the markups on cars, manufacturers were basically setting a fixed price, but customers have yet to adjust expectations. They still want a deal. Seven percent on a $60,000 car is only around $5,000, which gives salesmen precious little wiggle room to please that picky driver and close a sale.

until they cough up the final figure that their client might accept. Then make an offer of 5 percent less than that.

Pricing real estate, even for pros like Appel, is far from a scientific process. After decades of experience, his advice for sellers is always to start low, making a home's price seem too cheap to resist. This tactic cues an irresistible burst of dopamine (buyagra is just as effective in real estate dealings). "My philosophy is, if you underprice every property, the market will finally tell you what it's worth," he says. Sparking that scuffle is easy, in other words, provided you are brave enough to do one thing: radically under-price it.

Unfortunately, a new study suggests that seasoned vet Appel might be utterly wrong. It looked at fourteen thousand single-family homes, sold in New Jersey, Delaware, and Pennsylvania over a four-year period between 2005 and 2009. The research shows that an Appel-style approach is a crucial misstep, especially in zip codes already dogged with mortgage delinquencies. High-listing prices consistently boosted the final sales tally, largely a tribute to the resonance of the reference point. Remember the power of sharp pricing to suggest value, or a bargain? It holds true for homes, too, as another study that analyzed twenty-seven thousand transactions across two states confirmed. Whole number prices on a home were off-putting, and deterred a price-boosting bidding war. The survey looked at similar homes in certain areas, comparing their starting list and final sales prices. One zero at the end of a listing lowered sale price on average by .72 percent, while three zeros cut it by .73 percent. Take two identical homes on the same development, one priced at $485,000 and the other at $484,700. The latter one would sell for a higher price; in this case, researchers found, for around $1,380 more.

Taken together, such studies offer a two-point strategy for sellers. First, slightly overprice a house to set a reference point high enough that the haggled final number feels like a bargain. Then make that figure as precise as possible—say, $382,743—to reassure potential bidders of its fairness.

As we've seen, recent decades have been marked by the rise of market-based pricing, where what's charged is dependent on a sense of surfeit or scarcity. With the constant oversupply, naturally such a system is pushing prices down. Real estate has always operated in this way, with a cycle that repeats each year, reliably driven by the behavior of both buyers and sellers. Many homes are put on the market after January 1, but buyer numbers don't pick up until early spring, per real estate tracker Trulia. Asking prices then peak in May, but sale prices crest in July; by the end of the summer, the inventory still left lingering starts to go stale and markdowns commence. Impatient sellers and patient buyers succeed best. According to Trulia, in March, people are searching but there is less competition, while by November, excess stock will soften prices.

One final factor is worth bearing in mind as we mull the new all-haggle model that every retailer will soon have to adopt. Buyers and sellers have contradictory intentions when they enter that slow-burning cold war that is the closing process. Whatever the starting price, the former is keen to wrangle a discount by pushing the price down. He or she will use whatever tactics and legal strategies they can to chip away at the cost. The latter, of course, will do anything to protect or even boost what's paid (bring on those rival bids). As real estate shows, when prices are no longer fixed, they can go up as well as down. There's no limit on how low or how high those numbers finish—though there are a few hints.

Unfettering prices to let market forces decide the fair number might prove a pleasant surprise for either buyer or seller. The real estate world has been refining such a price-flexible process for decades, giving each side ample time to develop an arsenal of tricks aimed at helping to tip the rate in its favor. Those tips could prove useful for any shopper in retail's new haggle-heavy landscape.

First, let's look at sellers, the half that is keen to avoid discounting at all costs. Not every homeowner might put faith in the power of a sand-colored 4-inch plastic figurine of St. Joseph buried in the backyard, said by the superstitious to help speed a sale.* There are practical tactics that act as buttresses against downward pressure; indeed, entire ancillary industries that have emerged to help sellers safeguard their price against

---

* The origins of the superstition are murky—Joseph is the patron saint of unborn children, immigrants, and a happy death, among others. Even so, it's available for just $9.95 from www.stjosephstatue.com (shipping is free).

dickering buyers. None is more intriguing than home staging, the Kabuki act of prepping a home for visits by potential buyers.

The goal of such interior redesign is simple: Enhance a property's appeal and value, with minimum investment, to bolster against lowballing offers. An icon of the industry is Los Angeles–based Meridith Baer, a sixtysomething former actress turned jobbing screenwriter. She fell into staging when the owner of a house she was renting was so wowed by the makeover she'd undertaken of his property, that he turfed her out and put the house up for sale. The place was snapped up almost immediately. No wonder the broker who worked on the sale suggested teaming up so she could spiff up a few of the other houses on his roster in the same way. Without any formal training in decorating, architecture, or real estate, Baer has become the biggest and most successful real estate stager in the world, with almost seventy staffers and a portfolio of hundreds of houses in a given year. It's down to her special combination of flair for narrative and impeccable, yet universal, taste.

The ex-screenwriter now spins actorless stories, aimed at selling homes rather than tickets. Baer is hired to turn a house into a home that any buyer might crave, and in order to do so, she begins by creating characters in her mind on whose behalf she then executes her grand vision. "I might think: This is an heiress who just inherited a huge fortune, her family's always collected art, and this will be her Los Angeles home," she explained in an interview about one project. "It has to look like a home someone will pay anything for."

With fees starting at $10,000 per job, Baer's clientele is mostly moguls and Beverly Hills housewives—plus a passel of stars, like Halle Berry and Sharon Stone. They are keen to tap in to the 130,000 square feet of warehouse space she owns filled with trinkets that have an almost totemic ability to help sell a home, from two thousand old French lemonade bottles to some antique proctological probes. Baer even runs her own full-time workroom to handle any kind of custom upholstery. Everything she does is to help the seller maximize the price paid for the property, distracting a buyer from chasing discounts via a crave-worthy fantasy life. Baer's signature device is the "end of dinner party" scene: She purposely arranges half-finished desserts on fine china, with silverware lying just so on the kitchen counter. "I want it to look like someone just ran to answer the phone and they'll be right back," she explains.

Baer's career wouldn't even have been possible were it not for a fellow former actress, Barb Schwarz. Schwarz was working as a real estate agent in 1972 when she recognized the kinship between a home and a stage set. Treating a property like a theater designer would, by artfully accessorizing and creating a story from the basic bricks and mortar, she realized, could inspire buyer interest. Schwarz now runs both a staging business and the industry's ad hoc university, StagedHomes.com, which trains any would-be Baer in the art of interior redesign.

An experienced stager has one ultimate goal: Position the property so that buyers can more easily imagine themselves living there. It's both about establishing and erasing personality. First, stagers ruthlessly declutter and clean: no shampoo bottles or magazines in the bathroom, for example, and no family photos anywhere. A single snapshot of a lovable pooch or kitty can stay, but any toys or dishes or litter boxes are banished. A tile-grouting pen freshens every grubby bathroom or kitchen wall.

Next, it's time to tweak the decor: Figurative artwork is out, replaced with abstract canvases painted for the purpose if necessary (some stagers are dab hands). Only hardcover books without jackets are displayed on the shelves; paperbacks and creased covers can be messy. A stager might bring in furniture from her own storage space—a mirror and a loveseat rather than a sofa to give the optical illusion that a room is larger. They also arrange the room following the designer's Rule of Three: Pillows or decorative items always look better arranged in odd numbers (no pairs, thank you). One real estate maxim holds that yellow walls are a hard sell, but stagers know that all such bright colors should be softened with neutrals. Scuffed kitchen cabinets can be painted charcoal, both chic and dirt-resistant during multiple showings.*

---

* The only difference is when stagers are hired by developers to decorate model homes versus owner-occupied properties, according to real estate appraiser Jonathan Miller. "The furniture is undersized, around twenty percent smaller than it would normally be," he explains. "If you want to get a reality check, sit down in one of the chairs. I'm not a five-hundred-pound person, but you can feel it. It's almost like baby furniture."

Baer's fees can be as high as $150,000 per gig, but most stagers charge clients a few hundred dollars plus furniture rental fees. A fun idea, of course, but does it work? Absolutely, at least according to some ad hoc studies. One agent in California examined 2,772 homes that sold locally during a given seventh-month window; 120 of them were professionally staged. It took, on average, thirty-one days for untouched homes to sell in her study, but the staged homes sold within just two weeks. They also fetched 6.32 percent over the list price compared to 1.6 percent in the non-staged control group. Real Estate Staging Association (RESA), another industry body, claims that properties in 2010 sat on the market for an average of nine months. Once a stager had rearranged the home and it was returned to market, the average time until a sale was thirty-two days. Another metric even claims that for every dollar spent on staging, a homeowner sees a $4 return. Whatever the fine print, spending a few hundred dollars to prevent a buyer haggling a price down $10,000 or more is a wily investment.

Staging is never more useful than when a family has already moved out of the house. After all, if a prospective buyer walks into a home and sees it vacant, without furniture of any kind, it telegraphs one thing: that the owners are burdened with carrying double living expenses. This fact echoes through the empty rooms and makes it clear that the sellers are extra motivated to sell. Resulting lowball offers on an empty home slice an average 10 percent off the list prices.

To fortify against such markdowns, some homeowners go further than just hiring furniture—they install a fake family in the home. Dubbed *house managers*, these people are sourced and vetted by specialty firms such as Show Homes and Castle Keepers. Owners are usually charged a small fee, around $500, for the agency to find tenants, then house managers pay all utilities and a radically reduced rent (typically around 30 to 35 percent of standard market rates) to keep the house occupied: toilets flushing, lawn mowed, fridge full of food. Like real-life Bluths in *Arrested Development*, albeit a little less dysfunctional, they live in a smart house as discreetly as possible (thankfully, not exiled to the attic as Michael and his son were).

Most firms have a thirty-day minimum stay so that managing families are not uprooted overnight; stints typically last four to six months. Show Homes even personality tests would-be house managers: Are they flexible and tidy enough to cope with this lifestyle? Successful house managers come from all walks of life. One professional basketball player from the Minnesota Timberwolves decided to test drive a few pads in the Dallas area when he was traded to the Mavericks. He enjoyed the experience so much that he kept house managing even when next traded, this time to the New Jersey Nets. Retirees often enjoy the convenience of living in a warmer climate during the winter, then taking temporary accommodation up north as house managers in the summer when visiting their grandchildren, for example. If a couple has financial problems but is keen to keep their kids in a certain school system, they can sell their own home to pay down debt while moving into a new place nearby as house managers.

One Dallas-based TV producer has gone even further. He launched a firm to make mini films for upscale sellers, hiring actors to "live" in the space with scripts written to focus on a home's standout features. A dinner party scene draws attention to the gourmet kitchen, for example (Paging Meridith Baer). Such movies would then be showcased on the house's own website, the real estate agent's listing, and across social media.

But perhaps hopeful sellers should all just invest in a few apples and cucumbers at the supermarket next time. Several years ago, Chicago's Smell and Taste Research and Treatment Foundation was working with a few claustrophobic volunteers, and researchers were testing to see if any kind of scent could calm their symptoms. Surprisingly, certain smells did indeed alter the subjects' perception of space. Green apples and cucumbers combined calmed those claustrophobics by suggesting a larger space, while barbecue smoke had the reverse effect. Some developers have already leveraged those results. Firms like D.R. Horton have used fans to diffuse the smell of fresh baked apple pies in show homes. Adding a fresh cucumber to the recipe might eke out a few extra bucks. Indeed, few real estate agents will wear fragrance when meeting clients, a testament to the power of smell.*

* A quick digression into the strange and fascinating world of scent marketing. Smell is the only one of our five senses that bypasses the headmaster-like frontal cortex; rather, it has a pipeline to the limbic system, the earliest and most instinct-driven part of our brains.

Just as those ancillary industries and tactics have emerged to help sellers, a little bit of preparedness and observation can help buyers outfox such flimflamming. All it takes is patience and research to strong-arm a large discount. Start by looking at how long a house has been on the market.

Time is as unkind to the value of a house as it is to a hard-partying supermodel. Like a winter coat still sitting in a store after Christmas, houses that have been on the market too long are primed for a mark-down. Rarely will an explicit reduction be made, as that's too blatant a signal of a seller's urgency. But in normal conditions, most experts esti-mate that if a house goes unsold after a dozen showings and up to twenty-five days on market, it's around 10 percent overpriced and offers should be adjusted accordingly. By the time a house is on sale for ninety days, that percentage could rise to 15 percent.

Real estate agent and blogger Ardell DellaLoggia also recommends investigating the mortgage held on a property to see what an owner owes. Anyone whose monthly mortgage payment exceeds the average rental rate for a similar property is under pressure to sell, and the buyer is more likely to snag a bargain. You can also research if the owner has bought a new property yet, and what they spent: Two mortgages are a drain on anyone's resources. Since the real estate bubble burst, all-cash offers have also become more appealing; brave buyers can offer significantly less if the sale isn't contingent on complicated financing. It's even worthwhile seeking out homes where someone has died. Agents are legally mandated to disclose that information, and the squeamishness of some supersti-tious types can offer an opening to the hard-nosed and tight-fisted.

Staging, too, can be sidestepped. DellaLoggia recommends first going to the bedroom and rooting around in the closets. If you find men's or

---

Would-be presidential candidate Lee Myung-bak of South Korea launched a fragrance, Great Korea, that was intended to inspire hope and victory. Spritzed at rallies and polling booths, he won by the largest margin of any candidate since the current election system was intro-duced in 1987. The US army is a major customer for scent-marketing firms, too: When staging battlefield simulations, it's easy enough to replicate architecture, climate, and the local people of, say, Kabul. What is lacking, though, is the smell of battle: dead bodies, vomit, burning buildings. Soldiers trained in unscented scenarios perform 30 to 40 percent better; with smells piped-in, the number rises to 85 percent.

women's clothes exclusively in a family home, that's a subtle hint that divorce is the reason for the sale, and a likely spur to accept a low offer (just double check that the sellers aren't a gay couple, though). Examine the labels on the hanging clothes, too. "You can tell by the quality: If you don't see any crappy clothes, and they're all perfectly spaced, you know the agent or stager brought those in," DellaLoggia says. After all, even millionaires shop at Old Navy these days.

Next, head to the kitchen and check the fridge. If there's a milk carton, check the expiration date: However homey the place might seem, a months-old sell-by date is a tip-off that the entire setup is a sham. There are structural clues that can prove helpful, too. Freshly built handicapped ramps can signal an ailing owner, again likely to be keen to offload the property. Other homes have an architectural Achilles' heel: If the interior and exterior are mismatched—an antebellum mansion, say, gutted to monochrome minimalism—there's a far smaller pool of buyers for such a home and less overall competition lowers the final price.

Then again, you could just sign up for Housetipper.com, the Groupon for real estate. A part-time project started by an established Coldwell Banker broker, the site sets up relationships with developers, realtors, and ancillary businesses to offer cut-price offers. Just like Groupon, there's a minimum number of buyers that's required to turn the discount live, though the time limit on such big-ticket deals is weeks rather than two or three days. One LA firm has offered a $40 coupon for a $4,000 rebate at closing, while a Chicago realtor's $50 Housetipper promo guaranteed $2,500 in cash in the same way (provided it was within twelve months of buying the coupon and the transaction was $350,000 or more). Housetipper isn't limited to home sales, either: You can even get a $1,700 stainless steel refrigerator for just $51, or $1,200 worth of solar paneling for $48. Groupon itself trialed a similar cashback-at-closing deal in Chicago, but after grabbing headlines rather than sales—just over two hundred people signed up, earning the firm barely $2,500—it quietly retreated from this sector.

Real estate is a reminder that most shoppers are more primed for the new bargain (and bargaining) era than they might realize. Flexibility allows prices to go up as well as down; smart buyers and sellers can manipulate that movement in their favor. Is that the only risk for shoppers, though? Unfortunately, as Groupon demonstrates, there are other very different challenges that can emerge in an all-sale world.

The Grouponzi Scheme?

Things should be going so well: Groupon is perfectly positioned to dominate a world obsessed with deals. Yet it seems increasingly unworthy of that $16 billion valuation, as the business model seems to be more Grouponzi scheme than viable business. Shares that sold for $20 on the first day of trading had jettisoned a staggering 80 percent of their value just twelve months later.*

Some of its challenges are unique to the company, rather than its concept. Its daffy CEO was a huge burden, until he was unceremoniously ousted in February 2013. Andrew Mason is the ultimate kidult, having cultivated a studied wackiness that renders him the wrong kind of joke. Professional goof-offs, such as claiming to have experimented sleeping in his clothes so he could wake up a little later each morning, for example, or staging an employee bonding game that somehow involved slashing open stuffed bears with knives, became a liability to the multinational that his firm had become. Typical was the faux PSA ads it ran during 2011's Superbowl that prompted VC legend Guy Kawasaki to tweet: "Groupon, you suck . . ." In one spot, former Oscar nominee Timothy Hutton was reduced to making bad taste gags about China's oppression of Tibet being offset by a great fish curry deal at a Tibetan restaurant (hopefully, Hutton has fired his agent and isn't planning a trip to Beijing any time soon).

Mason's unprofessionalism was never more evident, though, than when one of his outré all-staff e-mails was leaked to the press during the firm's quiet period, and almost derailed Groupon's entire IPO (one analyst called it "the botch up of the century"). In that e-mail, Mason boasted

* Perhaps the founders should have been smarter than to siphon off thank-you payments to themselves, as large as $380 million, while the company floundered in this way.

about a bizarre assortment of the firm's achievements, from its British arm selling $2 million of mattresses in one day to jokes about how its desperate overseas clones were resorting to kidnapping Groupon employees' first-born children.* Eventually, it wasn't madcap antics that cost him his job, but mismanagement: After the stock plunged 25 percent in a single day, Mason was frogmarched out. His reaction was characteristically juvenile, comparing his tenure at Groupon to a 1991 video game, "Battletoads." "If Groupon was 'Battletoads,' it would be like I made it all the way to the Terra Tubes without dying on my first ever playthrough," he said in his farewell letter, then added with atypical sincerity, "I'm OK with having failed at this part of the journey."

Even without Mason's meddling, Groupon may not thrive. For all its pop culture punch, the company is a flimsy operation as riddled with built-in vulnerabilities as Lindsay Lohan (and just as much its own worst enemy). In a world of too much stuff, the ease with which Groupon can help business liquidate excess should be lucrative. Unfortunately, the premise it promises—that increased volumes will offset diminished margins—is painfully flawed. McKinsey Consulting has analyzed this relationship, and its bean counters showed that sales require a massive 20 percent uptick in volume to counter just a 5 percent reduction in selling price. Imagine the enormous bulk-buying needed to offset the 50 percent discount that Groupon strong-arms on its vendors. It's almost impossible in a world where, as we've seen, supply is constantly outstripping demand. When the firm does occasionally manage to generate frenzy, even that can backfire. Take one Santa's Grotto, deluged after an overenthusiastic copywriter boasted of a winter wonderland complete with train ride on-site. There was neither, but subsequent grinching and overcrowding led to

---

* The mattress world is a strange one, and a business that's long operated almost entirely via rotating sales. "Mattress Store Experiments with Non-Blowout Sale!" joked *The Onion*. The staff is unconcerned about this tide-turning approach, though. "If it doesn't work, we'll just go back to the tried and true methods," says one. "And blow the doors off this place next weekend with a conventional, all-out super sales spectacular." The parody is pointed. According to one retired furniture magnate, the "Going Out of Business" sales, in which mattress firms trade, are rarely monitored by local municipalities. Permits for such sales last only sixty days, but the furniture magnate would regularly extend the promo for a year. With good reason, too: As soon as the GOOB signs appeared, sales volume tripled, remaining at twice the normal levels as long as those signs were up.

swearing matches and threats. One elf was so upset at the treatment she received from half-price parents that she resigned.

There have been other splashy problems with unsatisfied merchants, including one waffle spot in Washington, DC, that blamed its shutdown after just three months on an ill-judged Groupon deal. "The margins are only going down. They've already hit up everybody who is the lowest-hanging fruit from a merchant standpoint," grumbles analyst Sucharita Mulpuru, as much a cynic about this company as about Gilt Groupe. In an attempt to sweeten agreements, Groupon's own margins are being squeezed—some national merchants are reported to have wrangled 5 percent rather than 50 percent returns to the deal site on a promo. Groupon risks destroying its suppliers, and so the entire business, by selling them a flawed concept of ROI.

It's less a retail Robin Hood, giving ordinary people access to pricey treats they otherwise couldn't afford, and more commercial ebola, multiplying deals to a level that's lethal to the businesses offering them. The UK arm has been so overeager to scoop up new shoppers that it was knuckle-rapped by the government's consumer watchdog for misleading information. One involved a paintball operator that denied participants the promised (and paid-for) lunch, while another caught a restaurant claiming a "74% OFF" promo that was calculated only against the menu's priciest item.

Another issue centers on the fact that Groupon is based on an idea, not wholly owned intellectual property. As a result, there are now an estimated five hundred Groupon clones—one hundred of them in the United States alone—and climbing. Even more businesses are chasing the same limited number of customers and pressurizing the same vendors. Yipit.com does nothing but aggregate that daily haul, while Unsubscribedeals.com allows regretful overenthusiasts to whittle down their inbox clutter. DealsforDeeds.com helps you feel better about spending less by allocating a sliver of takings to a local nonprofit, while DealsGo-Round.com is like an eBay for unwanted discounts, where you can sell a soon-to-expire coupon to someone else who wants to use it sooner than you might.* Every one of these sites is vying to become the Amazon of discount—of course, Amazon has its own version, too, as well as a sizable investment in Groupon's feistiest rival, LivingSocial.com. LivingSocial has carved out its own identity by focusing on experiences rather than products, and on premium or luxury price points: 46 percent of its users are college graduates, versus just 25 percent of Internet users as a whole. Of those subscribers, 49 percent are more likely than average to earn $150,000 or more (no word on the penetration of *New Yorker* subscriptions).

These daily deal sites also sit alongside Gilt Groupe and its rivals, the flash sales that shill their markdowns with an infomercial-like urgency. Along with Gilt, RueLaLa, and Ideeli for fashion, there's MyHabit (another Amazon offshoot) or OneKingsLane.com for homewares, and Fab.com for half-price hipster goods. Though few, if any, of these deal merchants have yet proved their business model's long-term robustness, their short-term success is evidence at least of good timing. They also cater expressly to that oh-so-millennial desire for instant gratification, those brief attention spans and hunger for newness. One psychologist even believes that deal sites are benefiting from the shortfall between the straightened budgets on which twentysomethings today must live, and the materialistic expectations formed by overgenerous boom-time parenting.

The five-hundred-plus competitors have helped birth Groupon Fatigue, a coinage from a joint study by Rice and Cornell universities, where the relentless onslaught of deals has caused shoppers to pull back (as we've seen, less rather than more choice encourages us to open our wallets). The litany of negative neologisms emerging more recently hints

---

* The unexploited niches grow rarer, with the launch of the likes of ExoticDeals.com; it features a new adults-only deal every sixty-nine hours, of course. Coupawz.com is Groupon for pets, while WeedMaps.com curates local deals aimed at marijuana aficionados—though it misses the chance to offer snack food coupons alongside dispensaries' BOGO deals. Glenn Beck even took enough time out from worrying that our supposed moral meltdown is at the heart of America's economic troubles to set up his very own deal site, Marketplace.theblaze.com. It has a special Emergency and Survival channel, aimed at tightfisted would-be Ted Nugents, which sells reduced-price treats like MyPatriotSupply.com's $24.95 personal water filter cut down to just $24.95.

at how pop culture has come to view the concept, too. Businesses risk committing Grouponcide, going broke offering deals that are needlessly generous. They are bedeviled by Groupon Sluts, who consume with no brand or store loyalty, zombies driven solely by discounts. A date might be only Groupon Cute, not sexy enough to spend too much money impressing. Worst of all, who would want to be known as the Groupon Couple among their friends, the pair who is constantly boasting of discount Date Night activities like kayaking, wine tasting, and balloon rides? There's even a blog, The Bad Deal, set up to spotlight and shame some of the sharper practices that have emerged in the Grouponified world. Some Harvard economists went further and identified a looming problem that's one of Groupon's largest challenges: As more consumers use vouchers, they will become the norm. Discounts don't matter, they suggest, when there's literally no such thing as full price.

This sense that there's always a sale can make shopping an exhausting process, as you constantly fret that you could have found a better price. An all-discount world is one where buying is a time-consuming process, and sales can even backfire if shoppers feel unfairly treated. Was there a coupon you missed that everyone else used? Maybe Amex cardholders got an exclusive markdown and you paid with Visa? Didn't you read somewhere about a 10 percent discount if your name started with M? Such relentlessness could make it refreshing, relaxing even, to pay full price, as long as that meant you didn't have to worry that a sale might start tomorrow. Surprisingly, in this era of markdown mania, that's exactly the approach a tiny clutch of intriguing companies still takes.

6

Discountphobia: The Mainstays of Never Marking Down

Logo Tattoos, J.C. Penney's Retail Suicide, and How to Spot a Superfake

There's a new word jostling for place in the lexicon, an ill-defined concept emerging in response to the pressures of marking down: *discountphobia*.

> discountphobia *noun* (from Medieval Latin *discomputare* to discount + Greek *phobos* fear) Rabid fear of ever reducing a price, an allergy to sales or deals, irrational hatred of markdowns.
>
> Antonyms: bargain fever
>
> Usage: In a Grouponified world, isn't such discountphobia financial suicide? How could a few unsullied businesses all but resist that unstoppable, shopper-centric trend?

Yet that was long the case in the movie industry. Matinee and senior specials have been decades-old traditions, but other pricing promos for film fans were as likely as an Oscar nomination for Adam Sandler. The impasse was down to the dysfunctional and distrustful relationship between distributors, the studios that make the films, and the movie chains or exhibitors. Rival halves of the business bickered over every aspect of cinema operations. The studios carped that ticket prices were too high, and called the exhibitors greedy; since lousy popcorn was the majority of profit, anyway, why not slash ticket prices to encourage more than one visit a week? In retort, AMC et al complained that they had fixed costs to cover, such as building cutting-edge multiplexes. *Make better must-see flicks, Mr. Studio Executive, and moviegoers wouldn't focus on price.* Given such hostility, it's not surprising there was a logjam around promotions. Neither the studio nor the cinema was prepared to swallow the cost of cutting prices.

It didn't help that there were logistical issues, too. Cinema workers resemble low-waged clerks at supermarkets, and a coupon of some kind is a variable fraught with problems. For one thing, dealing with a discount slows down the cattle-herding process on a busy Friday night. Not to mention that a disengaged box office staffer might misunderstand or misapply a chit, causing embarrassment or denting profits. Caught in between these spat-prone siblings are the ordinary moviegoers (until pat-downs are mandatory, though, at least it's simple enough to smuggle in contraband candy).

So there was a mold-breaking move when distributor Lions Gate goosed a film that it fretted might underperform in spring 2011 by partnering with Groupon. The $11 ticket to the Matthew McConaughey vehicle *The Lincoln Lawyer* was reduced to a real-world price of $1. In other words, if the promotion was successful, for every $110 million grossed, the movie might truly bank just $10 million in real money. Lions Gate was prepared to offset that cost in exchange for creating a potential franchise hit. The promo earned brickbats from box office watchers, but a domestic gross of $58 million made the film successful enough to spawn a planned sequel. The fact that Lions Gate didn't rush to repeat this gimmick, though, is telling.*

---

* It was illegal for a supplier to remotely control third-party pricing stateside until 2007, when the Supreme Court struck down ninety years of antitrust laws. It ruled that manufacturers have the right to protect their product's image via price, a practice called *resale price maintenance.* The case centered on a boutique in Texas that had been denied the right to sell a line of Coach-lite handbags when the manufacturer disliked its overly deep discounting. Ruling 5–4, the majority opinion said that too much discounting would erode the profits needed to provide good service. The dissenting argument estimated that it would cost a family of four $750 to $1,000 extra a year in dollars spent on consumer goods, or around $300 billion in

Much like the beasts of Hollywood, beauty was also a sales-resistant industry—in this case, for strategic rather than squabblesome reasons. Long ago, L'Oréal, Estée Lauder, and their rivals realized that a 50 percent off sale didn't just damage margins but wreck the mystique of the products. Instead, miracle cream pushers foisted gifts-with-purchase on the customers, as typified by Clinique's Bonus time, when loyalists would wait to stock up on refills and get extra goodies for free. Sadly, in the last decade, beauty has blotted its P&L with excess stock, much like everyone else. Beauty brands, too, have succumbed to selling half-price hope in a jar on Gilt Groupe, or even off-loading excess to Perfumania, a staple of many outlet malls across the country.

In a Grouponified world, then, shoppers stand center stage, surrounded by overstock that means they can finagle a deal on anything. Discountphobia should have been eradicated throughout the world—but that isn't quite true. Four contrarian companies remain determined to avoid discounting, whatever the cost, clinging to full price as ferociously as a Beverly Hills matron grasps her youth. Their promise to customers remains simple: It's safe to buy something today without worrying about a half-price sale tomorrow. The companies form an oddball quartet: a computer giant (Apple), a firm selling frocks and bags (Louis Vuitton), a coffee conglomerate (Nespresso), and the world's worthiest dolls (American Girl).

However their products may differ, the quartet shares an intriguing approach to business. This is a cunning strategy: It's as customer friendly as a shopping 3.0 buyer would require, yet markdowns are not its central tenet.

The First Step to Pantsformation

A few things are obvious walking into an American Girl store: It's huge (42,000 square feet over three floors), it's retail crack for any girl under

---

total across the country. It's probably the first and last time Supreme Court Chief Justice John Roberts ever worried about the merits of handbags.

ten (while their bored teenage brothers sit playing video games slumped on the floor in the corner), and it's very, very pink.* For the nonnegotiable price of $105, you can take home a historical American Girl, grounded in a certain period from the slave-era South to Watergate (Julie is flagged as a child of the early 1970s by her hippie braid) and packaged with a book that tells her empowering backstory. There's a portrait studio for keepsake snapshots together, and a hair salon where the doll's braid can be teased and styled in dozens of different ways. Some tykes might shun such historical flimflammery and opt instead for a rubber Mini Me, the so-called My American Girl. Lined up in vitrines like an army of plastic zombies, each offers a different combination of hair, skin, and eye color that children can browse to match their own complexions. It resembles a vintage Benetton ad, only shinier and a tad more soulless.

What isn't so clear at first glance is that the store really sells just a single toy. Look closer and you'll see box after box of near-identical dolls, each just gussied up in a different outfit. Such a ruthless limit on stock is one reason the company can always avoid marking them down. "Oh no, our dolls never go on sale," says a busty woman, frowning, her black hair as glossy and implausible as the toys that surround her. The 18-inch dolls, snub nosed and two toothed, all have the same soft body and stiff limbs. The white ones all have identical faces, while the scant selection of other ethnicities have slight tweaks, mostly flatter noses. The American Girl company needs only a few molds to churn out thousands, if not millions, of these chipmunk-cheeked toddlers. The implied economies of scale are obvious—especially since newish owner Mattel shifted production of American Girls to China without a whiff of irony.

American Girl was founded by a former teacher and news anchor, Pleasant Rowland, in 1986. She started the company to introduce a distinctive alternative to busty Barbie in the form of wholesome girlish dolls, aged nine or so, sold complete with their own storybooks foregrounding pluck and morals. It didn't hurt that Rowland owned a printing firm, either, so

---

* Also obvious is that no one trusts an adult male dawdling solo in a doll megastore. Duly noted: Borrow a toy-minded Sherpa as an alibi next time.

there would be synergy with her existing operation with that new undertaking. The line launched with a trio of dolls but has exploded in the twenty-seven years since, with teams of historians dedicated to ensuring accuracy in even the smallest detail. For example, when two BFFs, one black and the other white, were launched against a backdrop of boozy, floozy-filled nineteenth-century New Orleans, staffers even counted the city blocks between their respective, fictitious, homes to ensure accuracy in their backstory.

No matter how huge the roster might grow, though, it always uses the same basic molds to minimize those enemies of full price that bedevil retail today: overheads and -runs. American Girl hasn't passed those cost savings along to the customer, though: Prices for the dolls themselves have risen steadily from $74 in 2000 to $95 in 2010 and $105 in 2012.

American Girl's inventory is typical of any discountphobic brand. Stock must be lean and without much variation; little, if any, should be seasonal. Year in and year out, the product can remain much the same, sitting on the shelf patiently until it sells to someone, anyone, at full price. In American Girl's case, it offers only one time-sensitive toy: the annual, limited-edition Girl of the Year (2012's was McKenna, whose sporty spunk synced handily with the Olympics and whose story also handily involved a wheelchair bound tutor as a sop to the Paralympics). These dolls usually sell out long before December 31. If they do, it's easy enough to churn out a few more; if they don't, returning the doll to the factory for a new head next year is just as straightforward.

Just as American Girl juggles stock adroitly to avoid end-of-season sales, so do the other three discountphobic companies. Take a look around an Apple store and tally the number of products in stock: surprisingly few, especially not counting third-party accessories. Sure, you can opt for larger memory in that iPhone, or upgrade the processor in your laptop; an iPad can come with or without 4G. But these are minimal differences, mostly just tweaks to the innards, limiting SKUs to a manageable number. Apple's approach is borderline formulaic compared to the boastful built-to-order model that felled Dell and Gateway.

It's far more profitable, too. Consider Nespresso, which spends millions each year emphasizing the nuances of each of the sixteen flavors it sells, the possibilities of taste boundless. Nonetheless, each is sold in the same, identically shaped pod.

As for Louis Vuitton, the ready-to-wear designs of the label's creative director Marc Jacobs offer ample PR, but this collection is basically a marketing expense, akin to 3-D advertising. No one is supposed to want to buy MJ's outlandish clothes; rather, they're intended to stoke enthusiasm for the firm's true moneymaker, high-margin products like leather goods. Around 80 percent of the brand's stock of those is perennial; it's profitable happenstance that monogrammed bags are timeless and trans-seasonal. If an LV-logo tote doesn't sell in December, it will still be in fashion come February; there's no need to use hefty discounts to clear shelf space for new deliveries. Clearly, the first step in immunizing an operation against discounts is simple: Keep the stock lean and evergreen.

So let's imagine we're mulling a brand-new company, prepping a fancy business plan to show to investors. This company will be an icon of shopping 3.0, with a single mission: to be the anti-Groupon, avoiding sales at all costs, exactly as these brands do. We don't care what we make, as long as it's markdown-proofed while still irresistible to buyers. Perhaps that decades-long wardrobe staple, the white T-shirt? A company called Tees 'R' Us has potential, sure, but it's hard to swiftly brand such simple garments. Clothing is good, though, especially menswear; it's less trend driven and more perennial than the women's market. We'll need a gimmick: What about the perfect pair of pants, guaranteed to fit flawlessly, never to bunch or crumple at the waistband? Initially, let's offer a pair of chinos in standard sizes; the only decision a shopper need make is between three or four colors. In our business plan, we'll call this revolutionary company Pantsformation.

What's the next precaution to take against markdown proofing? How do we insulate our firm entirely against the Too Much Stuff syndrome? So far, we've limited the SKUs to keep inventory lean, but we also need fiefdom over volumes. The way to do that is to control every aspect of the manufacturing and selling process. We'll monitor each pair of pants from factory to selling floor to shopping bag. It's a practice known as *vertical integration*, and involves directing how, where, and when the product is sold with an iron fistish firmness. No one exerts a tighter grip in that way than Louis Vuitton.

Vuitton's Secret

A few years before the Euro meltdown that plunged Greece into Dickensian poverty, LV had picked Athens as the site of its next flagship store, a brand wonderland that would communicate the cachet of French craftsmanship to the Athenian hoi polloi. Not long after it opened, a fat-walleted businessman came into the store and eyed its stock greedily. Grabbing a sales assistant, he tried to wheedle a bulk deal on a couple of items. The staffer demurred, so the wealthy local upped his offer. "What if I buy five pieces, or pay cash? Does that get me a discount?" he puffed. Still no luck. "Okay, then. Give me the whole store. Everything. Do I get a volume discount then?" His question was overheard by one of the brand's senior management, parachuted in to inspect the newly opened store. That exec stepped in to help the sales assistant. "Excuse me, sir, but we'd be delighted to sell you the entire shop," he said, smiling. "We might just need a few moments to tally the cost. But it will be full price, with no exceptions." It's a testament to the lure of Louis Vuitton that the man left a few minutes later, having coughed up retail for a single bag.

That high-ranking exec repeated the story proudly to colleagues many times, as the perfect illustration of Vuitton's dedication to charging full price. Such posturing is possible only thanks to the brand's obsession with vertical integration.

The practice dates back to the 1970s, when an outsider was tasked to run the leather maker for the first time. Henri Recamier had amassed fortune and experience in equal measure as a steel magnate, and he brought both with him when he took over Vuitton, then a fusty and family-run brand. Recamier landed the job only because he'd married into the clan, and so was tapped by the Vuitton matriarch as her successor, the first non-blood relative to steer the firm. Nonetheless, he was stunned when he turned his pragmatic industrial eye on the luxury world. The business model was dramatically uneven: It was retailers, Henri noted, who made the real money, marking up leather bags by 100 percent or more while manufacturers struggled. Nixing that greedy retail middleman—in other words, opening wholly owned stores or controlling concessions—would mean Vuitton could keep that money for itself. So that's what Recamier did. His move doubled profit margins overnight: As conventional luxury firms remained at the traditional 15 to 20 percent, his reinvented company hit 40 percent or more.

Forty years later, Vuitton runs glossy ads starring Mikhail Gorbachev and Madonna and launches splashy collaborations with artists like Takashi Murakami. This is a distraction, though, since LV is largely obsessed with two things: efficiency and control (well, that and making lots of money). Unlike many designer concessions, the LV mini boutique in your local department store sits on leased space, a retail cuckoo squatting on the selling floor. Vuitton can staff and operate it directly. Stock isn't sold wholesale to the store, which could then bundle it into season-end sales. Rather, it's controlled entirely by the headquarters in Paris. One story above all best illustrates Vuitton's focus.

In 2005, at the height of luxury's new mass-market frenzy, the firm was facing a problem. Strangely, given that this was the era of surfeit, demand was outstripping supply. It was damaging the brand's reputation; shelves risked being emptied as soon as stock arrived, especially if shoppers spotted any hint of the year's unexpected hit, a denim monogram bag. Quickly, LV turned to McKinsey's bean counters and asked for help in weatherproofing production against such problems in the future. The consultants toothcombed processes that had remained unchanged for decades, and quickly spotted the inefficiency of Vuitton's craftsman-style model. McKinsey reorganized the factory floor into small teams that sat at U-shaped work stations; sewing machines were on one side, assembly tables on the other, so workers didn't even need to stand up to pass piecework along to the next person in the production chain.

The impact was instant. At the beginning of the year, thirty craftspeople spent around eight days producing a signature logo tote—after McKinsey's intervention, it took only six people just one day to produce the same item. Whereas most luxury brands have a thirty-four-week lead time on production, Vuitton's shrank to just six. This gave it more in common with a mass manufacturer and retailer like Zara, which famously owns its own factories so it can tweak production runs in real-time response to sales upticks or downturns.*

Operating with such leanness has another bonus: It reduces the risk of excess stock at season's end. If something isn't selling, Vuitton is nimble enough to halt production quickly. McKinsey even meddled with store practices to tighten the process. Should a customer decide to buy a bag, it decreed, no sales assistant should waste time ducking back into the stockroom to fetch one. Rather a full-time picker was billeted there to wrap whatever was requested in precious tissue paper and send it up to the shop floor.

As Recamier had realized forty years before, the equation for success at full price was simple: controlling the channel meant you controlled the price. Without a middleman, margins are higher, offering a plumper profit cushion during downturns. This practice also confers exclusivity, since you can buy a given product only from an authorized dealer where price is fixed. There's no risk of your standing in the store, Smartphone in hand, and Googling for a better deal online, that new and pesky practice known as *showrooming*.† "Its entire history, Vuitton has never gone on sale. No matter how much clients want to hem and haw, you don't budge," one floorwalker told me proudly. "The people who work at Vuitton, we love that we can say that." If only Vuitton had been able to resist the lure to shift production to China and expand for extra efficiency; as we'll see, such greed creates a lethal chink in this precision process.

The takeaway for our pant company here involves operations: Pants-formation should own its stores, whether virtual or brick and mortar. It should plan to buy or build its own factories, too, as soon as budget allows. No one else should be permitted to make or sell our product

---

* In comparison, H&M, Forever 21, and most other fast fashion retailers rely on outsourced factories with six-month turnarounds, meaning that around 80 percent of inventory is non-negotiably locked-in before the selling season even begins. If that denim bag is an unexpected best-seller, in other words, tough luck.
† The same impulse drives Macy's to sign up brand name endorsers such as Donald Trump or Tommy Hilfiger to produce exclusive collections for its stores that cannot be compared with stock elsewhere.

without Pantsformation's oversight. The other three refuseniks profiled here echo Vuitton's obsession with vertical integration. In 2012, twelve years after Nespresso opened the first of its chain of cafes-cum-showrooms-cum-shops in Paris, three hundred stores were projected worldwide (watch your back, Starbucks). Whatever concessions remain— including the one in the former bargain basement at Harry Gordon's Selfridges—can opt out of sales elsewhere in the store, and are staffed by the manufacturer. Similarly, a parent can buy American Girl dolls in only two ways: via www.americangirl.com or in one of its dozen freestanding stores from Houston to Miami to Minneapolis. Apple's approach to vertical integration is perhaps even more glittering than Louis Vuitton's. Until 2001, it relied on what was called the Authorized Reseller program, where stores could apply for the privilege of selling one of Steve Jobs's precious gadgets. That year, the notoriously controlling computer maker went one step further and opened its own stores. How it runs those retail spaces is another lesson in how to salesproof Pantsformation.

The Core of the Store

Don't think of your retail destination as anything as ordinary as a *shop*. A brand keen to sidestep discounts must create temples, places of pilgrimage that are as much about opening new markets as closing a sale. Apple doesn't even bother putting its name on the façade; instead, it uses just the logo, glowing brightly like a retail Death Star. This is a place operated for those in the know, it seems to say. The success of such stores was a particular point of pride for Steve Jobs—admittedly, hardly a humble man at the best of times. "This store grosses more per square foot than any store in the world," he boasted of Apple's glass cube–topped flagship on Fifth Avenue in Manhattan. "It also grosses more in total— absolute dollars, not just per square foot—than any store in New York. That includes Saks and Bloomingdale's." Perhaps, but Jobs wasn't really making a fair comparison: In a shopper-pleasing gesture, he decreed Apple's location should remain open twenty-four hours a day, 365 days a year.

The rapid emergence of Apple stores was also, at least in part, down to good timing. The dot-com-driven millennial downturn made it easier and cheaper to find space in 2001, since rental rates had cratered in its wake. Apple's financial exposure was reduced this way but still there was resistance when Jobs mooted the plan. After all, it was around the same time that Gateway's retail operation was imploding. Jobs pushed ahead, though, convinced he knew better than everyone. Yet again, he was right, especially after he hired Ron Johnson to helm the nascent division. Poached from Target, where he was vice president of merchandising, Johnson spent six months workshopping Apple store's concept with Jobs in a secret warehouse near Cupertino. The first Apple Store opened in May 2001 in Tyson's Corner, Virginia.

Johnson can take credit for much of the stores' success. It was his idea, for example, to lay each space out in a customer-friendly way, focusing more on activities that gadgets enabled than on the models themselves. Headphones would be displayed with iPods so a browser could road test both; a cluster of computers might be teed up to show how to make and play movies. Johnson was fortunate that Jobs understood the importance of quality, too: Apple is said to spend around $200 per square foot outfitting its stores, where other mall retailers such as the Gap spend about half as much. Those display tables weather hard daily use so well because they're solid wood; usually designers opt for veneer. The glass in store windows is specially made to be non-reflective but to offer high light penetration. Laptop screens are painstakingly displayed at a 70-degree angle, though such precision isn't just down to Jobsian finickiness. At that angle, Apple found, customers instinctively reach out and adjust the screen from a standing position, forcing them to touch and engage with the computer. WiFi is free for anyone, and terminals are set up like a gratis Internet café for browsing and checking e-mail.

Even Jobs made a few mistakes at first—notably, underestimating how the original floors, designed in the same pale wood as the display benches, would scuff and age. But his solution was even more sumptuous. A year after Tyson's Corner opened, Jobs revised the corporate stylebook and opted for gray Italian marble floors, the same kind he'd spotted on the sidewalks in Florence, Italy. An ersatz concrete replica wouldn't do, he barked. It had to be real marble, and identical everywhere, so Apple tapped a single family-owned quarry in Italy as its supplier. "We select only three percent of what comes out of the mountain, because it has to have the right shading and veining and purity," Ron Johnson said later. "Steve felt very strongly that we had to get the color right and it had to be a material with high integrity." The results are impressive: In an average mall, an 8,000-square-foot Apple store logs sales above $5,000 per square foot. Compare that to an 80,000-square-foot department store like Macy's, where sales per square foot hover around $300.

It's all the more impressive given the tough trading conditions for brick-and-mortar retailers, lumbered with overheads that their online-only rivals can avoid. Each of our four sales-shunning brands approaches retail with an unusual mindset: A store, they reason, has many uses and only one of them involves selling products. More than that, the physical store is a showroom, for touching and feeling the beauty of each item. It's a place of pilgrimage where would-be acolytes can linger and soak up the brand's essence. Consider Louis Vuitton. Think of how many times a monogram-toting twentysomething points to a bag and says, "This? Oh it's my favorite Louis," with a slangy familiarity that implies kin more than customer. That emotional connection has grown from the brand's effort to expand beyond being a simple place to shop. The gigantic LV outpost on the Champs-Elysées in Paris has been more than just a retail outlet since 2006. The seventh floor is home to the Espace Culturel, which stages edgy contemporary art shows, underlining the brand's reach beyond fashion. Elsewhere, Vuitton flagships have been dubbed *maisons*; they're full of touches that de-emphasize the commercial component. Take one of the newest to open, in Sydney, Australia. Nothing as tacky as a cash register is on display—those are tucked away behind a false wall. A VIP area (codenamed Constellation, as in star) is so secluded that it has its own air-conditioning. Why should the posh and the plebs even share the same oxygen, after all?

Nespresso didn't open strict stores, instead opting for hybrid shops-cum-cafés to emphasize that dreaded marketing buzzword, *lifestyle*. Come here to buy a Nespresso machine, the store suggests, and you can hang out with fellow devotees, a caffeinated clubhouse. Nespresso even refers to its regular buyers as a Club. There's also a café at American Girl Place (again, note the name, which minimizes suggestions that you're here to spend money), where devotees can celebrate a heavily themed birthday party. The biggest stores originally included a 150-seat theater where for $25, fans could enjoy kid-friendly musicals like *The American Girls Revue* and *Circle of Friends*, complete with a five-piece orchestra. Only a nasty spat with Equity led to their quiet closure. To celebrate its twenty-fifth anniversary, the firm teamed up with Celebrity cruises to offer a week-long trip to the Caribbean aimed at American Girl fans. The package included cooking classes, chats with authors of some of the books, and a giant birthday party. The ship sold out in forty-eight hours.

The lesson for our potential pant firm is clear: Opening a test store in some suburban mall isn't enough. We'll need to operate a brick-and-mortar store that transcends traditional retail. A huge flagship on Fifth Avenue in New York with a stage set for concerts would be ideal; musicians could come in occasionally and sing the praises of how much they love our pants. That's a great idea though perhaps a little pricey for our VC-friendly business plan. Rather, let's create an appointment-only space, hidden away from the street and decorated more like an apartment than a shop, with sofas and soft lighting. Its purpose will be advice and guidance, so any man can come to try on the pants for himself and prove the fit is perfect. If he wants a beer while he's browsing, we'll have a few on ice.

So far, the factors that shelter a brand from a blizzard of sales are straightforward enough: keeping stock simple and controlling channels to avert price-denting excess, and pleasing a picky shopper by offering a place to linger that feels more than a traditional shop. The next trait all refusenik brands share, unfortunately, is a little more nebulous. Think of it as the Would You Tattoo? test.

Would You Tattoo?

It's one of waggish photographer David LaChapelle's most iconic images: Rapper Lil' Kim looks coyly at the camera, naked but for a quiff of blonde hair, her hands strategically posed to keep the picture G-rated. All she wears is a full-body tattoo of the Louis Vuitton monogram pattern, repeated over and over. Kim's tribute to the brand (run by her BFF and fellow inking enthusiast Marc Jacobs) may have been CGI, but others have gone further; the Internet is awash with fans' permanent tributes from a single LV insignia to full sleeves or an entire head. Vuitton so admires this gesture that the models' necks were covered in faux logo tattoos during its menswear show for Spring 2011.*

Hipster nerds have made the same commitment to Apple—though its ubiquitous white headphones are akin to a temporary tattoo that millions wear every day. Doubtless a few edgy tweens have scribbled an American Girl logo on a wrist or an ankle in black pen in frenzied devotion to their favorite doll. Only Nespresso doesn't boast fans proudly showcasing their loyalty in ink—well, at least not yet.

Why would anyone volunteer to be an unpaid, lifelong advert for a company that he or she doesn't even own? No longer just buyers, those tattoo-sporting superfans have essentially volunteered to become advocates for the brands they adore. It's like the luxury world's version of the cultish self-improvement program Landmark Forum. Each of these companies is selling more than its product; it's a sense of PLU me-too-ness. Apple embodied that promise in its long-running Get a Mac ads, costarring John Hodgman (schlubbily personifying the Windows PC) and Justin Long, the dapper Apple avatar who looked like he'd just stepped out from behind a Genius Bar. Every viewer, it implied, would rather be a Mac than a sadsack. Owning Apple product inducted anyone into the same cult of cool.

---

* The label isn't always so forgiving, as artist Luis Gispert found out firsthand after producing a collection of photographs that spotlit the subculture where cars were outfitted in (supposedly fake) branded materials like Burberry, Gucci, and especially Louis Vuitton. "If you have Louis Vuitton, you're the man," he says. What stunned Gispert most of all wasn't the subjects, but the reaction to his project from the luxury brands. Silence from Chanel, Gucci, and co., but Louis Vuitton's lawyers threatened a cease and desist. At his meeting with the team, Gispert saw a "telephone book–thick dossier of all the creative people they've gone after for using their logo." Eventually, the threats receded under the fair-use statute. Then again, one sourcing agent told Gispert that some of the fabric used in such upholstery wasn't fake but overruns from monogram-printing factories in China that sold on the black market. Perhaps LV's snittishness wasn't entirely unfounded.

The implicit prestige that the firm sells, though, comes at a price. Apple laptops are often three or four times as expensive as their PC counterparts, but this is somehow comforting rather than worrisome. The cost of many luxury goods doubled in the *Sex and the City*–powered decade after 1998. Vuitton relentlessly pushes ever higher with annual increases that pursewatchers monitor obsessively. American Girl dolls now fetch 40 percent more than in 2007. Nespresso boutiques display prices (always in reassuring whole numbers, much like American Girl) in such small type that it almost feels like the store is apologizing for having to disclose anything so unseemly.* For these premium products, it's cash for cachet.

Such allure is explained by the theory of the Veblen good. Thorstein Veblen was a nineteenth-century economist who published an influential book titled *The Theory of the Leisure Class*. In it, he outlined the rise of what we might now call the status symbol. Economists, though, honor it with his name: A Veblen good is anything whose desirability increases in tandem with its price. In other words, the more expensive it becomes, the more we crave it as a symbol of our own social rank and power. As much buying in as buying it, it offers gilt by association. No wonder fanatics of such brands would go as far as permanently inking themselves as devotees, marking their status with a symbol.

Countless studies have shown the irrational and elusive power of such a feel-good good. In one study, researchers found that when students paid full price for a can of Red Bull, they were able to solve a larger number of puzzles after guzzling the drink than peers who'd paid less for the same soda. It enhanced their confidence, if not their innate brainpower.

A team at Stanford University asked volunteers to sample several Cabernet Sauvignon wines that were priced from $5 to $90, then told them to note their favorite. The trick was that there were only three varieties in total, randomly ascribed different price points. Nonetheless, the $90 bottle consistently topped the list regardless of the true caliber of its contents. In other words, a high price tells us to believe in quality.

---

* The prices are printed in numbers so tiny, in fact, that most fortysomething buyers squint as they fumble for spectacles in store—doubtless an inadvertent but handy way of keeping the demographics fresh, too.

In yet another scenario, volunteers were asked to try a fake medicine, Veladone-Rx, that was supposedly an opioid pain reliever much like codeine (it was a placebo). What scientists wanted to test wasn't clinical effectiveness but the impact of the cost. The medicine was offered to one set of volunteers at $2.50 per pill, and to a second set at 10 cents, a bargain basement price. Money might not buy you happiness, but it seems it can buy you pain relief; in the former group, almost everyone reported that the medicine worked as expected, while only half of the ten centers said Veladone-Rx worked at all.

It's almost illogical that premium pricing would immunize a brand against markdowns, but the aspirational quality of a Veblen good confers such exemption. Identifying with a brand in this way, helping buyers to stand out, is more useful than ever in a world of Too Much Stuff. Turning Pantsformation's trousers from a commodity into a sale-proof status item is simple: We should charge more, aiming to be an overnight Veblen good that shoppers yearn to see and be seen in.

It's important, though, to emphasize premium rather than price, to be costly but never showily so. American Girl's current dollmaker-in-chief, Ellen Brothers, always defends how much she charges for her hunks of plastic, whose price hikes have happened in part to shore up their Veblenness. "We've never shied away from that price point. It is quality, it's age-appropriate and historically accurate," she said. "It's so much more than a toy. It's emotional engagement; it's a friend; it's a history lesson; it's a keepsake."

Following the Veblen template when pricing our perfect-fit pants, let's offer casual chinos for $90, a little more than double a standard pair at Banana Republic. If only we could ask our staff members to undergo a logo tattoo on a prominent position—lower arm, ideally—before their first day at work. The next best thing is giving them a quirky title to band them together as a posse, a club that customers can aspire to join. How about Ninjas? Then we can train them in depth to explain the product, its built-in value, and uniqueness.

After all this, one final lesson remains to be applied to Pantsformation like a sales salve. It isn't about the selling process, but rather how cherished a shopper is made to feel once they get home.

Calling the Shots

Every morning, countless Americans trudge bleary-eyed into the kitchen, fumbling for a pod or two at their Nespresso machines. The drink will jolt them awake with a pulse of caffeine, an accepted part of their pre-work ritual and a daily reminder of how crucial this neo-espresso has become. A few hours later, over lunch, the phone rings. The voice on the other end is a chatty Nespresso staffer. She's checking in about whether you're satisfied with the coffee quality the machine is producing. Oh, it seems to be sticking a little, does it? She'll be glad to send a temporary replacement to use while the original model is examined by their technicians. Is there a Nespresso boutique nearby, she asks? She just wants to offer a quick reminder that it will always deliver extra pods, whenever needed—although if only you lived in Paris, you'd be guaranteed fresh stock at your door within just two hours. Thanks again for being a Nespresso customer, she says, before hanging up. Opinion solicited, the Nespresso loyalist feels respected and valued by that little gadget that sits on the countertop. That call telegraphs one thing: Nespresso really cares about each and every one of its customers. In an era where shoppers hold sway, it's a wily move.

Such anti-telemarketing is what the firm dubs a nursing call, and contributes to why Nepresso can shun discounting. The company maintains a relationship with buyers long after they've left the store. Such slavish, almost cultish service helps both keep prices high and shoppers happy; more than half of the firm's 7,500 staff worldwide is employed to directly work with customers, and 50 percent of new Club members arrive at Nespresso via a friend who's already signed up. That's a brainwashing rate that even Scientologists should envy.

Compare this to the Apple Care program, which provides unlimited technical support in exchange for a small fee. Apple Care was a masterstroke in protecting the full price of the brand. Thank Ron Johnson again for the last-minute addition of another crucial aftercare element, Genius Bars, to the store blueprints. He'd taken his prototyping team on a two-day retreat. One discussion centered on the best customer service they had received—time and again, team members cited luxury hotels like Four Seasons or Ritz Carlton as paragons. Johnson blended the lobby bar and the concierge personnel found in both hotels to create the hangout-cum-help-desk now known as the Genius Bar. It helped turn Apple into the antithesis of the traditional electronics store, where customers and salesmen were antagonists.

Johnson was lucky that the mainstreaming of computing had broadened tech know-how from antisocial nerds to skinny-jeaned twentysomethings. It provided him with a passel of sociable, knowledgeable staff. The cheery onsite team could tackle almost any problem, thanks to the good pay and training, including four weeks at the store and a month at headquarters in California. Johnson wanted to make Apple's retail spaces feel welcoming and cool, full of young, smiley types rather than hucksterish men in cheap ties bombarding browsers with glib patter. "All that the [traditional] salesman cared about was a fifty-dollar spiff," sniffed Steve Jobs.

American Girl's approach to nurturing customers is equally attentive. The hair salon at American Girl Place offers a quick onsite aftercare program, but it goes far further at the Wisconsin head office. A sizable chunk of the warehouse is dedicated to a doll hospital, complete with admitting station. Rows and rows of replacement heads sit at the ready, wrapped in tissue paper and ranged in boxes like Christmas ornaments, should a dog-eared or -chewed doll need radical transplants or an impulsive pixie cut need rectifying. There are dryers for clothes and basins for washing, plus walls covered in letters from pleading little girls asking for their dolls to come home looking like new. Similarly, Louis Vuitton will always repair any authentic bag a customer brings back to a store. Small problems, like a new zipper pull, might be fixed onsite, while more intensive renovations will be sent back to the factory for an estimate. No matter what the charge, it will be cheaper than shelling out for an entirely new bag.

All of these aftercare services are personal and attentive, intended to reassure a Veblen good-buying customer that the price was worth it after all. For Pantsformation, why don't we instigate a no-questions-asked-anytime-anywhere return policy. Don't like the pants anymore after a few weeks' wear? Send them back. Shortened a chino and the silhouette seems off? No problem. Girlfriend complained they were drawing too many admiring glances? Totally fine. The Ninjas will be tasked with lightning-fast online customer service, too, answering questions and making suggestions in live chats. We'll also launch online promos, fun games where models wearing our pants are hidden on other sites; vouchers will be offered to anyone who can find them. We'll encourage shoppers to chat and bond about such promos at a special fan site.

It's such a great business plan, what venture capitalist could resist investing? If only the company didn't already exist.

In 2007, Stanford business school grad Andy Dunn faced a conundrum: He couldn't find trousers that wouldn't gape in the rear waistband. Instead of continuing a fruitless search, he cofounded a company to make one product, the perfect-fit chino. With waggish charm, the team called its company Bonobos, in honor of the monkeys known for their butts. Since the start, he and his squad of Ninjas (yes, that's staffers' real soubriquet) have built a thriving business that, three years after its founding, was averaging $1 million a month. Fans of Bonobos's $88 chinos, a premium-priced treat, bombard the brand's Facebook page and participate in its digital promos with breathless gusto, less casual shoppers than unpaid evangelists. Dunn was careful to make sure that his communication with customers did not feel like hard sell. Regular e-mails, for example, are full of funny content as well as straight-up promotions. Dunn hasn't yet offered a prize for anyone willing to get the firm's logo permanently inked on their body, but give him time.

After years of tweaking bonobos.com until it was totally shopper friendly, Dunn moved the brand into brick-and-mortar retailing. He took an unusual approach, choosing to focus on building a half dozen so-called Guideshops, aimed quite literally at pointing men toward the product that flattered or fit. The first was carved out of 700 square feet in the Bonobos office in Manhattan's Chelsea; there is little sidewalk-level evidence that it's even there. There are no walk-ins; instead, would-be buyers can make forty-five-minute appointments to browse various styles, sipping a beer if they wish. Ordering, though, is handled digitally, so there's no on-site inventory to fret about—a smart move, since in-store transactions averaged $360 each time, double the online equivalent.

When Bonobos wanted to expand distribution, Dunn didn't strike a third-party deal and lose control of its distribution channels. Rather, he paired up with Nordstrom, another icon of good customer service, to create in-store boutiques as part of a $16.4-million deal.

Strangely, though its operation would suggest markdowns are unnecessary, Bonobos embraces deals, discounting old styles online and hosting scrum-like sample sales at its NYC headquarters. Since the refusenik stance is an enviable position for retailers, simultaneously protecting margins and making shoppers proud to pay more to be part of the club, why would Dunn stoop to slashing prices? One answer is that the firm expanded beyond its original pant-centric mission to offer a full line of men's clothing. As ever, with more inventory comes greater exposure. There's likely another reason, though, especially given Dunn's brilliance: It's as much down to strategy as need. He has clearly realized that in this shoppercentric era, entirely denying devotees the chance at a discount is unsportsmanlike. It will backfire.

The other four brands also make very rare, extremely discreet forays into discounting. Nespresso and American Girl both maintain prices on their main products (coffee pellets and dolls) while allowing adjunct items (loss leading machines, clothing) to be off-loaded.* The dollmaker hosts an annual warehouse sale and liquidates returns as a charity fundraiser for the local children's museum near its Wisconsin office. Apple, especially since the exits of both Steve Jobs and retail chief Ron Johnson, has staged some minimal promotions on Black Friday, and has long offered up to $200 off a new Mac to students, faculty, and staff as part of its educational discount program. The iPhone, Apple's sole partner product, wavers in price partly due to the conventions of the cell phone sector and partly because Cupertino isn't in complete control. Apple also sells refurbished and warrantied versions of its products at apple.com.

Only Louis Vuitton categorically refuses to slash prices for ordinary customers. It does stage a sample sale, but that event is highly hush-hush. Staffers are loath to even discuss it for fear of being uninvited,

---

* The coffeemaker might have to revise such strategies since its patents began to expire in 2012. It also quietly tolerated ancillary products such as Coffeeduck's refillable capsules, which offer an ongoing way to enjoy the machines at a cheaper cost.

since only a select few senior-level execs are allowed to rifle the stock when it's sold off at a temporary space in the LVMH tower in midtown Manhattan. "I try not to tell people I'm going, or they bombard me," one longtime attendee confides, explaining that supposedly only those of director level or above are invited. Entry is by both photo ID and corporate business card. Calling it "brutal" and bemoaning the three-bag maximum, the attendee's memories of the sale are far from fond. "I've had to sweet-talk a woman into giving me the last monogram on the floor, and it wasn't even one of the better shapes." What isn't sold is destroyed. LV's price inflexibility is brave, but in the new retail landscape, it's a risky proposition. Shoppers want and expect discounts, and rescinding that soi-disant right will force them to be even more resourceful.

Apple's Ron Johnson learned this lesson the hard way when he defected to a lower-end firm and tried to export his beloved discountphobic strategy to the mass-market. His stint at J.C. Penney offers a cautionary tale of underestimating, and misunderstanding, his customers.

No More Penney Pinching

Ron Johnson's retail résumé is unarguably impressive. In addition to the plaudits he earned at Apple, Johnson was a major part of the team credited with burnishing Target's cheap chic image in the 1990s via a series of smart deals, the pioneering collaborations that first earned Target cachet, such as homewares from Michael Graves. When wobbly mall staple J.C. Penney unveiled him as its new CEO in November 2011, Wall Street swooned.

Johnson wasted little time reassembling his Target dream team at Penney's headquarters in Dallas. Notably, he tapped Michael Francis to be Penney's president, a man widely heralded as a creative visionary and with a flair for headline grabbing. For instance, it was Francis who hired David Blaine to break out of chains in Times Square and resurface at a Brooklyn Target. Another time, Michael cheekily plastered the subway station nearest Macy's with all-red advertising. He wanted to help cement the discounter's association with the color, ahead of any rivals who might lay claim to the same shade (as we've seen, a smart man indeed). Michael's job was to translate Ron's vision into workable retail practices. No small task, given the radical plan envisaged that would transform every aspect of the store.

Johnson-era advertising needed to be entirely reimagined by a fresh agency: more color and more abstract, Norman-Rockwell-meets-Benetton, with a clear bull's-eye on Target's back. Predictably, Johnson hired Minneapolis-based Peterson Milla Hooks, an agency which had long toiled for his former employer, to execute his new ad plan. A three-year program would see all 1,100 of J.C. Penney's stores reconfigured around a top-secret new layout that involved a central service desk and social area known as a Town Square. It wasn't even J.C. Penney anymore: Its official name would be jcp (all lower case, at all times). Johnson made one unarguably smart decision: a focus on exclusive product, as Apple does. The stores would soon be filled with Penney-only merchandise from tie-ups with the likes of Vivienne Tam and Marchesa for fashion to Martha Stewart for homewares.

Johnson's opening salvo, though, and the one that he intended as a defining gesture, involved sales. After his time at Apple, where markdowns were so shunned, Ron must have been horrified when he arrived at Penney's. Seventy-two percent of revenue had come from products marked down 50 percent or more, and only 0.2 percent from full-price items. In 2011, the department store had run 590 different sales, or more than one for every day of the year. The new CEO saw these programs as messy and profit denting, and set about eliminating them. Not once did he seem to pause to wonder, or ask, how customers felt. Johnson trumpeted a pricing tourniquet that he guaranteed would stop potential profits flowing away. The idea of sales, even the very word, was banned.

The new jcp would be simpler and fairer, he promised, with no more coupons or one-day promotions. Color-coded categories denoted "monthly values"—promotions like jewelry for Valentine's Day—and Best Prices, the new name for final clearance, dribbled out on the first and third Fridays of each month to coincide with payday. What really mattered, Johnson promised, was Every Day prices. As he revealed this shake-up in

January 2012, he promised these would be 40 percent less on average than in the previous calendar year.

Johnson wanted to bring the price on the ticket far closer to the price a shopper actually paid: A $13.99 T-shirt that had been rung through for around $6 in 2011 would now be $7 from the start. He saw lofty aims in his makeover, even tying it to a State of the Union address by President Obama. "And the word I kept hearing [in the president's address] over and over again was 'fair, fair, fair.' We need more fairness in this country," he said. "And I believe that. And that's at the center of what we are to do at J.C. Penney." He imported Ellen DeGeneres, who proudly recalled one of her first jobs as a Penney clerk, to topline the relaunch. Again, he elided any concerns that customers drew relish or thrill from gaming a store through a sale.

Unsurprisingly, some seasoned observers were skeptical. "It's the dumbest thing in my lifetime, a disaster. We've trained Americans for the last sixty years to want bigger and bigger discounts, bigger savings and we can't say, 'Time Out.' The consumer will say, 'You're nuts.' One retailer can't change the American attitude," predicted veteran retail pollster Britt Beemer. "They'll be back doing the same old thing in six months."

Unfortunately for jcp, Beemer was exactly right.

In fact, less than six months after that press conference, Michael Francis was publicly and suddenly axed in a brazen act of scapegoating. The word SALE was then aggressively reintroduced to the store's lexicon. It was a reaction to losses of $163 million that accrued in the single first quarter of Johnson's new policy. Even poor Ellen DeGeneres disappeared into the retail ether, relegated to sit on her talk show sofa once more.

Johnson hadn't followed the template of Bonobos (or Pantsformation). Certainly, he'd promised more exclusive items, but there was no true vertical integration: jcp still relied on third-party vendors to provide its stock. As a middleman more akin to a distributor, suppliers like Levi's or Polo wielded power over pricing and supply. Furthermore, Johnson could slash product assortment only so much; by its very nature, a department store is diversified. Indeed, it's built on a premise of providing almost anything a shopper might need. Yes, Johnson planned that his reimagined jcp stores would have Apple-style amenities, social areas including a *mendergarten* for bored husbands, and a Genius Bar–style service desk. But such amenities would take some time to roll out company-wide; most shops looked the same on February 1, 2012, the day sales were outlawed, as they had twenty-four hours earlier. Of course, absolutely no one thinks of jcp as selling Veblen goods. It's just a great, reliable place to buy some cheap socks. Customer care wasn't a focus for Johnson either: His biggest staffing shift was telling employees they could wear smart jeans instead of starchy uniforms.

The strategy Johnson decided to follow is known among retailers as EDLP, or everyday low prices. Invented by Walmart's Sam Walton, himself a former Penney's trainee, EDLP centers on the idea of discounts and deals that can be swapped out for a fixed cost if customers trust the seller. EDLP is effective only on highly commodified, replenishment items like milk, where price is the sole driver. Used on fashion pieces, or any aspirational item, it dents the appeal. Walmart is a somewhat misleading template, too: It really relies on what might be called EDLP-plus. Walmart guarantees those low prices every day, but it also sparks a buzz of buy-agra with its cheery yellow Rollbacks, a fancy codename for a conventional sale.

If only Johnson had looked a little deeper into history, he'd have seen the corpses of companies already felled by an EDLP plan. The 1992 effort by American Airlines, when that mythical $199 LAX–JFK fare first appeared, simply led competitors to undercut the fares, damaging everyone's profits and driving AA to ditch EDLP within six months. In 2001, Kmart's then-CEO announced he was cutting back on coupon circulars, which he likened to "heroin needles" for customers; a year later, the firm was filing for bankruptcy. When Macy's bought four hundred stores from May company in 2005 (including regional heavyweights like Marshall Field's and Filene's), it tried to wean customers away from coupons as an experiment. By Christmas 2007, after seeing some same store sales drop as much as 63 percent, Macy's CEO was apologizing and reinstituting coupons. "People love these coupons. They love thinking they got us," current CFO Karen Hoguet admits. At least she understands that in the current, shoppercentric world, giving a customer a sense of triumph—or even the illusion of it—is a canny strategy.

What should have most worried Johnson, though, was how familiar the story of Sears in the early 1990s should have sounded. A fresh CEO was brought in with grand plans to create "Stores of the Future," cutting everyday prices on its signature brands like Kenmore and Craftsman by 30 percent or so. For six months, the company hemorrhaged money until promotions were desperately reintroduced. Sears never recovered. When that CEO finally stepped down, the company that had been America's largest retailer at the start of his tenure now no longer even owned its namesake tower in downtown Chicago. This happened long before overproduction swung the pendulum of power away from retailers— imagine the severity of losses had he tried this stunt during shopping 3.0, as Johnson foolishly did.

Turmoil at jcp's Texas headquarters was a tip-off that all wasn't going well, even from the outset. To the new management team, promotions were expensive, costly, and inconvenient. An estimated 30 percent of staff at headquarters had long been dedicated to overseeing sales strategy and execution—and Johnson was happy to ax those overheads. "They were hiring and firing people by the day. Everyone was so new and so confused and freaked out all the time," says one consultant who nimbly weathered the regime change. She was nonplussed by the retailer's strategy when she first encountered it, much as Johnson was. "Price crappy shit at forty dollars and have it on the floor for three weeks to a month in some hidden corner? Then only advertise it once it had gone on sale? 'On sale' was 'retail.'" The longer she worked with Penney, though, the more she understood its everyday effectiveness. "J.C. Penney was profitable when everyone else was losing money."

Such corporate roiling was reflected at retail: Once sales were banned, store traffic slumped 10 percent, on average, in the first quarter. Customers who did bother to browse were spending less or nothing at all, and same store sales in 2012 were down 25 percent overall. Johnson tried to buy himself time by no longer reporting monthly sales, but Wall Street was pressuring him to show results—growth, of course. Stock that had hit $43.18 just after Johnson's plans were first implemented tumbled almost 40 percent to $26.75; the largest single drop by a company on the NASDAQ since 1980.

Such pummeling was a little unfair, since a Deutsche Bank study showed that on a random assortment of items, Johnson's jcp was indeed 9 percent cheaper than Macy's and 26 percent cheaper than Kohl's. Even though jcp's prices may have been lower, it didn't matter. The new team had overlooked the emotional, chemical attachments to bargains. It's the dopamine, stupid. Ron's Marie Antoinette attitude to his shoppers didn't help either. Wary of interviews from his days at media-hating Apple, he holed up and so allowed unimpressed analysts to shape the story. "I wouldn't assume they like the [old] pricing strategy. I think they're insulted by it," he said in a rare speech. "We want our pricing to be fair and square. If a woman is out of town the week of a sale, that's not fair." Never once did he trot out real jcp loyalists in front of the cameras to offer their endorsement of his approach. He forgot that, more now than ever before, the customer is always right.

Johnson clung to his EDLP strategy like a retail life raft, slashing commission wages for staff in furniture, shoes, and jewelry as a cost-cutting stopgap. He even scalped Michael Francis, only to see stock sink a further 6 percent as analysts pooh-poohed the move. "Since Ron Johnson was unlikely to fire himself due to early runaround missteps," one snarked, "he appears to have decided to swing the ax over the head of the person he hand picked as president." By mid-May, just fifteen weeks or so since demonizing discounts, Johnson admitted defeat. He announced some extra Best Price Fridays, swallowing his considerable pride in the process. "It's just been kind of confusing. So we're moving away from the word 'monthlong value' because no one really understood . . . what we intended to do," he said, sighing, "It's a sale." By November of that year, jcp was printing an old-style circular touting forty-eight pages of Black Friday–only deals. A year after his arrival, in January 2013, Johnson finally capitulated entirely, reinstating the aggressive promotions he'd pilloried as so unfair. He even started using the classic reference price trick of displaying manufacturers' suggested price alongside jcp's on the tag to ram home the power of the discounted stock.

Johnson's return to a discount-driven retailing plan came too late to save his own job, though. His biggest champion had been activist hedge fund investor Bill Ackman, jcp's largest shareholder.* Having hand-picked Johnson to perform an Ackman-approved makeover he remained a loyalist until early April 2013, when he publicly grumbled that there had been "too much change too quickly, without adequate testing." The execution of the new plan, he added, "has been something very close to a disaster." No wonder, given that Johnson had presided over a staggering annual loss in 2012: $985 million, of which $552 million came in the fourth quarter alone. The company's stock lost more than half its value during his Ahabian quest against discounts, while its credit ratings slalomed junk status. In response, the board finally junked Johnson himself in April 2013. It must have smarted that he was replaced by Penney vet Mike Ullman, the very CEO Johnson had unseated.

jcp's misadventures show the problems a company can face when it tries to reinvent its business model without discounts. It's financially lethal to ignore the sway that shoppers hold today. They demand discounts and will chafe at being refused. Mass-marketeers will never be able to thrive by aping the strategy that works so well for Apple or American Girl. Upscale companies have their own challenges, though, ones that are direct byproducts of their impressive successes in keeping prices high and tight.

Superfake It 'Til You Make It

If sales are now a right rather than a privilege, what will entitled shoppers do when denied them entirely? They will rebel. Determination, and perhaps a smidgen of desperation, will drive them to bag an alternative to Vuitton: not a different brand, though, but a fake. Unsurprisingly, no

---

* Ackman is notoriously ferocious and unsentimental about his investments. After snapping up a chunk of Target stock he tried and failed in 2008 to take control of the board and force it, effectively, to dismantle the company and unlock the value of the real estate beneath its stores as dividends for shareholders. Undeterred, he switched attention to J.C. Penney, which failed to prevent his stealth takeover.

label is more bedeviled by this problem than LV, the king of counterfeiting. In the EU, Vuitton was the single largest brand among fake accessories seized, worth €213 million (around $276 million) and making up a staggering 29 percent of products confiscated. It isn't just a European problem, either. LV's price sensitivity is the reason Canal Street in New York has long been filled with iffy monogrammed totes. Recently, though, such shoddy clutches have been elbowed aside for an entirely new kind of knockoff, one that blurs the boundaries between authenticity and ripping off: the superfake. This cheap alternative to that discount-resistant designer treat is only technically not real. It is yet another casualty of greedy overproduction.

Remember how Carrie Bradshaw helped outlet malls mushroom with her insouciant dropping of both designer labels and thousands of dollars? Jennifer Hudson's thankless bit part in the first *Sex and the City* movie saw her character earn a name, Louise, simply so her boss Ms. Bradshaw could punningly induct her into the cult of pricey purses—hers was a "Louise Vuitton." Now, more people than ever want to carry this season's It bag. Firms have overreacted to that demand, and expanded aggressively: hiring extra craftsmen, for example, or shipping production to larger factories in China.

The greater the volume of items produced, of course, the easier it is for some to go astray, unnoticed. In this case, it isn't about oversupply driving prices down. Rather, oversupply makes it harder to police and track quantities of any given item. A few totes can vanish from a mass production line unremarked on. The greater the number of workers involved, the more anonymous they become and the easier it is for an errant staffer to stay late in the atelier for a few nights to make up a duplicate purse to sell on the black market. A regular fake is an enthusiastic attempt to replicate a white-hot design. A superfake is a bag made by the original manufacturer that somehow—perhaps stolen from the factory or made then sold by unscrupulous staffers—ends up selling on the black market.

Susan Scafidi is a Fordham University professor who specializes in fashion law and is one of the foremost experts on this rising phenomenon. Vuitton superfakes are impossible to distinguish from the real thing, she says, for good reason: The materials and craftsmanship are identical. "These may not be the bags that went out the front door of the factory at noon," she explains, "but they're the bags that went out the back door at midnight." One industry insider confirms that much of Louis Vuitton's signature monogram canvas is produced in the PRC.*

Far from the prying eyes of the bosses in Paris, a factory might be contracted to deliver perhaps five thousand of one design. Built into such an order, of course, are overruns; perhaps a bag will be slashed by the Xacto knife as a shipping box is opened, or there will be a few loose threads that make it second quality. What the manufacturer is authorized to do with such excess stock, though, is the quandary. In the past, it might have been dutifully destroyed. Now it's just as likely to be "lost" in shift changeovers. The fact that Vuitton long ago abandoned some of the harder to replicate artisanal detailing on most styles, such as hand-stitching, has only made this easier.

Such a bag is classified as a fake by legalese: The trademark holder whose logo is stamped on the inside did not authorize its sale. To an ordinary shopper, though, it's the real thing, only on sale, and far from department stores' reach. Compared to the thousands that an original LV might cost or the $50 price of a conventional fake, superfakes sell for a few hundred dollars. They sit, appealing in the middle of the trio (think back to our Goldilocks pricing-style rule). Workmanship isn't the giveaway on such superfakes, as each is identical to the item sold at Vuitton's own store. The only flaw is the serial number inside. A batch of superfakes will share the same one, like monogrammed identical sextuplets. While shoppers' eagerness to wrest a bargain whatever the cost has driven this market, there are other factors, too. The penalties for counterfeiting are soft compared with, say, drug smuggling. Margins are also higher than for narcotics or firearms, and the market is enormous. "Not every woman on the street wants an illegal weapon, but every woman wants a handbag," says Scafidi.

The superfake phenomenon is most keenly felt by Louis Vuitton, but

* On the next trip to the mall, take a look at the label inside a piece of clothing, and note the country of origin. In reaction to the backlash against Made in China and its perceived lower-quality standards, some brands have started to opt for the equally legal but disingenuous Made in PRC. The People's Republic of China, of course, is the country's official designation.

other brands suffer, too. Take Hermès. It sates shoppers' demands for discounts via an occasional sample sale open to the public, anathema to Vuitton. Trying to snag one of its signature must-have bags at a mark-down, though, is impossible. Don't bum-rush that event in hopes of un-earthing a Birkin (named for Jane) or a Kelly (as in Grace). The sample sale stokes, rather than calms, such frenzy among buyers, controlling and limiting sale even at full price. Like Vuitton, though, Hermès suc-cumbed to the lure of expansion, and so exposed itself to superfakery. In its case, volume production wasn't shipped to China. Instead, Hermès upped the roster of staffers trained to make these designs. In 2012, there were two thousand or more craftsmen, up from a reported four hundred or so in the 1990s. When a bag sells for a third of the annual wage of such a worker, it's easy to be sympathetic to their skullduggery. "Hermès pays them around €30,000 a year and a bag can sell for €10,000. If it takes twenty hours to make one, it almost behooves that craftsperson to make a fake and sell it," explains Michael Tonello, a former purse dealer and author of a tell-all about Hermès, *Bringing Home the Birkin*.

The company's greedy overexpansion—trying to sell to a larger num-ber of people while keeping employees on low wages—has made it vul-nerable to homemade superfakes. An impoverished, newly hired artisan can turn resentment into cold cash. It's easy enough to buy leather from the same tanneries on which Hermès relies, since they're outside ven-dors. The hardware is a little trickier—made in Switzerland, it's shipped in by armored truck—and the stamped logo is written in a company-owned font. Still, resourceful artisans have found ways around even these roadblocks. In 2012, French police busted an €18 million (or $23 million) ring of a dozen fraudsters manufacturing fake Hermès bags in secret workshops; several of the accused were employees of the house. Superfakery is spreading faster than ever, and, ironically, now bags of higher quality than the originals are sometimes produced, at least ac-cording to experts. Chief culprits in this case, where the workmanship can be too good, include Balenciaga's Motorcycle bag and Alexander Wang's accessories.

The rise in such couture counterfeits has made business even trickier for outfits like Ben Hemminger's Fashionphile or reputable resellers like

Tonello. Dishonest customers can do one of two things: sell a superfake Birkin on eBay or return it to Hermès for a no-questions-asked refund. If they've managed to buy a doppelgänger for the real thing, they can then even opt to sell that on eBay and double their money. The rise of such counterfeit products is the reason top-tier retailers have rescinded the authentication service they long offered. Vuitton and others will no longer allow a customer to bring a bag to any boutique to be verified as genuine. It's just too risky—and it's all Vuitton's fault.*

Resisting the pull of markdowns in an era of shopping 3.0 isn't easy. Given the effort, is it worth it? Certainly, given the right circumstances. Handled with precision, such price reliability can create a trust or bond between shopper and seller that is equal parts nostalgia and profit. Giving bonuses, whether nursing calls or free in-store art shows, helps buyers justify the premium they're paying; they'll be feelin' Veblen good. Yet a total refusal to acknowledge retail's new norms can be far more damaging in the long term than a few "20% OFF" signs. Can jcp rebound from its disastrous sortie away from sales? Will Vuitton pay the ultimate price for its discountphobia, a flood of not-quite-counterfeits damaging trust and permanently undermining its cachet? If the superfake industry continues to evolve apace, don't be surprised to see parent company LVMH blink. In fact, in early 2013, there were heavy- and well-sourced rumors that it was mulling a first-ever Louis Vuitton outlet, tasking an agent with finding a space stateside.

It isn't just Americans who see the allure of these superfakes, though. The Japanese mafia, or *yakuza*, has been reported to use intimidation to pressurize Fashionphile-esque stores into passing off superfakes as genuine. They then sell the cuckoo-like purses on the syndicate's behalf to brand-mad Tokyoites, funneling significant profits back to the gangs. In China, similarly, the superfake is spreading beyond handbags. The Middle Kingdom has always been a country with a very flexible relationship to copyright and intellectual property. Nonetheless, when employees at twenty-two Apple stores were told in late 2011 that they weren't

* Ben Hemminger has responded by corralling a set of freelance experts whom he's trained to do in-depth analysis of any bag brought in for consignment—think pocket money for boutique staffers or a hobby for top-tier collectors.

actually working for Cupertino proper but rather in full-scale brick-and-mortar fakes run by unscrupulous entrepreneurs, they were stunned. The ersatz stores were lovingly detailed replicas, down to that iconic logo on the glass-fronted stores.

As anyone who has ventured into an expat Chinatown can attest, shopping there is a master class in hard bargaining (and exotic-looking produce). Surely, then, the rapidly expanding consumer market in mainland China would race to embrace the markdown mania that has engulfed the United States. What about the rest of the world? Are Americans penny-pinching outliers or pioneers?

7

The World on Sale: Bargaining at the Bazaar and Other Stories

Why Germans Couldn't Use Coupons, How the Japanese Learned to Love Bargains, and a British Royal's Discount Mania

By the late 1990s, Shanghai had become a shabby city, a shadow of its opium-era self and a symbol of China's decades-long decline. Paving stones on the waterfront strip known as the Bund were chipped and uneven, the red-and-white-painted railings a relic from Communist times. The Peace Hotel, once an anchor of the strip and an opulent Art Deco pile, was run-down and institutional, its lobby grubby and unloved. The only place to buy souvenirs was the dusty, government-run Friendship Store; in clothing shops, forlorn fiberglass mannequins still sported molded hair, their built-in berets emblazoned with Communist-approved stars. It wasn't unusual to see locals nip to the corner store in pajamas, either, a quirk of the city that made Beijingers, long rivals, laugh. Just a handful of skyscrapers marked the new development area, Pudong, across the water. The ritzy Portman hotel seemed like the only easy place for a Western-style breakfast of coffee and a muffin, but both tasted as if made by someone whose closest encounter with either was on TV. Thousands of bikes barreled down the street like determined metal ants, making crossing the road a terrifying prospect.

Just over a decade later, Shanghai is almost unrecognizable. The Bund is stroll-worthy and tourist-ready, a tinny "Happy Birthday" melody inexplicably piped over the public speakers at hiccupy intervals. The waterfront was gussied up, like much of the city, in preparation for 2010's International Expo, a modern version of the World's Fairs that America staged in the nineteenth century. The Peace Hotel is now operated by Fairmont, which painstakingly restored the lobby (no photos, it warns, to discourage gawping groups of tourists). The Friendship Store is long gone, elbowed out to make room for a gleaming new Peninsula Hotel, with a futuristic mall attached full of international designer names; the only pajamas on show are at Chanel. Dozens of skyscrapers jostle for prominence in Pudong's neon forest, an area now so arriviste and energetic that expats have nicknamed it Pu Jersey. Outlets of java chains such as Starbucks and Costa dot street corners as in every global metropolis, coffee and snacks cloned from London or New York. Sports cars careen through the streets, paying little attention to the Stop signs and making crossing the road a terrifying prospect. Well, at least something's still the same.

Shanghai's transformation isn't surprising. The economic boom in China over the last decade has been well documented. Both industrial and revolutionary, it was a do-over of Europe's nineteenth-century transformation. In that short time, the country has rocketed up global GDP rankings, climbing from sixth to second, ahead of Japan and behind only the United States. That stratospheric rise dates back mainly to one day in December 2001. Back then, America was enduring tough economic times, mired as it was in a post-dot-com downturn and economically and emotionally stunned, in equal measure, by 9/11. Its strategic position wobbly, America finally acquiesced to China's fifteen-year quest to join the World Trade Organization. The onetime Communist megacountry's membership in capitalism's key body began just before Christmas. It was a crucial fulcrum in the shift of power.

For China, the appeal of the WTO was obvious: fewer barriers to trade, including lower export and import tariffs, plus looser foreign investment. It presaged a cultural shift for the country, luring rural workers to cities in much the same way as the Industrial Revolution had done in Europe almost two centuries earlier. Freer markets for China's goods generated a need for labor, which necessarily led to higher wages in real terms; between 2000 and 2007, they grew by 50 percent. In other words, goods could be manufactured more cheaply and efficiently in China for the developed world, while simultaneously creating a domestic market for those same products. It seemed like the perfect equation.

If only that were true. Until China emerged from its economic isolation, America had effectively policed global markets and determined the cost of raw materials. Now, though, there was competing demand from a (more) booming economy, pushing the value of raw materials higher than the US could afford. Traditionally, when sales were sluggish stateside, they could be juiced by a round of price slashing, and then offset by a unilateral reduction in costs. That was no longer so easy. As discounting started to spiral over the next decade, it got tougher and tougher for America to recover. In real terms, purchasing power diminished. Stateside margins grew ever thinner, caught as they were between escalating costs (China became a rapacious rival consumer of commodities, pushing prices of cotton up to $85 per bale in 2010, a fifteen-year high) and those accelerating markdowns. The answer to diminishing margins: layoffs and more layoffs, which led to people becoming more afraid to spend. Rinse, repeat.

This power shift has squeezed the middle class more than most. In the United States, the net worth of that social cluster has plunged by an average of 26 percent over the last five years, and median family income, adjusted for inflation, is lower than in 1998. There's even a new marketing buzzword to describe this phenomenon: the *Consumer Hourglass Theory*. This strategy instructs companies to focus on highest- and lowest-end customers and ignore the shrinking middle. Great news for Neiman Marcus and H&M, tough news for Banana Republic.

Simultaneously, the middle class in emerging nations has multiplied. In China, yearly earnings have increased tenfold since 1980, and 25 percent of the population now should be considered middle class. That's 300 million more people in that category—more than the entire population of America—and the number could rise to 700 million or more in the next decade.

No wonder the way we shop, from Shanghai to San Francisco, has radically changed. The clearest signal of that is our attitude to discounts. When it comes to retail, the world has long been divided into halves. Developed nations such as America or Japan were less bargain driven and haggle prone, full of fair pricing laws.* Emerging economies like China or India hacked at prices like Weed Wackers, their retail more free-for-all than free market. In the decade since China entered the WTO, that division has been blurring. In fact, developed nations and emerging economies have slowly been swapping places: as the developing world becomes more prone to, and proud of, paying full price, so mature markets no longer find discounts déclassé. It's a retailing *Freaky Friday*, with economic rather than comic results. How did we trade places as well as goods with these emerging markets? What does it mean for the future of discounting stateside?

Individuals Versus Collectives

Before retiring and turning her attention to botanical painting, Sarah Maxwell was an economics guru, a professor at Fordham University, and author of the pricing manual *The Price Is Wrong.* Maxwell was intrigued by the difference between her countrymen and the shoppers around the world. "Normally Americans are not terribly good at bargaining, but in other societies it's largely a game," she told me. To examine those differences, she initiated a study to compare shoppers in Brazil and India (both discount-loving cultures) with their promo-phobic counterparts in Germany and the United States. She wanted to answer one question: Why did the world's attitude to deals and discounts divide into halves? Maxwell's findings offer an elegant and surprising explanation.

First, Maxwell sought to understand the psychographics of each country. How did a given society think of itself? Was it an individualistic or collectivist culture? In the former, citizens exist separately but equally

---

* Even the English lexicon is a tip-off to the squeamishness that Anglo cultures have developed for negotiating, and the wariness we feel, rich as it is in words that describe sharp-dealing—we can be swindled or fleeced or bamboozled or hoodwinked.

in the same sphere; while in the latter, they consider themselves first part of a given peer group, which is then a subset of society at large. Think of this as the difference between building a house from Lego or Duplo bricks; the end result is the same, but the components are of very different sizes.

America indexes highest in individualism, unsurprisingly, earning 91/100 on a standard test. Most Western European countries, including Germany, are near the top of that same ranking, ranging from 60 to 80. The one-among-many, Duplo-style mindset is embodied by India or Brazil, which rank low on the individualism scale (Maxwell's research didn't include China, but such group-think is central to Mao-style Communism).

Maxwell cross-referenced the individualist versus collectivist findings with another concept: power distance. Big power gaps between groups, whether in influence or wealth, lead to what's known as a hierarchical culture. When those perceived gaps are smaller, we get a flat society. Collectivist countries tend to have large power gaps between those groups. Life and people are tiered and ranked, as embodied in India's centuries-old caste system that sifts people from holy Brahmins to untouchable Dalits. Conversely, individualistic societies tend to have flat cultures; everyone considers him- or herself entitled to the same choices and chances as any neighbor. It's this somewhat contradictory belief in fairness and freedom that fuels both the American Dream and Occupy Wall Street.

Maxwell then workshopped her theory about cultures' innate approach to prices in a real-world test. How did volunteers in a collectivist culture with wide power distance differ from those in a flat, individualistic country in their reaction to prices? One reaction was universal: Everyone felt indignation about being overcharged, or believing a perceived peer received a discount when they didn't. The key word, though, was *perceived*.

An Indian shopper didn't consider everyone browsing next to her a peer. Hiking the cost for an upper-class shopper, Maxwell found, was seen as fair. "The shopkeeper will charge me higher prices because he knows that I can pay" said one wealthy participant, shrugging. "[The price] depends on the kind of clothes you are wearing, the purse you are holding, the kind of vehicle you have arrived in," agreed another. Context is smaller in a collectivist culture; people expect equality only with a given group of which they deem themselves part. A Brahmin banker would balk if a Brahmin lawyer were charged less for a washing machine than she. A deal on the same white goods for a Dalit shopkeeper, however, would seem logical.

Members of an individualistic society, such as the United States or Germany, have a radically different reaction. They consider everyone a peer. If society isn't divided up into small groups or chunks, its citizens compare themselves to every other single member—a factory worker in Michigan might feel kinship with a fashion designer in Manhattan, for example. No wonder individualistic societies have long found it irksome and impossible to process the idea that someone else might be charged a different price. Finagling a bargain was almost rude, and discount-mindedness a discourtesy to your fellow Americans.

Even now, there are ample real-life examples of this dichotomy. Chinese shoppers have adapted their centuries-honed skills in street haggling to modern retail—like an ambush Groupon, flash-mob discount shopping has been a social media phenomenon. Sites such as Teambuy.com.cn or 51tuangou.com allow users to coordinate a time and place to arrive together at a store. Once in place, up to five hundred people will demand a deal on the same items—say a TV and DVD player—with a 30 percent reduction the ultimate aim. In Guangzhou in southern China, for example, the Gome electrical megastore was invaded at 4 p.m. on a summer Friday by a horde of deal seekers who collectively bargained for markdowns on cameras, and flat-screen TVs. "It was great. We just bought an apartment and this way, we can afford nice things for it," said one ambusher, Fairy Zhang.*

In individualist societies, most of them mature markets, there are stringent regulations around discounting. It might be controlled by law

---

* Hong Kong has even systematized its discounts according to one senior executive at Lane Crawford, the local answer to Bergdorf Goodman. Stores there have responded to the deluge of demands for discounts by centralized card systems that work much like frequent-flyer programs. "You qualify to be a VIP at Prada, for example, by the amount you spend each year," the exec explained. "As long as you spend over HK$170,000 [around $22,000] you keep your discount of 10 percent."

or just by social mores. Traditionally America and France police pricing using regulations. Massachusetts, for example, forbids any promotions around alcohol, but Groupon flouted the Massachussetts law with usual frat-boyish charm, offering $100 voucher good on both food and drink, before the regulators rapped its knuckles and forced it to amend the deal. In France, rules go further. The annual *soldes* (or sales days) on the calendar are actually mandated by government bean counters. Unsurprisingly, Brits relied on the power of chilly disapproval. For years, stiff upper-lipped types at grocer Marks & Spencer worried about the bad taste of marking down food that was close to expiration, and only recently did the company change a decades-old practice of discreetly donating such wastage to charities.

The traditional schematic, then, was straightforward: Collectivist economies, like many of the emerging markets, saw variable pricing as a shoulder-shrugging fact of life. Individualistic economies, or those found in the developed world, restricted deals and discounts, a response to locals' flat earth–style fairness. Once China joined the WTO in 2001, however, those strict divisions began to blur. Supply and demand equations were being rewritten, like malware hijacking the world's economic motherboard while Too Much Stuff syndrome bubbled in the background. The conventional, and clear-cut, schism started to crack. In some countries, this change even rewrote the law.

High Beta, Low Morale

Until 2001, coupons in Germany were as illegal as cocaine. It was all thanks to a pair of arcane rules, the *Rabattgesetz* and the *Zugabeverordnung* (or Discount Law and Free Gift Act). These regulated prices to such a draconian degree that stores could reduce tags by only 3 percent or less and could not give anything away with purchase (no BOGOFs).

The origins of such laws are sobering. As the nascent Nazi movement metastasized through the Fatherland, it used every tactic available to express its racist policies. Since many of the larger retail operations and department stores were Jewish-owned at that time, and used their market clout to undercut smaller, Aryan-run corner stores, Hitler decided to suffocate the Jewish retailers economically. He claimed that the cooperative setup by which the Jews had thrived was a "leftover of Marxist economic models" and enacted these strange laws behind that smokescreen.

The laws persisted for seventy years, until global market forces—both the looming Chinese boom as well as the new Euro currency that allowed online, cross-border price comparison in European markets—forced the German government to act. Were not the origins of such protectionism so overtly racist, it would be almost comical how long it took Germany to rescind those laws. The jobs-worthy court cases it produced have a spoofish tone. Quelle, the Teutonic Sears, tried to offer shoppers the chance to donate money to an AIDS charity every time its own-brand Visa card was used at the store. A German appeals court sniffed and denied the promo. A similar story involved heavy-duty shopping bags, for which a small fee was usually levied. A drugstore tried to fete its birthday by giving away such totes, worth 75 cents, and was blocked since such a tactic was judged to be a free gift.*

In 2004, another restrictive rule was nixed: the *Gesetz gegen den unlauteren Wettbewerb* (roughly the Law Against Unfair Competition), which regulated when sales could be held. Per this edict, a German store was considered to be breaking the law when it staged markdowns outside of two permitted circumstances. Stores could use sales to clear stock at the end of a season, or to mark the anniversary of the founding of the business—if, and only if, that anniversary was divisible by twenty-five. One thing that's never changed: Teutonic exactness.

Ten years after Germany finally succumbed to sales, it's clear that the driving force behind such economic maneuvering was as much

---

* Twofer deals on steins of beer during Happy Hour were unheard of—that's a BOGOF promotion, banned by *Zugabeverordnung*. Even international companies were flummoxed, sometimes surreally so. American Express could operate its reward program, but not tell anyone that it did on the basis that it "creates the impression that they are offering something attractive, yet the customer does not know what exactly—if anything—he will receive." Ditto Lands' End and its iconic return-anytime-for-any-reason guarantee. The net result of a three-year-long battle in the German courts in 1999 was that it could operate at that same level of customer service. It just couldn't tell any Germans that it did.

psychological as financial. Only one thing could override the ingrained approach to prices that Maxwell examined: fear. Financial clout used to rest entirely with America and its peers, but now control was moving eastward. China's WTO membership helped make the fight for and price of commodities ferocious, just at the very time that developed economies were at their weakest. It was a lethal coincidence. One study of the world's economic center of gravity showed how it shunted from the mid-Atlantic in 1980 to close by Izmir in Turkey by 2008; it's predicted that it'll be somewhere along the India-China border by 2050. A staggering 72 percent of GDP growth worldwide in the three years since 2008 was in emerging markets. The IMF predicts that number will continue to astonish, leveling out at around 60 percent through 2017. No wonder China overtook the United States as the world's biggest food and grocery retail market for the first time in 2011, worth $607 billion versus our $572 billion.

The people in China and its emerging allies, like India and Brazil, can feel this momentum, too, displaying a buoyant optimism that contrasts with the developed world's fear of what the future might bring. "They have a sense of confidence about their financial future," notes Yuval Atsomon, a McKinsey consulting principal who just moved to London after six years of living and working in Shanghai. The emerging markets, Atsomon admits, may not be as wealthy yet, "But their lives are getting better and better on a fairly fixed trajectory and their attitude pretty much follows that path. And those consumers are going to drive three quarters of global consumption growth in the next fifteen years."

This changing economic reality is more powerful than the cultural norms to which we've become accustomed. That new-monied middle class in Beijing has a different mindset from its counterparts twenty years ago, one that's more individualistic than ever. Its snobbish attitude to markdowns is all too familiar, as these shoppers embrace the allure of full price with gusto. The Middle Kingdom's middle class is behaving much like its counterparts in the West once did. Newly time poor, with dual-income families, they are surrounded by enticing and reliable Veblen goods. Premium prices are reassuring for ordinary Chinese people especially first-time buyers of items like cars (60 percent of the market are newbies) or laptops (likewise, 30 to 40 percent). Paying full price is a guarantee of safety and quality. A recent McKinsey study of the middle class in Shandong, one of the wealthiest and largest Chinese provinces with a population of more than 95 million, found that 30 percent would stretch their budgets to pay a premium price for a supposedly better product. Imagine anyone, anywhere in America saying that right now.

Westerners are still relatively wealthy, in fact. The problem is that we don't *feel* confident. Former *Wall Street Journal* columnist and stalker of rich people, Robert Frank, called this "high-beta wealth," a nod to the term used for high-risk stocks that yo-yo in value. There's a jittery sense of the future for many developed nations now: uncertainty, austerity, even worries of default.* Those who once felt secure enough to live without budgeting in America, who saw full-price pride as a marker of social and financial standing, are now panicky enough to succumb to deals. This skittishness underlies every development chronicled in this book. It's sobering to realize that we can still feel this way in an era when shoppers have never wielded more power. We should feel jubilant, rather than jumpy.

One nation above all is uniquely positioned to show how such financial woes drive a yen for discounts. A onetime thriving country that has staggered for two decades under heavy financial pressures, this developed nation is surrounded by upstart, emerging economies keen to usurp its position or power. In an era when the consumer is more in control than ever, a trip to consumerism's spiritual home is essential. Welcome to Japan.

Land of the Falling Prices

Tokyo is a schizophrenic city. The images of it on TV and film—squirming with people, neon signs blazing, so futuristic it looks like Paris reimagined

---

* In the Great Recession of 2008–2010, millionaire investors saw 20 to 30 percent of their net worth evaporate, and nearly one in five lost up to 50 percent of their riches. Compare that to how in the 1960s and 1970s, when economies slowed down, the one percenters lost, on average, well, 1 percent less in net worth than the average American. What changed, Frank suggests, was the Wall Street–fueled boom of the 1980s; where once wealth was drawn from dull, reliable sources, commodities like timber or mining, it's now speculation and stocks that boost portfolios. Government regulations were loosened in America and birthed the era of leveraged buyouts and pirouetting financial plans that befuddled an ordinary investor but could make or lose a fortune for Gordon Gekko and co.

by Martians—are unfair. Far from *Lost in Translation*, most signs are in both kanji and Roman letters; the subway announcements alternate instructions in Japanese and English. Much of its skyline is low-slung and human-scale, and city center neighborhoods like Harajuku are honey-combed with backstreets, still lined by traditional, two-story houses (albeit mostly converted into cafés or stores).

One neighborhood, though, embraces and embodies every cliché of movie Tokyo: the brand wonderland of Ginza, where luxury labels jostle for prominence with a pouty insolence. It's a forest of glittering buildings, each of them a retail temple. Chanel? It has its own skyscraper, complete with quilted façade. You don't have to leave the nine-level Gucci megaplex all day since it has its own restaurant to keep you refueled between sprees. As for the Hermès flagship, the 65,000-square-foot temple to spending seems to pulse like a spaceship in neutral, ready to lift off at any moment.

This city was a lottery win for the luxury market in the 1980s, when heritage brands flocked to the home of Sony, desperate to slake the thirst for indulgence of that cashed-up, quality-minded Japanese consumer (sound familiar?). Indeed, the country is now so synonymous with premium product that, according to the *Economist*, 85 percent of the women there own at least one Louis Vuitton product. Most interloping Western brands were canny enough to realize that they should charge the maximum possible for the privilege of buying into luxury's exclusive club. Vuitton items here could fetch prices up to 50 percent higher than in Paris, while Prada premiums might top 65 percent. There was little strategy behind such a stance. Brands did it "because they can," one McKinsey consultant explained, and were able to get away with it thanks to "a relative lack of price sensitivity and transparency and a disproportionate focus on the quality of the item and the shopping experience over the price."

Certainly, there was some justification for the markup, since luxury import taxes to the island nation could reach 50 percent or even 60 percent. Truly, though, pricing was done largely on a Veblen-good principal. Like China's emerging middle class today, Japanese people in the 1970s and 1980s *wanted* to pay more, and would gladly save up for that splurge. The boom time seemed boundless. Even department stores didn't offer deep sales, and they were run much the way Vuitton manages its concessions. Shops such as the Saks-like Mistukoshi were more akin to malls where they rented space to big-name tenants. Overruns and dead stock, therefore, were absorbed by most brands (as Vuitton continues to do today).

"In Japan, we don't go to barbecues, or go surfing, we go shopping," says Ron Sternberg, an American marketing exec who has lived and worked in Tokyo for almost thirty years. "Japanese would be too embarrassed to buy something at a discount as they're very status conscious. If you were born and raised in Tokyo, you would rather die three times than walk into a department store and ask for a discount. Nobody bargains on a status symbol. It's just not done."

The only exception was the annual orgy of *fukubukuro* each New Year. These bargain-priced lucky-dip bags acted as the local answer to Black Friday loss leaders: Each pouch's contents guaranteed to be worth more than the price paid. Stores could off-load last year's remaindered merchandise this way, in alignment with the Japanese superstition against starting a New Year with detritus from the past. A good deal and good luck bundled together. These were so crucial a retail tactic that even a deal-phobic brand like Apple was forced to participate in this promo, offering grab bags with headphones, T-shirts, or iPod touches for 33,000 Yen (around $420). Until July 2000, snaffling a killer *fukubukuro* was really the only way to find a great deal in Tokyo. That's when Gotemba Premium Outlets opened and helped change the way Japanese people shop.

The outlet's launch was the culmination of a decade-long adjustment in local attitudes. Japanese business culture is notorious for its unwillingness to ax workers—it would rather reduce wages for everyone than give out a few pink slips. So as the financial markets imploded in Japan in the 1990s, predating the rest of the developed world's meltdown by almost twenty years, it presented a new opportunity. Dogged by deflation, the country's salarymen's wages were sagging even if their desire for designer goodies was not.* It's a mood that sounds familiar to anyone in

* Japan's aging population doesn't help—by 2050, 40 percent of the country will be over sixty-five compared with just 11.6 percent in 1989. Senior citizens, who usually live on fixed pensions, are keen to maximize spending power. They vote for politicians who will keep the

America right now. Gotemba's canny owners identified this attitude shift and decided to capitalize on it for the first time, cloning the look, feel, and layout of the outlet village from successful Western counterparts like Woodbury Common.

They were proved resoundingly astute from day one: Traffic snarled in a two-hour jam. In just the first two weeks, 800,000 shoppers descended on its campus—the mall's owners had expected it to take six months to reach that level. Gotemba's custom-built sewage treatment system was overloaded not once but twice, and Porta Potties were shipped in as an emergency measure. More than a decade later, Gotemba shuts down only once a year, for twenty-four hours each February, to check the electrical system.

The best way to get to the mall from Tokyo is by train (those traffic jams are still brutal during weekends). The 10:50 a.m. on Saturday is listed as being a Romancecar—disappointingly, the name refers to amorous, armrest-free seats inside each caboose. For around $60 per ninety-minute round-trip, the train shuttles eager shoppers north—splashes of bright green paddy field hiccup in between the drab urban sprawl. The mall itself sits in the shadow of Mount Fuji, but on a warm, wet day in June, it's hard to see. Muggy and suffocating, the air feels like an outdoor steam room. A free shuttle bus trundles from the local train station, chugging along a nondescript ring road; a grubby *pachinko* building is the only street-side highlight. Gotemba the town is clearly far less luxe than its biggest attraction with blue-collar visitors drawn here for a day of gambling and tonier types colonizing the outlet shops.

It's startling, then, to see the Gotemba shopping village appear. Despite the *Desperate Housewives*-meets-*Stepford* all-white architecture and English-language signs, the mall takes a distinctively Japanese approach to discounting. Under local law, it's illegal to require a certain discount from stores, so 25 percent is "requested." Most retailers, though, slash prices by 40 percent or so, even more during the brick-and-mortar flash sales that they stage. Bright yellow signs in Adidas swing from the ceiling:

---

yen high on international markets, making imported goods as cheap as possible. The only way to kickstart the country's torpid economy, of course, is the exact opposite strategy.

"30% OFF 13.30–16.00"; a whistle blows and they're pulled down on the dot at 4 p.m., using handheld hooks. There's the usual lineup of outlet staples—Coach is the top store, as it is in many malls stateside, plus Gap and Nike—but there are also less-familiar names.*

Tinny K-pop blasts through the speakers inside Samantha Thavasa, where the half-price purses look like the designs Hello Kitty would produce were she hired to helm Tory Burch. As for Nikon, it offloads old models at its outlet here. The camera maker offered a 3 million Yen bag (around $38,000) as a limited-edition *fukubukuro* promotion and sold two of them, a headline-grabbing stunt akin to the outlandish offerings in the Neiman Marcus Christmas catalog (remember the $25,000 cupcake-shaped car with customizable toppings, which could zip along at a mighty 7 mph?). Gotemba stores occasionally offer *fukubukuro*-like lucky-dip specials at other times of the year.

Kazushige "Kaz" Okuma runs the Gotemba operation. He returned to Japan a few years ago after spending much of his career stateside helping oversee outlets there. Such expertise makes Okuma adept at translating both languages and culture. He's also a smart and gossipy guide. Were the mall a harem, Kaz would be the proud sultan; he decides which store is underperforming and kindly asks it to make way for a newer, fresher tenant. Stores here are refreshed more aggressively than in America or Europe to keep luring locals back with novelty. The "90% OFF" signs in Escada are a tip-off that it's been mothballed—and though the Maison Martin Margiela outlet is a constant under-performer, Kaz says he'll keep it open as good PR, since that's the only such outlet in the world.

There are other differences between Gotemba and its sibling spots in Western countries. For example, Japanese shoppers prefer whole numbers, so the discounts here can seem arbitrary: "43% OFF" screams one banner. Even food is marked down: A grab bag of Häagen Dazs pints at its outlet is 2,000 Yen, 42 percent off. What's more, the stores seem far less warehouse-like. Staffers are as solicitous as at the full-price counterparts

---

* LVMH has a multibrand outlet, inexplicably called Meleze, which has racks of goodies from each of its labels—all but one, of course. Even in today's Japan, Louis Vuitton never discounts.

in Ginza, well versed in clienteling the cheapskates. One Coachette smiles broadly as she hands over an extra 20 percent discount card, and chats about the different local styles. "There are some special things, smaller bags. People only want to carry valuable items here," Okuma says.

Almost nothing here is second quality or defective—that goes too far for Japanese sensibilities—but it also means that made for-outlet merchandise is even more widespread. The Prada store, which, Okuma notes, outperforms any sister shop in the country, including the full-price flagship, has shelves of ballistic nylon bags. These are one of the brand's signature styles, of course, and a fashion classic that has long been a staple of the full-price stores. None of those on show here, though, was ever sold elsewhere but Gotemba. "In the factories in Italy they can't fire people so easily, so they have to give the factory workers something to do. That's what they told me," Okuma explains, nodding to the stock that litters the shelves. "Bottega did it first, but now Prada is doing it and so is Gucci." Indeed, at the Gucci store, there are Double G waxed calf bags for around 51,400 Yen (or $650). In small letters, the Italian-language tag says "outlet borsa" (or "outlet bag").

There are relics of Japanese premium pricing, of course; Gotemba outlets sell some items sans discount. The snazzy Nikon 1 mirrorless camera is full price (around $500) and occupies a hefty chunk of the store, while Bulgari has non-discounted jewelry. It's a smart strategy, handily reference pointing those bargains even lower, but one that few American operators would allow. "When Bose started, they wanted to have a demo room here. They didn't care about selling so much—just for people to learn about them here and then go back to Tokyo to pay full price," Okuma recalls. The store was retrofitted to sell a few items, but it's still as much showcase as shop, with little marked down. For instance, the brand's signature headphones are just discounted 5 percent.

Bouts of rain pummel shoppers all day, but the weather doesn't dampen the crowds. After all, there are bargains to be nabbed. Clearly, these Japanese shoppers have little of the discomfort of deal hunting that might once have dogged their parents. There are few foreigners amid the throng; barely a dozen all day, wandering among the crowds and drawing demure stares from the locals. As in much of Japan, an island nation that has sat in self-imposed isolation for centuries, *gaijin* (foreigners) are a rarity. This couldn't be more different from our next destination, which has sat at the fulcrum of the world for two millennia and teems with visitors. Tokyoites, so typical in a mature market of the 2000s, are learning to love a deal with uncharacteristic gusto. In Istanbul, though, something quite different is happening.

Grand Bizarre

Turkey has been an economic bright spot of the last decade. It's one of the seven economies (alongside China, India, Brazil, Mexico, Russia, and Indonesia) expected to contribute 45 percent of global GDP growth over the next ten years. It expanded at 7.5 percent between 2002 and 2006, the fastest rate of any OECD member country, with per capita income in the decade from 2000 more than doubling, from $4,200 to $10,000.

Of course, that economic boom might be ascribed to the commercial nous so inherent in the Turkish psyche. Indeed, perhaps no place in the world is as synonymous with deals as Turkey's largest city, Istanbul. A Biblical-era trading post that's been commerce obsessed since its founding, this city-state once had a near-monopoly on commodities, straddling the Silk Road by land and the only water route between the Black Sea and the Mediterranean. A center of buying and selling between Europe and Asia, its suburbs still sprawl on to both continents.

Turkey has also long been famed for fabric- and carpet-making, and remains prominent as one of the world's top textile producers; the labels inside clothes at fast fashion chains bear the words "Made in Turkey" as often as they do "Made in China." Indeed, the rowdy markets that remain a feature of every neighborhood now groan with product that didn't even make it to an outlet mall. Just off Istikal Caddesi, the main shopping drag in the city center, two entire streets are dedicated to nothing but cut-price factory overruns. Beyoğlu Pasajı, an underground passage, sells mostly men's, while the cul-de-sac alleyway of Terkos Gikmozi is a jumble of women's labels like Pull and Bear and Stradivarius, both owned by Zara (H&M, interestingly, buys up its overruns from all the

Turkish factories to ensure the branded pieces don't end up here). T-shirts and tops flutter like pennants, hanging from chains on the tarpaulin-covered roof; most cost around 5 Turkish lira ($2.75). The dusty black Gucci V-neck is clearly a knockoff, despite a ratty certificate of authenticity dangling from the hanger.

None of those neighborhood markets compares, of course, to the Grand Bazaar. This is the spiritual home of sales. Its purpose is clear from its name—in Turkish, even the word for bargain, *pazarlık*, includes the word for market—and this giant complex has been mecca for markdowns ever since it was built more than five hundred years ago. After the Ottomans overwhelmed the dwindling Roman population in what was then Constantinople, Mehmet the Conqueror quickly set up a trading complex here, with thick walls and a gate for security. Astonishingly, Mehmet's building still survives at the heart of the market, and is where many of the most prestigious jewelers and gold-hawkers trade.

Arriving at the Grand Bazaar is an overwhelming experience, as disorienting as falling down a retail rabbit hole. Familiar as it might be from so many movies, its sheer scale is bewildering. There are more than sixty so-called streets zigzagging under coverings, jigsawed together as the Bazaar expanded, unplanned and haphazard, during three hundred years of economic booms. It feels like stepping into an Escher drawing. Gauging the exact number of stalls or shops is impossible, but most estimates put it around three thousand. The place smells not of cigarettes, but of people who smoke—sweat and tobacco. Men artfully pirouette through the crowds carrying trays with chains, or laden down with glass thimbles of hot, sweet peppermint tea. Tinkle, tinkle is the noise, every time someone stirs. It's Friday, so clusters of well-dressed men gather to wash their feet in the fountain before prayer time at the mosque. Their trouser legs rolled up, the men seem small and vulnerable amid the heaving crowds.

Rounding a corner is a Magic 8 Ball of shopping: You never know what you might find—an entire stall dedicated to musical instruments, say, or one that drips with glass lamps. Most of the shacks, though, sell clothes or accessories, all of the branded items undoubtedly counterfeit, a large part of Turkey's estimated $6 billion annual contribution to the global knockoff market. Browsing the bric-a-brac here is the best way to

Braille a brand's current hotness: The more frequently you spot its fakes, the greater its mass-market cachet. Perennials like Hilfiger and Polo are joined by vast stocks of Mulberry and Burberry (or Burbery, according to one unfortunate stall); the red-sequin D&G baseball cap is impressive and gaudy enough to be an original. The whole place has a furtive cruising quality that feels like shopping in a singles bar. Much of the merchandise from stall to stall is the same—after all, no counterfeiter can sell own label product, since his or her business is predicated on replicating what others make. Haggling over price, then, is the only way to differentiate. Voices pipe out hopefully as shoppers pass by. "Excuse me, where are you from? Can I help you spend some money?" asks one. "Can I ask you something?" adds another. "My friend, have a look!" "Yes, sir, can I help you?" "Good price, sir, not too expensive—" A pause. "Oh, okay, okay, less less, forty lira."

Thankfully, the glossy-haired and grinning Nirvana Asaduryan, a local travel agent, is on hand. "My soul clears here," she says and sighs. "My father owned two jewelry stores, so since I was seven or eight I've breathed the air of the Bazaar. It's good, you know, a child raised at the Bazaar makes more money than one born wealthy." Asaduryan is a wide-eyed, enthusiastic veteran. Walk around wearing sunglasses, she suggests, to deflect the constant attention from stallholders. Remember, they will size up the size of your wallet from how you're dressed, just like an Indian store might levy a premium on a Brahmin. So no to a Rolex or Cartier watch, yes to shorts and cheap sneakers.

Nirvana stops in front of a tiny, closet-sized store crammed with ikat-printed scarves folded neatly, running up the wall to the ceiling. The sign reads: YAZMACI. "It's all handmade, the Prime Minister's wife buys here—and if the owner is in a bad mood, he won't talk to you," she warns. Murat has a sad-sack, bloodhound face with deep bags beneath his eyes, but he offers tea—*tinkle, tinkle*—so clearly he's having a good day. At least he was until a trio of bossy British women appears, each wielding a chunky DSLR camera and over-perkily chirping, "This would be great for my blog!" Murat pauses to talk to them; the blondest stiffens her shoulders and readies for negotiation. "How much is this?" she asks. "It's thirty-three lira a meter," he responds. Clearly, she's jonesing to bargain.

"Can you do a different price?" Without missing a beat, he says, "Yes, thirty-five lira a meter." It's hard to tell if Murat is joking or insulted. Perhaps it's a little of both.

Yet amid the retail relentlessness, something doesn't feel quite right. After 2 p.m., the Grand Bazaar is busier than ever—but that's due to the cruise ships rolling in, Nirvana explains. Soon, the nagging problem becomes obvious. Looking around, it's hard to find a Turkish face among the browsers, other than the bossy guides who cajole snaking groups of gawkers down the busy alleys. In fact, every shopper seems to be communicating in English. One couple is arguing adroitly over a leather purse, the husband increasingly bored. "I do it for you. Normally it's two-ten, and the price for tourists is one fifty Euros. But I do it for you for one-ten, half price," pleads the shopkeeper. Spotty math aside, he still can't quite convince them to pay, adding, "No, no, I can't go lower." The husband looks close to coughing up the cash to avoid having to wait there while his wife argues any longer.

This is a shift, another signal of the blurring between halves of the world. Barely five years ago, there were still plenty of Turkish shoppers hectoring for half price with their countrymen. But now the Grand Bazaar feels like a great place for Brits, Americans, and other Europeans to hone their haggling skills before launching them back home. For the first time in five hundred years, it's truly much more a tourist attraction than a locals' haunt. Indeed, the Turkish government has introduced new regulations aimed at helping visitors make the most of the bazaars. In January 2012, a new fine was introduced for stallholders who were too noisy; the wardens who judged a call as overly loud could levy 500 Turkish lira ($280) per shout. Similarly, shopkeepers were urged to sign forms that guaranteed them as disease-free and to keep their hands and faces spotless. The whole place feels more Princess Jasmine than Scheherazade.

At the same time, Turks have begun migrating away from these age-old bazaars to the malls mushrooming around Istanbul. By the end of 2013, it's estimated that there will be 2,960 square feet of mall space to lease for every one thousand inhabitants of the city, or around 15 percent higher than the average across the EU. This is still Istanbul, though, and locals here haven't yet entirely abandoned their old instincts: Swanky department stores like Beyman or Brit import Harvey Nichols must still offer flash sale–like deals. The former charmingly calls them Butterfly days, where for twenty-four hours on the last day of the month, any sticker with a butterfly on it is 50 percent off.

Perhaps nothing spotlights how much attention is being paid to the Grand Bazaar by the West and other developed nations than the recent raid ringmastered by LVMH. In April 2011, Nirvana recalls, one of the firm's senior executives came to the Grand Bazaar. He spotted a replica of a Vuitton bag that was issued as a twenty-strong limited edition. Furious, he called the police not only in Istanbul but in Ankara, the capital and site of the government. (Tellingly, none of the other faked brands under the LVMH umbrella, like Dior or Fendi, sparked the same indignation.) "There were five hundred police at the Bazaar," Nirvana says. "Everyone selling the Louis Vuitton fakes was arrested. And now you shouldn't even mention the brand on the phone."

The police raided 137 stores, and those found in possession of fake Vuitton were hauled off to the new courts that have been set up to deal specifically with the widening problem of brand piracy. It's the reason that LV-branded goods are now almost impossible to find there. Hunting down a monogrammed bag now, as many of the Western shoppers are clearly keen to do, is like a fashion safari, each tote as elusive as a leopard sighting. A raid on that scale was unprecedented, but will likely continue. After all, more and more foreign customers are defecting from full-price boutiques. They are trading down to the likes of Fashionphile, perhaps, or trying their hand at haggling on fakes right at the Bazaar.

At least brand boutiques have nabbed a new customer to replace those veterans: free-spending Chinese who descend like luxury locusts on such shops whenever they travel. One report claimed there was widespread unhappiness among Japanese store staffers who sniffed at the aggressiveness of mainlanders on a buying spree, although the staffers were glad enough to take their money, of course. The Chinese middle class shores up its new Western-style affluence with behavioral changes. Ever since the United States finally relented and allowed China to enter the WTO, its citizens have been aping the behavior that was once associated with Americans. They've become less and less collectivist, and keener to display their individual merits or worth. One straightforward way to do that is to shop—proudly and loudly—at full price. To see what this means, and the influence such free-spending Chinese shoppers wield, let's take one more trip. This time, it's to the land of Burberry, Barbour jackets, and British reserve—specifically, England's capital: London.

The Power of the Peking Pound

The first hint is the red-blue-green logo by the cash registers in some of the city's poshest stores. Amex, Visa, Mastercard are familiar enough, but in the last two or three years there has been a strange addition to the list of accepted credit cards in store. Union Pay is China's homegrown credit card processor and it dwarfs the global names in the domestic market. As Chinese visitor numbers and spending habits ballooned, British retailers realized that most shoppers preferred paying with plastic to hauling suitcases of cash to a department store. Union Pay's rapid ubiquity at top shops across London telegraphs the importance of China's newfound love of premium to the UK economy today.

These visitors spend, and spend freely. They aren't just scouring the bargain bins for end-of-season deals (though they'll do that, too). Modern jet-set Beijingers and Shanghainese are ponying up for full-price treats to take home. Selfridges—Harry Gordon's legacy still thriving in Central London—has seventy-five Union Pay terminals and is offering Mandarin lessons to enthusiastic staffers. Rival Harrods already keeps seventy fluent speakers on hand to help foreign shoppers. True Brit brand Burberry pegged 30 percent of its sales in England to Chinese customers. Stores are no longer chasing the greenback, but the redback, China's renminbi.

No wonder, since the average Chinese visitor to the United Kingdom spends £1,700 (about $2,670), more than three times the average of every other nationality, around £567 (about $890). The Middle Kingdom's economic growth, and confidence it engenders, is one reason Chinese shoppers display such largesse. But it's also that they are wealthier, by dint of the government's one-child policy. The so-called 4-2-1 family structure concentrates inherited money rather than dispersing it, enriching the younger generation as grandparents die. Chinese cultural norms have boosted bottom lines, too. The tradition of bringing back gifts from trips means shoppers might buy a dozen Hermès scarves at once. Most Americans would max out at a couple of Hard Rock London T-shirts. The country's nouveaux riches are so culturally significant that they've even earned their own nickname, *bao fa hu*, which means "explosively rich." Think Trumpian bombast with better hair.

Chinese money sloshes around the capital. It underwrites cultural events, so that, for example, textile magnate Richard Chang's fortune was the emergency fund that propped up an exhibition at the Royal Academy by artist Anish Kapoor after a cash shortfall in 2009. Chinese milk firm Yili advertised on London buses during the Olympics to appeal to customers while abroad, and luxury menswear brand Bosideng has just spent £55 million (around $88 million) on a flagship store on London's arguably swankiest retail strip, South Molton Street. There, it joins the ten thousand shops the firm owns and runs back home. UK real estate developers are clearly eyeing the renminbi with their pricing strategies. One penthouse apartment in Dorset, Britain's answer to Maine, was offered at £888,000, deliberately using the number that's associated with luck everywhere in China. UK tourism chiefs were so keen to lure more visitors from the mainland that they sent a passel of look-alike royals to Shanghai to promote the country during the queen's Diamond Jubilee. It's a lucrative strategy, since a survey showed that 92 percent of Chinese visitors thought that "good brand names provide better value, due to quality," making them 54 percent keener than a Brit to splurge on a higher-priced item.*

These Chinese middle class tourists who are outspending their old-world counterparts right on their own turf is another symptom of the shift in global economic power. It's just like Tokyoites learning to love a bargain, and Western shoppers displacing locals from the Turkish bazaar. There's no longer a simple division between one half of the world that embraces bargains, and another that sees prestige in premium

---

* Deals still endure, albeit in some strange ways. One theme park in Guilin, China, launched a half-price promotion that was limited to women in short skirts (schoolmarm-style, it even specified the length—in this case it was 15 inches or *shorter*).

prices. The traditional lines between Western and Eastern spending patterns are blurring. Not everyone is surprised by this shift. In fact, some experts believe this was inevitable.

IESE professor Pankaj Ghemawat is one academic who foresaw the swap in global economic power. He tracks emerging economies and believes this stage is a natural correction, he says, rather than a seismic shift. "This is a return to the normal way in which twenty of the past twenty-two centuries ended, with China the world's largest economy," he explains. It was the last two hundred years that were the exception, rather than the norm. Before the Industrial Revolution, per capita incomes were largely equal worldwide around subsistence level. In 1820, China was responsible for 33 percent of world GDP, with Europe lagging at 27 percent. The latter's influence peaked in 1896, when it was responsible for 39 percent of output, versus China's 12 percent.*

By 2030, though, those numbers will reverse again, as the EU's share shrinks to 14 percent and China rises to 21 percent or just over a fifth of the world GDP. The strangest thing, Ghemawat says, isn't that the world is undergoing an industrial urbanization, but that it took so long to happen. As soon as China joined the WTO and saw its manufacturing base boom, the onslaught of capitalism inevitably squelched its traditional collectivism.

China, along with other emerging economies, is simply undergoing a delayed Industrial Revolution. In a rerun of the nineteenth century in Europe, pride in paying full price emerges alongside the middle class with which it's so associated. It's no coincidence that Aristide Boucicaut invented the price tag just as the middle-class shopper emerged two hundred years ago. The catch-up is happening at warp speed: Britain, where the first Industrial Revolution began, required a century and a half to double per capita economic output. It's taken China twelve years and India sixteen years to do exactly the same thing.† By 2025, 60 percent of

---

* The USA peaked at 34 percent in 1945, when China's share had shrunk to a piffling 5 percent.
† That one-child policy, which has enriched today's shoppers, is the only time bomb that threatens China's dominance. The supply of human beings—arguably the country's handiest natural resource—will soon no longer outstrip demand; once the generation of single-child-policy families reaches middle age, cheap labor will be ever harder to find. The one child policy began in 1979.

the one billion or so households earning more than $20,000 a year will live in the developing world. These economies will soon behave much as Westerners have done for the last two centuries, full of brash monied confidence. At the same time, the developed world will relearn its long-lost skills of bargain hunting, hobbled by weakening output. Just ask Kate Middleton.

The Price-Conscious Princess

While Chinese shoppers are luxuriating in full-price treats just over an hour away in Central London, English royals are shopping elsewhere. Bicester Village, a short drive from the city of Oxford to London's West, is another premium outlet mall, like Woodbury Common or Gotemba. It's comprised of the now-familiar low-rise white buildings that house a roster of the usual blue-chip brands with redlined prices: Gucci, Prada, Alexander McQueen. The only nods to its location are blue-blooded Brit labels such as Mulberry, Smythson, and Vivienne Westwood, plus two jaunty, red phone boxes, rare enough on ordinary English streets today.

Although Bicester Village opened only in 1995, less than twenty years later, more than 4.5 million shoppers are perusing its racks each year. In 2010, average annual sales per square foot were £1,400 (around $2,200), the highest at any such mall in the world. (It was no big surprise that there were plans to demolish a nearby supermarket and replace it with fifty more cut-price designer shops.) On a cold weekday in early February, there are still crowds thronging its alleys—no wonder, as it's still clearance season. Markdowns are more irresistible than ever: La Perla's lingerie is 75 percent off, and a bright red pillow at Ralph Lauren Home screams FURTHER REDUCTIONS. Valentino is offering UP TO 65% OFF FROM OUTLET PRICE, and the words are underlined for extra urgency.

Even here, some stores are more discreet, like Reiss, the minimalist midmarket workwear brand beloved by the Duchess of Cambridge, née Kate Middleton. She wore one of its dresses, a simple white number that cost just over $300, for her official engagement snap to the future king of England. Reiss has a smallish outpost here, selling both its men's and women's collections. A young honey-blonde staffer with English rose skin is cheery and helpful, wading through the piles of $40 sweaters. She knows the tabloids' beloved Waity Katie all too well. "She is here all the time—she was last in the shop two months ago," the staffer says. "When she comes to Bicester, you know, she's always with two girlfriends and you just see her browsing the racks. She doesn't look like she has security with her or at least you can't tell where they are. We love her." She rolls her eyes, "I mean it's not like one Asian prince—when he comes, he shuts that whole restaurant down and brings in his own waiters." It's a jarring, but memorable, image: The future queen of England has no problem snapping up half-price frocks on a casual shopping afternoon with friends—while a royal from a developing nation is so rich and obnoxious enough that he doesn't need to deign share a restaurant with the huddled masses.

Pax, Professor Ghemawat, but somehow this doesn't seem like a simple economic correction, one where a global Industrial Revolution returns us to the equanimity of two hundred years ago flattening out differences. Rather, in the shopping 3.0 era, it presages a permanent role reversal. Buyers are the center of the process for the first time, but worldwide they are reacting to that opportunity very differently. The financially wobbly (those living in the developed world) cling to discounts as their way of leveraging such clout. The comfortably wealthy (the freshman middle class in China et al) relish the privilege and choice the power confers. They don't shun bargains entirely—dopamine's power is universal—but they've become the only thriving market for full-price goods.

Stagnant growth in mature economies for the foreseeable future is likely to heighten, rather than dampen, such divisions. It's unlikely that the pendulum will ever swing back. By the mid 2020s, it's easy to imagine companies reconfiguring their operations to address the disparity. Imagine a luxury marquee creating a two-tier selling strategy, for example. One team would be tasked with overseeing the Luxe line, available only in China, India, and other booming nations. The line would feature elaborate detailing, an aesthetic nod to those cultures' traditional tastes. As important, it would be premium priced, Veblen-good style. An entirely separate group would design and market the V for Value line, aimed at America, Europe, and Japan. V would be a minimalist rip-off of that premium collection, stagily sold with every ticket touting the retail value versus its actual price. Perhaps they could even tap Queen Kate to be the face of the brand.

It's easy to picture that scenario in ten years' time, but what about the immediate future? How will the pandemic of discountmania change shopping tomorrow, or even next year, as sellers adjust to the buying public's growing clout? The best way to answer that question is to start with the past, or rather, the unhappy recent present of one of discounting's earliest pioneers. How did Filene's Basement become retail roadkill at the very moment that it should have been set on its most profitable path?

8

The Future of Bargain Fever

*The Rise of Showrooming but the Fall of
Filene's, What Question All but Guarantees
a Spot Discount, and Coca-Cola's
Weather-Dependent Vending Machine*

The last days of the giant Filene's Basement store on Union Square in New York were forlorn, retail's version of a busted starlet reduced to nothing but endless reality show guest spots. The company had already filed for Chapter 11 once, in May 2009, but dodged shutdown when swallowed by rival discounter, Syms. Theirs proved an unhealthy match. Two years later, both firms floundered and the last Filene's Basement stores were set to shutter on December 29, 2011. The discounting pioneer deserved a better end than this.

A week before closing forever, the Manhattan flagship was one of the final stragglers. It looked more like a crime scene than a department store. Photos of every fixture were tacked to a pin board like evidence; bankruptcy required liquidation of all the firm's assets, and prices were scribbled on Post-its pressed on each shot. Among the jumble, every component of the store had been ruthlessly stripped: $150 each, please, for the store's two wheelchairs but just $60 for the wooden box to recycle plastic bags. Every fixture was sold with clear removal conditions—YOUR TOOLS, YOUR DISASSEMBLY, YOUR CLEAN UP, YOUR HAND TRUCK, YOUR LOAD, YOUR HAUL, barked one placard.

One mannequin, so carelessly outfitted it looked as if she'd dressed in a hurry when her husband had come home too early from the office, had a yellow sticker slapped on her neck; she was worth just $50. EVERYTHING 40%-60% OFF LOWEST TICKETED PRICE, screamed the thicket of signs hanging, pinned-up, or on stands. There was so little merchandise of worth left by then, though, that there wasn't much worth selling: a few cheap towels, piles of rifled-through Nautica shirts, and polyester-lined jewelry boxes. Entire sections of the store were full of empty garment racks, jigsawed together like climbing frames. No wonder most of the shoppers seemed to have ducked inside to keep warm rather than to browse. A huddle of women sat in chairs by the window, chatting noisily on cell phones and ignoring the chance to shop.

Less than a year after this scene, Filene's and parent company Syms were joined on the discount scrapheap by Daffy's, once home to "Clothing Bargains for Millionaires." Its demise, in September 2012, was characteristically showy: The day after its store in Soho shuttered, all fixtures and signage torn down, one sheet was pasted to every street-facing window. CLOSED FOREVER, it howled with a tragedienne's histrionic flair. Three icons of cut-price chic collapsing near-simultaneously seems strange, especially when the rest of retail was forming itself in their image.* Perhaps that was the reason for their downfall. Who needs a bargain basement when the first floor is already 50 percent off? As competition for marked-down merchandise grows, it's simple fashion Darwinism. Yes, there is too much stuff, but now there are too many channels competing to offer it to picky shoppers (just ask Gilt Groupe). Filene's, Syms, and Daffy's were joining bell-bottoms and bustles on style's scrapheap. TJX, which owns TJ Maxx and Marshalls, and chief rival Ross are truly too big to fail, XXL-sized operations with enough

---

* It was similarly momentous in February 2013 when Barneys announced that its storied Warehouse Sales in NYC would now be primarily online, year-round, rather than twice yearly brick-and-mortar blowouts.

buying clout to navigate and dominate the newly competitive discount landscape.*

Then again, it could be that Filene's prices just were not aggressive enough. One recent study found that shoppers no longer trust the supposed original price claimed on markdown tickets at such discount stores. Conditioned to sales, they will mentally adjust that higher number down by 25 percent, assuming implied inflation. It's a byproduct of what the industry calls *insult pricing*, the same impulse that drives a convenience store to charge $11.99 for a pack of condoms when an identical item is just $6.99 at Target. A traditional luxury markup is 7.5 or 8 times cost. Why, then, was Spice-Girl-turned-fashion-flavor-of-the-month Victoria Beckham caught manufacturing her dresses in grubby but legal conditions in London for £60 (around $95) each then charging $2,200 at retail? That's a staggering twenty-three times cost. It isn't just premium brands like Beckham's, either. As long ago as 1997, in fact, Bloomingdale's and Macy's were fined a total of $300,000 by the state of Florida for misrepresenting full price, after complaints from shoppers that sale savings on furniture were overstated.

Does the ignominious end of Filene's make this a Norma Desmond moment for discounts? Will everyone become mired in markdown madness as they move from being the exception to the norm, from 10 percent to 90 percent off? Not at all, especially as Filene's failure was mostly down to financial mismanagement. Rather, this move toward everyday discounting presages a new way of buying and selling, that third era in retail we're calling shopping 3.0. Pricing will be as much a strategy as a tactic, with shoppers at the center of the process with real power for the first time. If 45 percent of products are already sold on promotion, what

---

* TJX had annual revenues of $21.9 billion in 2011, besting Nike, Xerox, and Halliburton, among others. As secretive as a sample sale run by Scientologists, one former staffer confided that TJX operates more like a retail partner than a closeout vendor: much of its inventory (around 85 percent) is current-season excess off-loaded by major brands to keep balance sheets lean—it's reportedly Polo Ralph Lauren's number one vendor. Don't be surprised to find Gucci, Prada, and others on the rack in some of its stores, either—especially the one next to the firm's headquarters in Framingham, Massachusetts. This is run as a test store, where ideas can be workshopped before rolling out nationwide. The former staffer says it's always kept stocked with top-tier merch in case CEO Carol Meyrowitz takes an impromptu stroll through the aisles on her lunch hour. Lucky her.

does it mean once discounting reaches 51 percent of overall volume, and a sale price is more standard than a full price? What implication does that have for prices at all? It will nurture four major changes that will change retail forever. The canary in the discount coal mine of the first is a bloodied but unbowed household name: Best Buy.

Showrooming Me the Money

Best Buy has 19 percent of the US electronics market and is free from major competitors (RIP: Circuit City, CompUSA). Pop culture is more obsessed with gadgets and technology than ever, making its sector one of the hottest in retail. Yet this chain still struggles. It's largely because it's being hobbled by the new discount-powered tactic that's the ultimate in consumer control: showrooming.

Such price comparison started at bookstores. With the rise of Amazon, local booksellers became more like libraries, coffee-scented places to browse before buying the same things online—and more cheaply. That was before the surge in Smartphone-ownership; once the Internet was accessible in your pocket, showrooming exploded. It became an instant convenience: Standing in front of that 42-inch TV in Best Buy, who wouldn't fire up their phone and check if there wasn't a better online deal? Unless they could offer exclusive, comparison-proof products, brick-and-mortar stores morphed from shops into showrooms. Overheads were constant but incomes dropped.

Among retailers, Best Buy hasn't handled this change well. In 2007, it installed kiosks encouraging shoppers to check prices at BestBuy.com. The gesture backfired when Connecticut's attorney general responded to complaints by starting an investigation. It turned out that prices displayed at the website shown in-store were deliberately higher than those on the public site so as not to undermine physical sales. A company spokesperson claimed that it was meant to act more as a catalog of each location than a website per se. The kiosks were designed to ape the online look, she continued deadpan, "to ensure that customers who were familiar with the national website could easily navigate the in-store kiosk to find what they were seeking." Such a shifty approach to shoppers is lethal in a new buyer-centric world.

Best Buy has blamed showrooming for poor financial performance over several quarters, especially since price comparison apps have emerged, including eBay's Red Laser. These apps use Smartphones' built-in cameras to snap an image of a UPC code then scour the web for better prices. Retailers will resort to extremes to circumvent this; stories have even circulated of shelf-edges being obscured expressly to obviate this. It gives the retailer a rather desperate, dog-ate-my-homework air.

It's becoming increasingly hard for stalwart brick and mortars like Best Buy to compete with online retailers. Amazon can slash prices as loss leaders; with few physical overheads, it also makes money from several revenue streams, like cloud data storage or the fees it charges third-party vendors to sell via its site. On December 10, 2011, Amazon announced a spiff for users of its Price Check app. Customers submitting physical store prices could receive up to $5 credit or 5 percent off three items. It was marketing genius, turning ordinary Americans into a zombie army capturing precious competitors' data. It empowered shoppers while also exploiting them.

Retail consultant Nikki Baird says her clients are panicky about the implications of showrooming, especially as Smartphone penetration reached more than 50 percent of American consumers in mid 2012. She notes that several CIOs and store ops VPs recently asked her, deadpan, if it was smart or even legal to install cell blockers inside stores. Such moves are like tinhatting with aluminum foil.

The impact of the fact that shoppers now carry a magic discount ray in their pocket or purse at all times is intriguing. For one thing, the ease of accessing information via Smartphone has helped power the renaissance of own-brand goods, or private label. These products circumvent showrooming. One of the best proponents of such a strategy is Trader Joe's. It is one of the supermarket sector's darlings because it limits household names to just 20 percent of stock; the rest is private label.*

---

* Those products are often made by brand-name competitors, one reason for its TJX-like media-shyness and ironclad vendor contracts that stipulate, "Vendor shall not publicize its business relationship with TJ's in any manner."

Nothing sums up its strategy better than the signature wine Two Buck Chuck (now, sadly, $2.99), which is exclusively made for, and sold by, the retailer. When Trader Joe's enters a new market, it will stage taste tests of Two Buck Chuck against $100 wines to prove its quality and grab publicity. It also carries just four thousand SKUs versus a traditional supermarket's fifty thousand or more, and as we've seen over and over, less choice is the best way to drive sales. Such leanness also means the supermarket can leverage larger volume discounts, making unit costs lower.

In fashion, Kohl's and Macy's rely on their own labels for 40 percent of sales; one of J.C. Penney's few bright spots in its recent makeover has been Ron Johnson's obsession with locking up exclusive product deals. Research firm NPD has tracked own-label clothing for decades. For the thirty years after 1975, it surged from just 25 percent of sales stateside to double that. Store brands in supermarkets made up more than 30 percent of the fourteen thousand or so new food and beverage products launched in 2011, double the previous year. And Target, so snitty with Amazon that it stopped selling Kindle devices in summer 2012 in retaliation over showrooming stunts, even sent a cajoling letter to suppliers that was widely published, demanding more Target-only products to preclude showrooming and so differentiate their store.

Private label may be one way to stymie such comparison shopping, but there are also opportunities in showrooming. If everyone is walking around a store, cell phone in hand, retailers have the chance to reach the buyer in a new way. Showrooming has birthed GPS-driven deals where, for example, North Face might send coupons or promotions to a cell phone user with its app installed nearby. Brouha is one service that allows businesses to communicate with customers in-store via RFID; similarly, Valpak's app will flash coupons for nearby companies if launched. Anyone using Aisle411 at Walgreens or Shop 'n Save can take advantage of the maps it offers to help navigate a store, while also picking up digital coupons.

Brands themselves can opt into promotions that unlock extra savings for the shoppers who interact more, say, by sharing certain finds with friends. American Express partnered with a slew of vendors, such as H&M, McDonald's, and Whole Foods, to create insta-coupons. Standing in a store, cardholders who had synced their Amex cards with their Twit-ter handles could hashtag tweets that would automatically earn them paperless coupon credit on their cards. Meanwhile, rebate giant Parago launched its own app, GoRebate, which scraped for money-back deals in a geographic vicinity. These programs turn a cell phone into a dowsing rod for deals. After all that, you probably deserve a drink—but don't pay full price for it: Use GoTime to hunt down the nearest Happy Hour.

Arguably the most successful of these location-based gimmicks is Shopkick, which combines a loyalty program with insta-deals. Retailers who partner with Shopkick are provided with a special device to install in every location. Like a dog whistle, this emits a special signal that is logged by a Smartphone's microphone as a shopper enters the store. It's far more precise than GPS-powered versions, which have a margin of er-ror up to 1,000 yards (translation: You could cruise past in a car, grab a GPS coupon, and then spend it online at home). Shopkick deals usually involve a discount, like the $10 off a $40 spend it secured with Old Navy—as well as reward points, which accumulate with use and can be spent on song downloads and movie tickets, or even donated to charity.

Another symptom of showrooming: the muddying of different chan-nels, real world and digital. To avoid losing a customer to a cheaper on-line competitor, some traditional retailers have started offering same-day collection: Order online and trot to a nearby retail outlet to pick up the purchase straightaway. It emphasizes the instant gratification they can offer that a dot-com rival cannot, as well as offering savings on shipping charges. Macy's, Sears, and even poor Best Buy all offer this hybrid shop-ping model. Walmart calls the program, with typical lingoish flair, the Endless Aisle. You can even pay with cash on collection rather than us-ing a credit card. It's smartly tailored to customers that other stores often overlook, say, those without bank accounts and those still wary of shar-ing data online. Just two months after launching, the cash-on-collection option already represented 2 percent of sales at walmart.com

More tellingly, the chain trialed a couple of walmart.com-branded stores in California. With small footprints in suburban malls, rather than the huge standalone stores more typical of the brand, they focused on key categories like toys and electronics. Nothing could be bought on-site: Shoppers were guided to walmart.com terminals in store, with shipping offered to that same store, a regular location, or the buyer's home. Reports have long bubbled up that Amazon would chance a brick-and-mortar store, likely in its home city of Seattle, though nothing has been confirmed (maybe they're workshopping it in a secret warehouse, Apple-style). Piperlime, the online subsidiary of Gap, had a pop-up store in New York's Soho in September 2010 that proved so successful, a permanent site was announced nearly eighteen months later. When San Francisco clothing start-up Everlane.com wanted to expand its reach, it didn't spend money on a viral video. Rather, it rented a storefront in Manhattan so potential customers could touch and feel the clothes. All orders were then made on iPads dotted around the pop-up. It wasn't showrooming, but browsing, brick-and-mortar style.

Everlane.com's founding principles center on one final, intriguing offshoot of showrooming: price transparency. Showrooming damages the trust between seller and buyer, both resentful of the other's attempts at control. If a firm offers complete price transparency, though, that gesture can make the same interaction both bonding and confidence-boosting. On the windows of Everlane.com's pop-up shop (proudly called "NOT a retail SHOP") in New York's Nolita, giant white letters spelled out its mission statement. IT'S A FACT, it says, YOUR DESIGNER CLOTHES SELL FOR 8 TIMES WHAT THEY COST TO MAKE. NOT AT EVERLANE.COM. Inside the store, the brand explained its promising premise in greater depth: An entire wall inside was dedicated to a flowchart-like graphic that broke down the cost of producing one of its T-shirts, stage by stage. Sewing added $1.35 in overheads, for example, and transport another 50 cents. The total cost, per this outline, was just $6, which Everlane marked up to just $15. At traditional retail, it trumpeted, the exact same T-shirt would cost $50.

Founder Michael Preysman, a VC refugee who is rather more geek than chic, is obsessed with prices. Specifically, he rants about how artificially inflated they have become in the luxury sector (perhaps he recalls Victoria Beckham's 2,300 percent markup). In founding Everlane.com, Preysman wanted to break that pattern, cutting out the middleman and selling directly online. It's a standalone riff on own label. He calculated that Everlane.com can make a viable profit using a multiplier of 2.5, and could pass on that saving to shoppers. After starting with a basic line of T-shirts, he's expanded into belts and bags; button downs, sweaters, and scarves are next.

Using price transparency to repair the bonds broken by relentless show-rooming isn't restricted to Everlane.com. Belgian boutique HonestBy.com goes into even more granular detail. Click on any item—perhaps a cotton wrap-shirt dress by Bruno Pieters—and you'll find complete transparency. Alongside material information such as the size or composition of the brand label and its carbon footprint, shoppers can also X-ray the price. Every line item used in manufacturing is listed and priced, down to a single safety pin for €0.03. Total materials are tallied with patterns, development, and branding. The raw cost of €111,30 is doubled for staff and admin costs by the designer; and doubled again for HonestBy.com's retail costs. Bruno Pieters, sold exclusively online, also passes along the savings.

It's the same thinking that led Michael Dubin to found Dollar Shave Club, a razor subscription company that grabbed attention, and sales, via a made-to-go-viral video poking fun at the inflated pricing of conventional brands such as Gillette. One of the drivers behind showrooming is customers' belief that prices are arbitrarily high. Dubin's company agrees. By selling directly, he offers four weeks' worth of blades for as little as $1 per month, including a free handle. He also cannily launched with three options, Goldilocks pricing–style, and doubtless earns the best margins on that best-selling middle offering.

Facing competitors like these, the smartest conventional retailers don't resist showrooming and how harshly it X-rays their prices; they challenge customers to best them. Buttressed by plenty of private labels, Lowe's all but dares shoppers to check prices, issuing forty-two thousand iPhones across seventeen hundred stores so sales assistants can facilitate comparison. British department store John Lewis, a consistent retail darling, pioneered the installation of WiFi in its stores. This was essential, given that the store's motto is "Never Knowingly Undersold." John Lewis takes pride in price matching—no wonder as much of its stock is high quality but own label. This protects the company from delivering too unprofitably on that promise of price matching. In fiscal year 2011, it continued to hardily weather the economic slump, with pre-tax profits leaping 20 percent to £367.9 million (or $593.3 million). Those figures remained as buoyant in its 2012 fiscal year, with gross sales up 6.4 percent to £8.73 billion (around $13.35 billion).

"It's part of a broader trend toward more transparency," says Oren Etzioni, who created a program that aggregates price histories to suggest when is best to buy, known as Decide.com. "You see it from the fact you can't kill people in Syria as easily as you used to, to the fact that your Congressman Wiener can't hide the fact that he sent lewd pictures, or real estate prices listed on Zillow.com, and CEO reviews on glassdoor. com." More than anything, though, justifying the price as fair is a strangely retro notion. It's really moving back to the cost-plus pricing that collapsed in the 1980s. Technology, and the way it vests shot-calling with shoppers, has taken us back to the future.

Cheap or Choosy?

Price versus choice, which matters more? That's the question at the heart of the second way in which the dominance of discounts is transforming the way we shop. This trade-off is the Buy a Vowel principle: Are you cheap or are you choosy? Think of it as a simple formula. More choice is more expensive, while less of a selection lowers costs. That's the reason Uniqlo offers two styles of jeans in ten colors apiece, rather than five styles in four shades, since it can negotiate harder on higher volumes, Trader Joe's–style. The Cheap or Choosy? question is informed by one of those truisms of behavioral economics, the science that explores our irrational attitude to money. Remember transaction utility or the Cab in a Rainstorm idea? It centers on the fact that the value of something isn't absolute, but boosted or reduced by a set of subjective circumstances. Transaction utility is an appealing principle for a business, but using it to guide pricing was almost impossible. How could you gauge a given customer's price sensitivity at any moment? It was impossible—at least until recently. Dr. Jinhong Xie, a University of Florida professor originally from Beijing, has just patented a code breaker for this enigma of behavioral economics. She calls it Probabilistic Selling Strategy or PSS.

Imagine you arrive at a buffet and you're starving. How much would you pay for that smorgasbord of salads? The price says $10, but it looks so delicious you're surprised it isn't $20. A woman stands next to you surveying the same spread. She's feeling queasy and might have a migraine coming on. Nothing really appeals to her, so that $10 charge seems steep. She leaves the restaurant, convinced she'd manage to eat only a couple of bucks' worth of greens. That café, unable to read your minds, charged both the same price. In so doing, it missed an opportunity with each individual, making a $10 sale that could have reached $22 if selective discounting were applied.

Xie is obsessed with this quandary. "A seller has two strategies: one is to charge a high price and only sell to people in the more favorable consumption space, or charge a lower price to sell to everyone. You either lose margin or you lose volume," she says, her voice rapid-fire. "But if everyone put a sign on their head telling how much they were willing to pay—well, if that was legal. Imagine how much profit you can get?"

Xie staged a series of experiments to better understand the relationship between price and choice. Using two umbrellas, identical but for the color—the first red, the second green—she started lowering the price to see how the volunteers would respond to the discount. She offered one caveat, though, as she tempted them with lower prices; the bargain deal activated only if the subject would forgo control of the color. Volunteers received a discount for lessened selection; they could choose to buy an umbrella, but not control the color in which it was supplied. Some volunteers had strong preferences for one of the two colors but many were glad to trade choice for a deal. Based on these findings, Xie developed a patented program that almost any online retailer can use. It's yield management with a dopamine-driven tweak.

Here's how it works. Imagine a typical clothing chain that must order its winter inventory six months ahead. For wool sweaters, it buys a cashmere V-neck in four colors: ten thousand each in red, green, white, and black. Unfortunately, by the time those sweaters hit the stores, glossy magazines have trumpeted the return of monochrome dressing, and the First Lady has been seen wearing nothing but black or white. Sales of red and green cashmere, then, are sluggish. Traditionally, that chain would have had two options: Reduce the entire line to help drive purchase, or just mark down those two colors. The problem with the latter tactic is that it highlights their unpopularity, making those slow sales a self-fulfilling prophecy. Shoppers know this price cut indicates slowdown and will likely hold out for even steeper price cuts. This solution also gives an unnecessary deal to the customers with a fondness for color; after all, not everyone cares what those damn magazines say. Not to mention, breaking price so visibly mid-season sets a bad precedent for future seasons.

Were Xie's PSS plan in place, the sweater problem would not exist. The program would monitor sales of each unit and trigger only if given certain conditions—if the red sweater is lagging more than one thosand units behind all the other colors, for example. Anyone buying that red sweater online as her first choice would be checked out as normal. A shopper who clicked on black or white, though, would receive a prompt as she placed it in her basket. "Are you sure you would like that sweater in black?" it would ask. "We'll guarantee the same size, but we'll take 30 percent off if you allow us to choose the color." PSS offers discounts only when they're needed, an opt-in rather than an opt-out. The strategy protects profit margins while simultaneously offering customers a clever promotion and keeping inventory lean. If every retailer used it for the online arm, it could eliminate the need for a 70 percent sale at season's end. It's old school Lucky Dip, with a discount as the lure. Psychologically, it leaves decision-making to the shopper, so it's a natural fit for the new retail landscape.

A few companies already use a similar model to PSS, though not Xie's unique patented process. At swimoutlet.com, its TYR Grab Bag swimsuit is discounted 60 percent thanks to a simple trade-off. "If you're not picky about color or print, this surprise of a suit is perfect for you! Just choose the size and we pick the print for you from this mixture of last season's favorites," the site explains. "These competition suits are a mixture of maxback and diamondback cuts as well as polyester or nylon/lycra fabric." German Wings, a European discount airline, offers Lucky Dip pricing on some flights, known as Blind Booking. Log onto the site and pick your departure airport, then choose a theme for the trip; gay-friendly, perhaps, or culture, or shopping. Your selection autogenerates a list of destinations on your chosen date. You'll see up to eleven places, from Manchester to Milan or Munich. Each time you exclude one of those cities from the booking, the price increases by €5, so what you pay in the end is directly governed by whether choice or cost is more important to you. Gilt Groupe tried its own version of this trade-off with what it dubbed Freefall during the holiday season 2012. It staged a series of 5-minute sales throughout the day where a limited number of products were set aside to be sold in a new way, with the price dropping as the minutes ticked by—patient buyers could risk the inventory depleting in exchange for a lower final price.

The Cheap or Choosy? trade-off will be a staple in the new retail landscape. Xie's innovation focuses on the cost-conscious consumer, Ms. Cheap. But what about Ms. Choosy, her diametric opposite, the person who is happy to pay more in exchange for the ultimate selection? To her, a premium is more than justifiable if it grants the ultimate in exclusive choice. In a world of mass markdowns, isn't the only way to charge full price by offering the chance and choice to buy something no one else will ever have? According to one thriving business run by a pair of Hitch-cockian blondes in Manhattan, the answer is yes. Or perhaps, given its couture-level customer, *mais oui*.

When Reykjavik-born Aslaug Magnusdottir was working at Gilt as head of merchandising for its VIP-skewing Noir imprint, she fielded one constant complaint. "Over the last couple of years I kept hearing from designers that beautiful pieces from their collections—often their favorite pieces—never made it to the stores," she said. "Because of the economic downturn, stores have become more and more risk averse, so many of those most special pieces didn't make it to the sales floor." Such moaning sparked the business she now runs with socialite-cum-stylist Lauren Santo Domingo. Moda Operandi provides exclusive choices on designs from brands like Thakoon and Alberta Ferreti—clothes that will never be offered to the ordinary American. In exchange for such access, her customers gladly pay full price. Are they Cheap or Choosy? Given that the average spending on posh frocks was $1,800 per transaction within six months of launching, it's a moot question.

The idea that became Moda Operandi was surprisingly simple: Offer exclusive designer merchandise by cutting out those department stores (although unlike Everlane.com, Magnusdottir is glad to split the added margins with its suppliers). Say a buzzy designer like Thakoon stages a show with fifty looks at Lincoln Center during February's Fashion Week. If he has a deal in place with Magnusdottir, the Moda Operandi team descends on his atelier the day after that show, and sets up an ad hoc photo studio, snapping models in that market-fresh batch of frocks. The entire collection appears online two days later for sale.

Perhaps only half of what's shown might end up in wide-scale production; those are the samples that gave a name to that showroom sale. If a designer partners with Moda Operandi, nothing need go to waste. For a short window—anywhere from three to twelve days—members can order anything they see, at full price. That dress that might have lingered in the showroom for months until it was sold off at cost can instead be bought and worn by the too-rich and too-thin anywhere in the world. Moda levies a 50 percent deposit on orders. Between four weeks and four months later—but, crucially, always before the collection appears in store—the precious garment is delivered and the balance due. The chichi site's members sacrifice discounts for access. It's basically a modern riff on a trunk show, a department store tradition where select customers are invited to preview a collection and air-kissed by the respective designer. At a trunk show, the only items on display are those the store deemed worthy of buying, and triggered into production. Moda turns Thakoon's runway directly into a shop.

What Moda Operandi offers has irresistible snob value: the opportunity to buy something from a darling designer du jour like Alexander Wang that no one else will ever have. Of course, sometimes it can backfire, just like a pair of glitter pants that Wang showed and sold via Moda Operandi. "None of the buyers had picked up on them, but when we made them available, people loved them. They became best-sellers," Magnusdottir explained. Best-sellers, somewhat conversely, are the one thing the firm must fret over. Who would be happy having shelled out full price for something only to turn up to the same benefit as a rival uptowner in the same togs?

Much like a comedian can now workshop jokes via Twitter rather than in a dank smoky club (translating retweets as chuckles), a designer can use this channel to see which of its pieces should go into production. For the first time, thanks to Magnusdottir's mechanic, labels can learn directly about their customers rather than relying on data from Bergdorf and other major retailers. Moda's financial setup—50 percent deposit, 50 percent payable on delivery—acts like a layaway. Doubtless, as at Fashionphile in Los Angeles, it has also helped some women sneak through expenses that would have seemed outlandish in a single sum. ("I've heard that from a couple of people. They've bought more expensive pieces because of it," she acknowledged.) To help overcome any fears about fit or quality, there's a staff of stylists on hand at any time to coach buyers.

With its focus on designer fashion at full price, Moda Operandi is the anti-Gilt. And Magnusdottir's entrepreneurial instincts were proved astute when Moda secured $36 million in its third round of financing including investments from both Condé Nast and LVMH.* Though Moda Operandi launched only in February 2011, there were more than one hundred thousand members worldwide by the end of that same year; and a partnership with Condé Nast's *Vogue* during Fashion Week to help spur click-throughs. The roster of fashion It girls, like Neiman Marcus vet Roopal Patel, who've been lured to help buff its credentials hasn't hurt either.† The constant clicking isn't just their high heels. But though Magnusdottir is insistent there will never be discounts, customers can return unwanted garments within three weeks of delivery (though they'll forfeit that 50 percent deposit in the process). Moda Operandi buys its stock outright, rather than taking it on consignment, so

---

* Another endorsement is that it's already inspiring clones, like British upstart VeryFirstTo. com. That rival has a *Monty Python*esque patina, though, since it regularly offers bizarre treats, such as buying thirty seconds of airtime on British TV to create a marriage proposal in advertisement form for £135,000 (around $206,500).
† Another on-call acolyte: *Project Runway* judge Nina Garcia, who perhaps should let someone else do her shill-tweeting in the future. She was widely mocked for a let-them-eat-cake-ish MO-boosting tweet that chirped, complete with hotlink, "This is the bag you can spend a few weeks' salary on and not feel guilty. It is going to last you a lifetime." Since that bag was a $26,500 Birkin, clearly her Lifetime salary would impress even Matt Lauer.

Magnusdottir has said it might need to stage sample sales in future. If Gilt Groupe is still in business then, maybe she can call in a favor.

"Is That the Widows and Orphans Price?"

In March 2011, Gap quietly trialed a new website: gapmyprice.com, an entirely deal-driven site. It was a discreet toe-dipping into a different way of selling, launched with little publicity. The standalone channel asked shoppers to haggle for items and challenged them to name their own price, Priceline-style. To get the discount, each buyer had to print out a coupon and redeem in store. There was even a "Winners" board showing other successful hagglers and what they paid, to both give it a social media tweak and encourage the nervous.

Admittedly, the product selection was small—around fifteen items from the current collection—and some of the discounts skimpy (one shopper secured a whopping 95 cents off a striped T-shirt). But it was an example of the third way that retail is being reshaped today. Just like that return to cost-plus pricing by Everlane and co, there's a throwbackishness to this shift. Until Aristide Boucicaut introduced the idea of a price tag, mere decades after Europe and America sprinted past the rest of the world thanks to the Industrial Revolution, haggling was a daily tactic for ordinary people everywhere. That long-lost instinct is being revived for shopping 3.0. "Americans may finally learn that price tags weren't put there by the big printer in the sky," says Herb Cohen, author of the haggling Bible *You Can Negotiate Anything*. We're returning to the centuries-old practice of name-your-price, the ultimate in shoppercentric retail.

EBay and Priceline reminded Americans a decade ago of that simple maxim, at least online: Prices can be negotiated. Having relearned such instincts so greedily, Americans are now exporting those same expectations and strategies to the mall. Since deals are everywhere, why not secure one for yourself by asking, ever so nicely, if there's any chance of a better price. Leverage lies with buyers now: As supply outstrips demand, those in a position to spend shouldn't blanch to haggle over white goods, for example.

As soon as the economy cratered in October 2008, one survey found that 56 percent of Americans had tried to negotiate for something other than a car. Half of them had secured a cheaper price just by trying. More tellingly, six months later, that proportion had risen to 72 percent with a four out of five success rate. A 2010 *Consumer Reports* survey offered similar findings, that two-thirds of Americans had finagled better deals in shops by haggling during the previous six months.

This is the impulse that has helped four Panera Cares Pay What You Want cafés thrive since the chain opened this quirky offshoot in May 2010. The power to pay, or not, is entirely with the diner. Reassuringly, given that this is a nonprofit offshoot, the firm says 80 percent of customers pay the suggested amount or a little more. This is also the theory behind Priceyourmeal.com, an eBay for restaurants. Diners place bids for dinner, as high or low as they deem its value, with a BuyItNow-style button for the hungry or impatient. One company, Pricing Prophets, even offers a service where clients can poll its database and crowd source the right price. A new golf buggy inventor received suggestions from $199 to $499, and so settled on around $249 for final retail.

More than ever, we all want and need to learn how to negotiate better. Thirty years ago, when Herb Cohen published his book, it was a groundbreaking best-seller. Today, it would be just one of many haggling field guides, each of them authored by a different negotiation coach with his or her own unique approach to driving down prices. What's most interesting, though, about this return to shopping in the pre–price tag era is how each of these coaches share an all-American approach to haggling. The method, however, has none of the abrupt standoffishness that makes many people shy away from even asking.

Take Nancy "Negotiation" Fox. Throughout her patchwork career, from running an art museum and a symphony to managing director of a watch company, there's been one constant: her love of haggling. Three years ago, spying the mainstreaming of discounting, Fox decided to turn her natural instincts into income and become a negotiation coach. She explains how she uses her discount techniques every time she makes a major purchase.

Smile and be persistent, Nancy says. Never raise your voice or take no for an answer. Fox's favorite gambit is "Is that the best you can do?"—an open-ended conversation-starter that she believes all but guarantees some kind of price wobble. "You can inject humor, too—'Is that the widows and orphans price?' or the senior citizens discount. Whatever you can think of—'Gosh, I'm not feeling very wealthy today price?'" Ask if there's a friends and family special, and if the sales assistant looks confused, you can pass it off as a misunderstanding. If that same staffer smiles and banters back, with a stagey wink, and says, "But you don't even know my name. After all, how can we be friends otherwise?" it should soon convert to a spot markdown.

Fox gleefully recounts how she reduced the price of a 36-inch TV set, originally $600. It was an hour before closing on a Saturday night at an electronics store, the perfect moment as sales people were tallying their commission for the week. As the man assisting her took one down from the shelf, she asked if there were any open-box models. If not, she wondered if she could buy the floor sample for 15 percent off. He agreed, cutting her costs to $510. Of course, Fox wasn't finished. At the register, when asked how she wanted to pay, she hesitated. Coyly, Fox admitted she had cash enough to cover the purchase, and would use that method in exchange for a 3 percent discount, the same margin a store would owe American Express on a credit card transaction. The manager resisted, since credit card monies were deposited in the store's bank account instantly. Cash, however, didn't appear in its balance until Monday morning, when it was manually paid-in. It meant the store would lose out on forty-eight hours' interest. Fox responded by using the calculator on her phone to calculate how much that sum truly was. It was $1.80, a minor cost to make a sale, surely? She walked out with the TV for $495.

Another well-known negotiation coach is Ed Brodow, who has the vaudevillian showmanship of a natural-born New Yorker and former actor (he's both). Brodow believes that retail negotiation should focus on win-win, an outcome where both shopper and store feel like they've been fairly treated. "If you go into Bloomingdale's and want to buy a certain piece of furniture, remember that the store needs to move the item because there's other stuff coming in. And they need to make their margins.

So the question is: How do we work it out so both of us get our needs met?"

Brodow has a three-point plan to script a response as soon as you learn any price: The Flinch, The Squeeze, and The Nibble (and no, he doesn't double up as a dating coach). The Flinch is one incredulous word that can mean so many things. It involves sputtering a single word: "What???!!!" "It's a subliminal thing because you're not really saying anything," he says. "What you're implying is whatever the other person is asking as a price is ridiculous." In other words, the meaning is twofold, either, *Are you kidding? That's too expensive*, or *Wow—what a deal*. However the salesman understands it, that word telegraphs one intention: your focus on price.

Then comes The Squeeze. This is the power of competition, showrooming in conversation. "Just say, 'Gee, I really like your product but your competitor could sell me the same thing or something very similar for much less.'" It shouldn't be long before there's some offer of a discount. Accept it casually and act as if the deal is done.

Next, it's time for The Nibble, the casual, *By the way, can I also have this or that?* No one wants to lose a sale, especially if he or she considers it confirmed. This last tactic is how you can get a free shirt with that suit, or free delivery on that sofa.

Michael Sloopka, another negotiation guru, is predictably even more polite; he's Canadian, after all. Sloopka teaches seminars that are geared to giving his students enough gumption to ask for a better deal. He stresses that the crucial mistake many people make when discount hunting is to say too much. If you tell that front-desk clerk you want 15 percent off the room, and he was about to offer 30 percent, it's a misstep. Instead, smile and ask the Under What Circumstances? question. "You run into an obstacle in life, whether it's an upgraded room or tickets to a ball game and I teach people to say 'Under what circumstances could I get a room with a view?'" As a shopper, it's about retaining control: Allow that hotel or store or restaurant to propose the discount or the solution, rather than suggesting it yourself for them to approve. Then again, you could just wait until it's all been automated.

Group Dynamics

The Coca-Cola weather-dependent vending machine is the discount world's answer to the aliens captured at Area 51: much debated, never sighted. "It was the Olympics in 1996, and Coke indexed the price of a Coke in the machine to the temperature outside, charging a premium— if it was ninety degrees, it would be two dollars, ninety-five degrees, it would be two-fifty," recalls Kevin Mitchell, head of the Atlanta-based Professional Pricing Society. Mitchell swears he remembers seeing a machine charging $3, far more than the standard price at that time. Three years after the Atlanta games, *The New York Times* reported that Coca-Cola was again discreetly testing such a device, using a simple temperature sensor and computer chip. Rivals scoffed at the idea. "What's next? A machine that X-rays people's pockets to find out how much change they have and raises the price accordingly?" snarked one.

More than a decade since that article, such a machine has yet to debut. The reason: The machine never existed, at least according to Coca-Cola historian Ted Ryan. He has trawled through his archives and can find absolutely no evidence beyond a throwaway comment from then-CEO Doug Ivester who said it would be a great gimmick, were it logistically possible. Nonetheless, the story fizzes back up periodically to much disdain.

The idea of changing the price of something throughout the day— offering a discount when a store is quieter, say, or tweaking what's charged according to a customer's willingness to pay—is one of retail's much-repeated quests. Inventory-driven pricing could slash overstocking in the era of Too Much Stuff syndrome. This, the fourth and most significant of the shifts induced in shopping by the rise of discounts is known as *dynamic pricing*. Thanks to recent technological leaps, it's finally becoming a reality. The tools to tweak pricing dynamically are showcased each year in New York, at retail's answer to the Oscars, the National Retail Federation (NRF) show.

Every January, the NRF commandeers the giant Jacob Javits Center in New York to showcase an orgy of new ideas. In 2012, those included

StyleShoots, a table tennis–like setup allowing almost anyone to professionally photograph clothes for online sale. Accessvia had an impressive airline-themed booth complete with red-suited "flight attendants" and suitcases; if only it were clear what it did (something to do with signs, it seems). Epson's booth was full of bulky, strangely retro printers that could cough out customer stickers in an instant. FRUSTRATED? NEED A SHOULDER? VENT HERE (SERIOUSLY!) chirped a jaunty sign in the café, though no one seemed to be kvetching.

The busiest section, though, was around a half dozen or so booths from ZBD, SES, and Pricer. Each of these firms sells electronic shelf labels, language-manglingly known as ESLs. They resemble handheld computer games from the 1980s, what Atari imagined the future might look like. By using these gadgets, though, supermarkets no longer need a sticker-packed gun to change prices each week. Instead, the week's specials can be entered on a central computer and the shelf label will update instantly. It can be changed as often as needed; once a week, as is traditional, or once a day, even once an hour. Such technology allows for price matching with online competitors, for example, but it also means that charging more for Coke when the mercury hits 90 degrees is just a button away.

Each of the products works slightly differently. SES uses an antenna to transmit data by radio, a low-frequency system similar to that used by submarines. The company is based in France, which has been one of the hotbeds of this technology for several reasons: The deep penetration of vast grocery hypermarkets, with Walmart Superstore–besting footprints, makes changing prices an especially onerous task. Add to that the fact that restrictive local labor laws keep wages high, and it's easy to see why French customers would be keen to adopt greater automation.

The industry leader, though, is emoticon-loving Pricer,* a Swedish firm with more than half the global market. Rather than using radio waves to transmit changes—which can pass through a store wall and turn on a nearby lamp, if misdirected—Pricer relies on less wide-reaching

---

* Bizarrely, its logo is ;-)

infrared technology. Pricer's product has been installed in more than seventy-five hundred stores across the world, and its network is adding one million labels each month. The basic ESL costs €3.5 or €4 (around $5) per unit, while the jazzy graphic version is more than double that. The ESL offers some welcome advances—one American client, Hulth says, uses the graphic version to pull prices from online competitors to short-circuit showrooming. In Spain, he continues, supermarkets that abide by laws restricting the sales of alcohol at certain hours can simply change the tag on liquor after licensing hours expire instead of pulling down unsightly grilles. Of course, Hulth admits, every price consultant hired to look at the potential for supermarkets has the same first question: "How many price changes can you do in one day?"

There have been ham-fisted attempts to introduce dynamic pricing in the past. Before ESLs, insta-price changes on the Internet were too tempting for some firms to pass up. In one notorious case in 2000, Amazon was caught adjusting the price on a DVD of Julie Taymor's *Titus* by culling a shopper's history for hints. A buyer who deleted the site's cookies on his browser that identified him as a regular shopper saw the price drop from $26.24 to $22.74. Amazon similarly slashed $51 off an MP3 player at the same time, at least if a customer had checked prices on a comparison shopping site. Amazon was using those cookies in much the same way that a bank levies a loan rate based on a customer's credit score. The company thought it could discreetly test how price conscious its deal seekers truly were, but the company underestimated the power of message boards at that time. Just imagine the deluge of derision had Twitter been available.

Amazon was soon overwhelmed with complaints and hurriedly backtracked. "It was done to determine consumer responses to different discount levels," said a spokesperson. "This was a pure and simple price test. This was not dynamic pricing. We don't do that and have no plans ever to do that." It offered refunds to customers who'd paid the higher prices, too.*

---

* Users have reported that some sites, such as ThinkGeek.com, Levis.com, and Coastal.com, still offer variable deals to members. Log in, leave an item in a shopping cart, and navigate away, they say, and a few days later an e-mail should appear in your inbox offering a special promo to help close the sale.

Nonetheless, an Annenberg Center study five years later examined this practice in great depth and uncovered other experiments, including a photo-equipment vendor that also changed its prices if the shopper's browser was storing cookies from comparison sites. The study also found that two-thirds of adult Internet users assumed it was illegal for retailers to charge different people different prices online (it's not) and 87 percent of people thought such treatment ought to be outlawed.

Though the mention of dynamic pricing produces such a flurry of resistance and suspicion, and can risk alienating muscle-flexing shoppers, it's already widely in use. Just look at the early bird special at a diner or how train fares rise during commuter hours. Loyalty cards at supermarkets or drugstores are proxies for dynamic pricing, too, changing the cost of an identical item for two people standing next to each other in a checkout line. Airline prices zigzag according to demand; easyjet, one of Europe's two biggest budget carriers, operates in a dynamic pricing model much like most airlines. Founder Sir Stelios Haji-Ioannou, an Anglo-Greek entrepreneur, has become a de facto evangelist for such an approach. Every one of the spin-off businesses that Haji-Ioannou set up in the United Kingdom followed the same model. Delivery from easy-Pizza was cheaper off-peak, while easyCinema offered tickets for just 20p (around 78 cents) if booked a month in advance, rising to £5 ($7.85) for last-minute purchases. Because the movie industry is highly sensitive about price, studios refused to supply first-run films in this model and easyCinema's concept was quickly abandoned. Crucially, though, consumers never complained.

There are several bars around the world—Le Wall Street in Reims, France, or New York's Exchange Bar & Grill, and Bar Dow Jones in Barcelona—which peg the prices of drinks according to a giant stock ticker on display inside (imagine how deep the discount would be on a J.C. Penney–pegged cocktail). Of course, in a tech hub like San Francisco, there have been extensive trials of this model—beyond bars. To ease congestion, the SFPark project varies meter rates between 25 cents and $6 an hour according to demand, while the San Franciso Giants baseball team managed to eke out extra profit in the 2009–10 season by selling seats for games with prices pegged to a set of factors that included weather and the popularity of the visiting team. (Would that make Dodgers tickets more or less expensive than normal?) The automated cab-calling app Uber operates what it calls "surge pricing"; riders get a discount if it's off peak, but the more requests for taxis that are logged, the higher per-ride charge will be levied. For the same ride on the same night, one San Francisco customer was charged $27 at the start of the evening and $135 hours later. Admittedly, this caused an uproar, but the app is still thriving.*

Thanks to the rise of ESL, though, dynamic pricing is moving into supermarkets and other brick-and-mortar stores. Strangely, it's surfaced first in once price-controlled Germany, where one supermarket uses electronic shelf tags to dynamically change pricing on products according to the time of day. If you're coming in for milk in the morning, the price may be different from the afternoon. There are convenience stores in Frankfurt where prices are decided at the register—so a chocolate bar could be discounted tomorrow if business is slow. Some vending machines in Japan have enacted Coca-Cola's mythical weather mechanic, installing temperature- or time-controlled pricing devices, without much controversy. According to Pricer, a Japanese customer is more concerned with accuracy in pricing than with equitability; and prices are often lowered after lunch on fresh items, to avoid shilling stale goods the next day to an unwilling clientele.

Pricer has an American client, a well-known gas station that it declines to name, which adjusts prices by day or night. And Hulth also says that consumers have been found to be less price resistant on Friday nights; browsing the supermarket after a long, hard workweek, they will be more free-spending, and some corporate customers have tried raising fruit and vegetable prices 20 to 25 percent at that time in response. The most fun example, he says, is a European Duty Free store that piloted a canny discount program using ESL technology. It programmed prices to

---

* Openly discussing dynamic pricing can be a tricky path for entrepreneurs. According to Shauna Mei, the Tracy Flickish mastermind of high-end doodad merchant Ahalife.com, her customers could expect prices to be tweaked according to their social status. "Why do we give a celebrity a free dress?" she told me, without irony. "Someone like you should pay less money than the homeless guy on the street." Thank goodness Hermès doesn't yet offer sleeping bags.

change according to the nationality of the most recent flight to land. By trial and error, the Duty Free store learned that Germans, for example, were more price sensitive to familiar products like beer. They would demand steeper markdowns on brews but be content to shell out higher prices on whiskey.

The looming issue with most ESL units is the displays rather than the discounts, as the low contrast is hard for older eyes to make out, so reading glasses need always be ready at the supermarket. Once that tech is upgraded, though, this barrier should come down. It will also offer a new shopper-powered way to wangle deals and make the idea more acceptable. "Dynamic pricing done for the retailer is bound to fail. Done for the shopper, it's bound to succeed. If I can go out and tell all my friends, 'Come in on the deal and we'll all get a lower price,' that is social leverage," says shopping guru John Ross. Pricer is developing social media integration for its graphical displays, moving beyond simply showing competitors' prices: Imagine integrating an ESL shelf talker with Facebook. Scan the barcode on a product, then sync to the brand's fan page and Like it. The number of Likes could then be recorded on the tag in front of you, ticking higher with each shopper's click. Every shopper then receives a special promotional price on that item as a thank-you gesture.

Think of it as ad hoc, impromptu Groupon, powered by the shopper rather than the seller. ICA Vanadis supermarket in Sweden has already trialed a similar program; the greater the number of customers who used their Smartphones to check in at a location during September 2011, the higher the product discounts. Brazilian department store Magazine Luisa ran a social media program that encouraged customers to take pictures of, or promote, an item they liked from the store on Facebook or other channels—if friends bought it, they got a kickback from the sale. It hasn't yet been trialed in this way in United States. Bloomingdale's does provide free WiFi but it counterproductively precludes such useful social media by outlawing photos in-store, so such fandom must be furtive.

As prices have started to see-saw so dynamically, whether on- or offline, it's also birthed a slew of companies, apps, and sites that help track such changes and so game the system. Camelcamelcamel is a nemesis for Amazon, tracking price history and sending alerts on whatever you've earmarked if there are significant drops. Oren Etzioni's Decide.com claws data on consumer electronics from across the web and uses an algorithm to predict when it will be cheapest to buy a given item. It plans to expand to other categories. Book a hotel stay via Tingo.com, and if anyone, anywhere gets a better deal on that same room, the difference will be automatically refunded to your credit card.

Services like Bitehunter collate deals from Groupon and the like, pulling them together onto a map of local markdowns, while Tweetalicious scrapes Twitter feeds for fleeting deals. Volunteers log and flag great discounts on sites such as SlickDeals, and the site even incentivizes their users by rewarding hard workers with tier status, like an airline frequent-flyer program or judo belts. The way to progress through the ten tiers, from Learner to Grand Master, involves tasks like scanning newspaper inserts and posting the deals for lurkers. No wonder Whalesharkme dia.com, which owns a cluster of deal-aggregating sites such as RetailMe Not.com and was founded only in late 2009, had revenues of $120 million in 2011.

Since it's now easier than ever to change prices in an instant, flash sale–like promotions are migrating to brick-and-mortar stores. It's turned the traditional doorbuster into a tactic that can be randomly applied to juice sales or traffic—and remember, joyous surprise is a powerful dopamine booster. This is one reason some of the outlets in Gotemba have two-hour-long promo periods in the afternoons, for example. Companies that partner with California-based tech firm Scout Advertising can have coupons generated during their slower trading hours. The app even watches weather locally to anticipate the dampening effect of snow or rain, for example.

Uniqlo launched its London flagship in October 2011 with what it dubbed the Happy Machine, which was filled with a variety of products that were released for three days at different times and with steep discounts. Flannel check shirts were £5 ($7.85) at noon, while shoppers had to wait until 7 p.m. for a £15 ($23.50) ultra-light down parka. Virgin Holidays sold premier package vacations on a first-come, first-served basis in a London department store for just an hour one Friday in July that same year. Supermarket Carrefour staged a Hora Magica or Magic Hour in Brazil that May, and two hundred families, all of them holders of the store's loyalty card, had VIP access to its store in Osasco and up to 50 percent markdowns on all the non-food items there.

Dynamic pricing, or even the hint of it, can still cause an uproar if shoppers feel it is being used in an antagonistic way. Struggling online travel agent Orbitz.com found that out all too publicly. After its tech gurus noticed that Mac users spent $20 to $30 more per night on hotels than their Windows-equipped counterparts and were 40 percent more likely to book a four- or five-star hotel, the company sensed an opportunity. Why not adjust the displays accordingly so the cheaper deals were foregrounded for the tighter shoppers, while those cashed-up Macheads, ready to splurge on a suite, could see pricier options on the first search page. Cost per room was technically the same, but Orbitz was employing the ethos of dynamic pricing, cherry-picking to whom it suggested the best prices. CEO Barney Harford's damage control media tour was apologetic. "In many cities, customers are overwhelmed by the fact that there's hundreds of different hotels and our goal with our sort and recommendation algorithms is one to be able to find a hotel that's right for them," he bleated, "I was just doing a test to somebody that was asking this question, oh, this hotel is cheaper on this site." Within a week of the story breaking in August 2012, the news had sliced around 10 percent off its stock price. Call it a discount.

Final Sale

If power rests with buyers for the first time, does that doom sellers to a helpless pandering on price? Certainly, using discounts aggressively, as airlines do, or scattershot (cough, Groupon), even with a furtive edge like Orbitz, will rightfully backfire. Newly emboldened shoppers will sneer at such tactics—then take the deal and move on. Businesses that turn the discounting obligation to their advantage, though, can still profit in this new system of selling. Tesco doled out bargains as a loyalty-builder, and became a billion-dollar global business in the process.

Secretive clienteling at upscale stores has become retail's version of a thank-you note. Offering shoppers the chance to be cheap or choosy both treats them as discerning and explicitly places power in their hands. One marketer is messianic about the opportunities amid this change. He is a believer that it can work to retailers' advantage more than to their detriment.

John Ross is a former Home Depot VP who went on to found his own consulting firm, Shopper Sciences. With power in buyers' hands for the first time, Ross believes that using data from point of sale is hopelessly outmoded. He focuses not only on those who spent money (consumers) but also those who browsed (shoppers). It isn't about maximizing each transaction, a belief he shares with Clive Dunn and Edwina Humby, but rather about building long-term relationships, treating buyers with respect. "The premise of the marketing process has abandoned the shopper at the front door," he told me. "From the moment someone runs out of toothpaste to the moment they give the store money, who's watching that?"*

In the future, the smartest businesses won't simply number-crunch their sales data, or consumers, to squeeze extra margins out of sluggish sectors. Rather, they'll talk to their shoppers and ask questions. Analysis that is qualitative (*What would make that item more appealing to you, ma'am?*) rather than quantitative (*How many of those items sold on Friday?*) will help sellers make better strategic decisions about price. If only jcp's Ron Johnson had spent a week working the shop floor, he might never have committed such half-price hara-kiri. After all, dopamine, which provides the physiological thrill to deals, drives and codes behavior. Stores confident enough to unclench and allow shoppers to proactively chip at prices will see those same buyers enthusiastically return. It's treating them more like peers than patsies.

---

* Ross has counted blue-chip brands like Chase, Exxon, and AT&T among his clients, all of whom tasked him with making them more shopper-centric. He relies on old-fashioned anthropology combined with new-fangled technology like Affectiva, retainer-like headgear that deciphers the reactions of volunteers while browsing. He says that the commonest way to discourage a shopper from buying is simple: a missing price tag. Most people would rather leave something than have to chase a staff member to ask how much. Aristide Boucicaut would be thrilled.

No wonder there has never been a better time to be a buyer: informed, empowered, entitled. What does that really mean? Lumbering under the burden of Too Much Stuff syndrome, oversupply colliding with under-demand, the retail world has inevitably tipped in shoppers' favor. This constant churning of prices has added a gleeful gotcha to every mall or supermarket trip, a black eye that makes stores bleed red ink. Shopping is, indeed, fun again.*

Buyers are no longer limited to whatever deal is on offer at the local mall five minutes' drive away. Each has the ability to compare costs in the palm of his or her hand; it takes only thirty seconds to see if there's a better deal elsewhere. As credit cards are integrated into mobile payment systems, this should escalate. Imagine a casual wave of a Smartphone deducting payment at point of sale, a soon-to-be commonplace sight. Who will be first to develop an app that sounds an alarm to prevent that shopper from overspending? There's a lower price elsewhere, your device might blare, displaying driving directions or the relevant URL in front of an embarrassed checkout clerk. Indeed, how long until one of the major outlet brands—billion-dollar Ralph Lauren, perhaps—admits that its lower-priced business is too important to seclude at off-price malls and daringly debuts a store on Michigan or Fifth avenues?

Sales have become so constant that sales and negotiation guides are booming. These code-cracking manuals outline the days, weeks, or months when a given item will be cheaper; charity races are in April and November, one notes, triggering sneaker markdowns. Fall prices are usually lower, it adds, to clear stock faster and make way for incoming winter boots. Who will be the first to identify the anti–Black Friday, the day to avoid the mall at all costs, when discounts are at their year-round scarcest. Perhaps they can call it Blue Monday? (Deal site data points to early October as a clear candidate for that dubious honor.)

There's one caveat, though: With great deal-making power comes equally great responsibility. If shopping has become a joyous game, it requires sportsman-like adherence to the rules of fairness—from both sides. Buyers who are too greedy or cheat the system will destroy the very sellers

---

* Apologies, Old Navy.

on whom they rely. This is the curse of *Extreme Couponing* or Groupon, both of which have badly bruised the retail eco-systems in which they exist. Sometimes, settling for 30 percent off may have to satisfy.

Everyone should benefit from an era where half price has become the new normal. Maybe it's buying a Sunday paper to double check for coupons each week or asking an assistant about a discount for paying in cash. It could be befriending a floorwalker at a favorite store, then querying when presale starts. Perhaps it's just promising never to hit checkout online without Googling for a code or two. Do it, just once and see what happens—the results might prove surprising. No one should pay full price for anything, ever again. Yes, that includes you.

Acknowledgments

F or the last decade, I've tried to write smartly about stupid things; this book is the culmination of those efforts. I hope it's been as satisfying to read as it was to write, even if it's permanently ruined my ability to feel anything other than ripped off if I'm forced to pay full price for anything.

Bargain Fever could never have come together without two incredible women. It was over brunch at the Breslin in Manhattan one dreary Saturday with Amy Koplin where I brainstormed the basic idea that would evolve into this book—for that, I owe her Bloody Marys and thanks, both in bottomless quantities. She has also been unstinting in her advice and guidance ever since, as both seasoned editor and friend; I could neither have started nor completed *Bargain Fever* without her. My agent, Erika Storella, and I must have singlehandedly kept the Colombian coffee industry solvent, given the volume of Juan Valdez we've downed between us in the last two years; she was the first person to have faith in my idea, and her enthusiasm helped bolster my belief that this could actually be a viable book. I owe both of them so much. Thank you and thank you.

Shout-outs to my roster of willing readers, who braved rough versions of chapters without complaint and offered savvy suggestions: Vanessa Colomar, Maureen Neary, Jamie Pearson. Lindsay McCormack was a fearless and enthusiastic researcher. As a publishing veteran, Clare Drysdale proved an invaluable sounding board. Alison Diboll's masterful wordsmithing is worthy of its own book. Drew Crawford was a peerless alibi during some undercover reporting. Andrew Litvin and Sedef Onar, you were both debonair deck shoe–shopping partners in crime. Thanks to the Moss clan in Yorkshire, especially Master Arthur, for providing me a rural bolt hole when my energy flagged.

Over the years, several of my editors at various publications have commissioned stories that helped buff my reporting credentials, and from which I've drawn as sources for this book: Thanks to Richard David Story, Clara Sedlak, Keenan Mayo, Adrien Glover, Vanessa Friedman, Gillian de Bono, Sarah Medford, Paul Croughton, Elizabeth Semrai, Julian Sancton, Tali Jaffe, Keith Pollock, Stan Parish, Jason Chen, Stephen Wallis, David Landsel, Sarah Medford, Amy Goldwasser, Jenny Comita, and Yolanda Edwards.

Thanks to the crack team at Portfolio: Niki Papadopoulos, who ponied up for me to start my bargain adventure in the first place, Adrian Zackheim, Natalie Horbachevsky, Christy D'Agostini, Annie Anderson, Will Weisser, and the rest.

A call-out to the crack team of volunteers who donated their expertise to help me look and sound smarter, better, and younger: Todd Bush, Mike Kelly, Richard Read, and Meg Nolan. There are no bigger PR superstars than Kelly Cutrone, Margie Cader, Chris Constable, Kristen Vigrass, Flint Beamon, John Melick, Emily Lawi, and Theresa McDonnell—but they know that already. Paul Sullivan, my fellow U of C survivor, I owe the germ of this journey to you. As both a sounding board and smart friend, Amy Spencer helped kickstart my writing career and has been a constant ever since. And Jim Kloiber, the champagne in Switzerland on day one was such a generous way to mark an indelible moment.

Thanks to the discount mavens who generously took time to talk to me, whether revealing couponeers' deepest secrets or dishing on the best way to squeeze a spontaneous bargain from a wary sales assistant. Of the more than 250 people whom I grilled, extra gratitude is due to the following, in no particular order: Teri Agins, Amy Arnsten, Ardell DellaLoggia, Paul Glimcher, John Ross, Neil Stern, Greg Furman, Robin Lewis, Marlene Jensen, James Dion, Nils Hulth, Larry Robinson, Jinhong Xie, Dr. David Lewis, Britt Beemer, Michael Tonello, Ellison Poe, Izzy Grinspan, Paula Rosenblum, Henry Coates, Steve Fritz, Sherri Kimes, John Morgan, Tim Loecker, Earl Ellsworth, Matthew Tilley, Kazushige Okuma, Ira Neimark, Nancy Fox, Colin and Lindy Woodhead, Susan Scafidi, Ashley Cox, Yuval Atsomon, Jonathan Citrin. Guney Oktar,

Adam Lynch, and Lisa Sun also went above and beyond the call of friendship duty. Their professional generosity was boundless, whether tramping with me through Istanbul's back streets, explaining the minutiae of real estate legalese, or even teaching me the rudimentary fundamentals of supply and demand over breakfast.

More than anything, though, a huge debt of thanks to the dozens of people who dished deliciously about life behind the bargain curtain without need for credit—you know who you are. Thanks for your kindness, trust, and candor.

For anyone who's reached this far, I have to finish with a tip of the hat to my long-suffering, long-distance parents: my mother, Joan, who deeded me both her love of books and of bargains, and my father, Derek, the most creative person I know. Thanks for everything. Next time I'm in London, lunch is on me—well, as long as we have another one of those free pizza coupons.

Notes

Note on Research

Bargain Fever is based on more than two hundred interviews, which I conducted between February 2011 and February 2013 in various locales, from Tokyo to just outside Tampa. I attended all the events that took place during this period and that I describe in detail. I have also used considerable secondary material from books, newspapers, and magazines, in addition to my own articles from the last decade spent as a journalist covering froth in all its forms.

Unless noted otherwise, all Internet-based sources here are based on the content available at the given address on March 29, 2013. If this content has changed or become inaccessible since then, previous versions may be available through the Internet Archive at http://www.archive.org/index.php.

Introduction

1 **My name's Mark, but I'm surprised my parents** . . . For the record, I'd like to apologize to my ever-patient mother for having mocked her obsession with stretching the pound from the moment I could talk. I'll admit it, without that, I would have lacked the foundations to write this book.

3 **Few would criticize** . . . "LA restaurant offers discount for dining without your phone," Air Talk, August 14, 2012.

3 **So pervasive has** . . . Laura Schreffler, "Dumped reality TV star Kate Gosselin lands a new job . . . hawking discount coupons," Mailonline, November 3, 2011; Don Kaplan, "Kate Gosselin's abrasive personality and expensive demands led to her being fired from CouponCabin blogger job: source", *New York Daily News*, October 17, 2012.

3 **"I just channel the friendliest . . ."** David Hiltbrand, "Would you buy insurance from her? Apparently Stephanie Courtney is the TV ads fun Flo." *Philadelphia Inquirer*, March 9, 2010.

4 **Even this wasn't always enough . . .** When I researched the extremes to which some will turn to earn a bargain, sacrificing Christmas seemed the most outré but far from unusual. One woman in Oklahoma, Norma Cole, told me she buys a turkey during the Thanksgiving sales, freezes it, and thaws it out on January 1, her family has de facto delayed Christmas Day. "After Christmas, you can buy the same things you would have before, only you've got it for half price," she told me, unfazed. Dot-com marketing manager Elaine Wu in San Francisco also saves her spree until the sales start. "Just because it's a day late doesn't mean it's going to be any less special or didn't come from the same sentiment," she says. "It just means that it's going to save us sixty percent." For the last decade, Wu has been calling Neiman Marcus on Christmas Eve to check details on opening times and doorbusting designer deals two days later. "It was a cultish thing, then, and the crowds were much smaller." She warns that it's very different now, though. "I mean, the shoe section looks like a war zone."

4 **December 26 is trending . . .** Bill Martin, CEO Shoppertrak, September 29, 2012, author interview.

4 **The number of Americans . . .** Greg Ellis, Salmon Research, February 28, 2011, author interview.

4 **Most tellingly . . .** Sherif Mityas, A.T. Kearney, March 1, 2011, author interview.

4 **Was it kosher . . .** Richard Pérez Peña, "College Offers Top Applicants Two-Thirds Off," *The New York Times*, September 28, 2011.

4 **There was only one catch . . .** "Ohio Animal Shelter Offers Discounts on Fat Cats," Foxnews.com, June 4, 2011.

4 **In January 2012, globe-trotting . . .** Popbitch, "For Chuck's Sake," January 19, 2012.

5 **One of the fiercest examples . . .** Mark Duell, "Black Friday Madness: Grandfather Body-Slammed by Cops, Man Tasered, Two Shot, Wal-Mart in Bomb Scare and Woman Pepper-Sprays Rival Shoppers on Day of Chaos," Mailonline, November 26, 2011.

6 **Supermarkets after World War II . . .** Sheena Iyengar, *The Art of Choosing*, p. 187.

6 **In 1980, there were six major blue jean . . .** Robin Lewis and Michael Dart, *The New Rules of Retail: Competing in the World's Toughest Marketplace*, p. 65.

6 **In 2012, there were 2.3 billion square feet . . .** Christopher Miller, "Self-Storage Properties," *Apartment Management* magazine, July 2008.

6 **Retail space increased at an average . . .** Robin Lewis, CEO Robin Report, April 11, 2012, author interview.

6 **The American population's average** . . . World Bank, http://data.worldbank. org/indicator/sp.pop.grow.

6 **In a new retail equation** . . . It was retail consultant John Ross who first shared the term *shopping 3.0* with me, in reference to his work on the difference between a shopper, who might just browse, and a consumer, who spends money on the same trip. Robin Lewis helped me understand the phases of retail to date, outlining the seismic shifts. I also owe a debt to British consultant Henry Coates, who was kind enough to first outline to me the issues of oversupply that have started to bedevil the retail landscape.

6 **Retail guru Robin Lewis** . . . Robin Lewis, CEO Robin Report, April 11, 2012, author interview.

7 **One business, Shopper Gauge, has even** . . . John Ross, Inmar, September 26, 2012, author interview.

1

9 **In less than two hours** . . . Unless otherwise noted, reporting and quotes are from a chilly but cheery night spent at the Clifton Park mall in upstate New York, November 24, 2011.

12 **Around 20 percent** . . . Mayo Clinic Press Release, "Mayo Clinic Researchers Tie Parkinson's Drugs to Impulse Control Problems," Wednesday, March 23, 2011.

12 **One man spent** . . . David Standaert, John N. Whitaker Professor and Chair of Neurology, UAB School of Medicine, September 12, 2012, author interview.

12 **Indeed in France a fifty-one-year-old** . . . Katie Moisse "Parkinson's Patient Wins Lawsuit Over Gay Sex Addiction," Abcnews.com, November 29, 2012.

13 **"the best reward system . . ."** Wolfram Schultz, Wellcome Principal Research Fellow, Professor of Neuroscience, University of Cambridge, August 29, 2012, author interview.

14 **Researchers used an fMRI brain scanner** . . . George Loewenstein, Herbert A. Simon Professor of Economics and Psychology, Carnegie Mellon University, March 20, 2012, author interview.

15 **Some scientists are chary** . . . Dr. Paul Glimcher at NYU is one of the leading skeptics. He believes that mapping chunks of our brain onto Freudian theories is risky and reductive, as he told me in an interview on April 30, 2012. "So neurobiology has managed to do nothing in one hundred fifty years except replace id, ego, and superego *mit das Nucleus Accumbens and das Insula?*" It gives him a chance to show off a mean German accent. Regardless, he's especially wary of the marketers who've turned fMRI and neuroeconomics into a lucrative schtick, notably Martin Lindstrom of BRANDSense. Lindstrom offers beguilingly insightful

theories that seem almost to X-ray the buying intentions of the human brain, all but turning the fMRI into a crystal ball. Most full-time scientists scoff at Lindstrom's work, but he's nonetheless widely cited. No wonder Glimcher likens the widespread use of such brain scanners to "handing out grenades to children in the Ugandan army."

15 **However, a genetic quirk** . . . Amy Arnsten, Professor of Neurobiology, Yale University, September 5, 2012, author interview.

15 **"It's losing that part of you . . ."** Arnsten, author interview.

16 **One recent study charted** . . . "Forget love, it's BOGOF that sets the heart racing: British (women) more excited over bagging a bargain than finding the One," Mailonline, February 18, 2012.

17 **Their jobs wouldn't exist** . . . Neuroeconomics only emerged in the last thirty years or so, when upstart academics began questioning the in-built weakness of conventional economic theory. With its sleek mathematical absoluteness, this system ignores one variable: how messy, biased and craven human beings can be. Relying on fMRI machines that track blood oxygen levels as indications of activity in a given region, its adherents apply those findings to economic models.

18 **Take a set of volunteers** . . . Dr. Paul Glimcher, Professor, Center for Neural Science, NYU, April 30, 2012, author interview.

18 **One price consultant often runs** . . . Tim Smith, Managing Principal, Wiglaf Pricing, March 22, 2012, author interview.

19 **Volunteers were offered two similar** . . . Glimcher, author interview.

19 **We're loss averse about more than just cash** . . . James Dion, President, Dionco, January 31, 2012, author interview.

20 **Another classic study that also illustrates** . . . Richard Thaler, cited in Garcia, Bazerman, Kopelman and Miller, "Worse but Equal: The Influence of Social Categories on Resource Allocations," *Harvard Business School Working Paper,* 2006.

22 **Price consulting became a career per se** . . . William Poundstone, *Priceless: The Myth of Fair Value (And How to Take Advantage of It),* p. 145.

22 **The industry-wide Professional Pricing Society** . . . CFO Staff, "Taxpayer Beware," *CFO* magazine, April 2004; Kevin Mitchell, President, Professional Pricing Society, March 12, 2012, author interview.

22 **One supermarket study in the 1990s** . . . Donnie Lichtenstein, Marketing Chair, University of Colorado, February 17, 2012, author interview.

23 **Commentators snarked when the 1,400-franchise chain** . . . Julie Jargon, "Slicing the Bread but Not the Prices," *Wall Street Journal,* August 18, 2009.

23 **An entire article in *The New York Times*** . . . Jodi Kantor, "Entrees Reach $40, and Sorry, the Sides Are Extra," *The New York Times,* October 21, 2006.

23 **"It's menu engineering . . ."** Larry Robinson, Price Point Partners, March 13, 2012, author interview.

25 **In 1978, seventeen years after launching Pampers** . . . Poundstone, *Priceless*, pp. 153–154.

26 **Two professors teamed up** . . . Duncan Simester at MIT and Eric Anderson at Northwestern worked together on this study, published in "The Role of Price Endings: Why Stores May Sell More at $49 than at $44," unpublished conference paper, April 2001. See also Simester and Anderson, "Mind Your Price Cues," *Harvard Business Review*, September 2003.

26 **One Morgan Stanley retail researcher** . . . , June 22, 2012, author interview.

26 **MIT's Duncan Simester, one of the professors** . . . Anderson, Cho, Harlam, Simester, "Using Price Cues," unpublished paper forming part of Cho's PhD thesis, December 2007.

27 **Chris McManus, professor of** . . . Professor I. Chris McManus, February 13, 2012, author interview by e-mail.

27 **When the postal service was invented** . . . Victoria Finlay, *Color*, p. 165.

28 **As baby boomers drive** . . . Paco Underhill, *Why We Buy*, p. 133.

28 **In the first round** . . . Kenneth C. Manning and David E. Sprott, "Price Endings, Left-Digit Effects and Choice," *Journal of Consumer Research*, 2009.

28 **Price formulas like these** . . . "Monster Raving Loony Party," General Election manifesto, 2005, www.loonparty.com. In Australia, where 5 cents has been the smallest coin since 1992, the .99 ending is still commonplace.

29 **A clique of French academics** . . . Nicolas Guéguen and Céline Jacob, "Nine-ending Price and Consumer Behavior," *Journal of Applied Sciences*, 2005.

29 **One price consultant even estimates** . . . Marlene Jensen, Pricing Strategy Associates, January 26, 2012, author interview.

29 **Rutgers marketing professor Robert Schindler** . . . Mark Roth, "Shoppers Fall for 99-cent Pricing Gimmick, Decisions Affected by the Left-most Digit," *Pittsburgh Post-Gazette*, December 26, 2006.

29 **"Any products with physical risk . . ."** Robert Schindler, Rutgers University, March 19, 2012, author interview.

30 **The chain claims** . . . Quentin Fottrell, "5 Retail Price-Tag Tricks," smartmoney.com, March 2, 2002.

30 **Take the one for Cami Secret** . . . Take a masterclass in pricing by watching the commercial in its entirety at www.camisecret.com.

31 **The human brain can hold only.** . . . Sarah Maxwell, *The Price Is Wrong*, p. 211.

31 **By 2013, though, there were a staggering** . . . Source: Procter & Gamble media relations, June 27, 2012.

32 **Iyengar has built her entire career** . . . She relates the full story of this brilliant but simple experiment in her book, *The Art of Choosing*, pp. 183–187.

32 **Iyengar has even studied** . . . *CBS News Sunday Morning*, interview transcript with Iyengar, April 25, 2010.

33 **The more products there are on offer** . . . This idea was first suggested to me
by Jonathan Cohen, Professor of Psychology, Princeton University, during a
telephone interview, May 2, 2012.

33 **The Midwestern supermarket chain Supervalu** . . . Robin Lewis and Michael
Dart, *The New Rules of Retail*, p. 134.

34 **Doubtless this is why one enterprising** . . . Mom of two, Laurie Black, listed
her services on Craigslist. "I love shopping and love shopping for other people,"
she touts her services there. "Lets help each other shall we?" She certainly doesn't
sound out of place, at least. More on Laurie: Alice Hines "Unemployed and Eager
to Shop on Black Friday . . . for You," Dailyfinance.com, November 4, 2011.

2

36 **Fortysomething April Blum** . . . April Blum, May 2, 2012, author interview.

36 **This breathless account** . . . Timothy W. Martin, "Hard Times Turn Coupon
Clipping into the Newest Extreme Sport," *Wall Street Journal*, March 8, 2010.

37 **Khloe and Kourtney Kardashian co-opted** . . . Kourtney touts her love of
coupon-clipping konstantly. See her kolumn on celebuzz.com. (Couldn't resist.)

37 **One of the longtime producers** . . . Martin Goeller, April 19, 2012, author interview.

37 **A relative newcomer to the cult** . . . April Blum, May 2, 2012, author interview.

38 **In 2010, 332 billion coupons** . . . NCH Marketing Services, 2010 Coupon Facts
Report.

38 **Percent of people.** . . . Matthew Egol, Andrew Clyde, Kasturi Rangan, and Richard Sanderson, "The New Consumer Frugality: Adapting to the Enduring Shift
in U.S. Consumer Spending and Behavior," *Booz & Co*, 2010.

38 **42 percent consider themselves** . . . John Gerzema and Michael D'Antonio,
"How the Crummy Economy Has Changed Spending Habits," *The Business Insider*, November 16, 2010.

38 **Average face values are rising** . . . NCH Marketing Services, Inc., Mid-year
2011 Consumer Packaged Goods (CPG) Coupon Facts Report.

38 **Affluent households, defined** . . . Brian Quinton, "Coupon Use Soared in '09
at All Stores," *Promo*, April 21, 2010. Data quoted is from NCH.

41 **News America is a subsidiary** . . . Peter Lattman, "Marketing with Muscle,"
Forbes, October 31, 2005.

41 **"Sometimes a woman . . ."** Val Stark, Education Director, ACP, presentation at
conference, April 24, 2012.

42 **"See the addresses . . ."** John Morgan, ACP, March 15, 2012, author interview.

43 **Meet the Million-Dollar Coupon Broker** . . . Unless otherwise noted, all quotes and reporting are from a day spent in Dade City shadowing Rachael Woodard, February 29, 2012. Wooden signs at the city limits proudly tout, "Named one of the top places to retire by Where to Retire magazine 2002"— which naturally makes a visitor wonder what happened to get it nixed from that same list every year since then.

46 **Take Nancy Kremin** . . . Nancy Kremin, December 5, 2011, author interview.

47 **Gault is the founder** . . . Teri Gault, February 15, 2012, author interview.

48 **Jill Cataldo is a typical** . . . Jill Cataldo, January 12, 2012, author interview.

48 **Pate set up a smart pyramid** . . . Chrissy Pate, April 17, 2012, author interview.

49 **Not all these cottage operations** . . . Karen Jowers, "Cash in More Coupons," *Army Times*, December 5, 2011.

49 **Eighty percent of *Extreme Couponing's* stars** . . . Martin Goeller, April 19, 2012, author interview.

49 **He pegs as much as 70 percent** . . . Matthew Tilley, Inmar, April 24, 2012, author interview.

49 **The zenith of coupon** . . . Tilley, author interview.

50 **"These wack-jobs . . ."** Matt Schwartz, "Bargain Junkies Are Beating Retailers at Their Own Game," *Wired*, December 2010.

50 **In fact, when one of *Extreme Couponing's* breakout stars** . . . Quentin Fottrell, "Extreme Couponing Star: I Was a Scapegoat," smartmoney.com, May 11, 2011.

51 **"In the last week, I saw one . . ."** Jill Cataldo, January 12, 2012, author interview.

51 **As for megamogul Rachael Woodard** . . . Rachael Woodard, February 29, 2012, author interview.

51 **It's just a few hours' drive** . . . Unless otherwise noted, all quotes and reporting are from a day spent in Fort Lauderdale with Sheriff Lamberti, March 1, 2012. With his bushy gray mustache and ramrod-straight back, Al looks like he was made in a factory that specializes in cops. Special thanks to Ben Popken for connecting me with Mr CHiPs.

52 **Populist and popular, he's proven** . . . Brittany Wallman, "Welcome for Jenne at BSO; New Sheriff Israel has no issue with visit by convicted felon", *Sun-Sentinel*, January 19, 2013

54 **A fraud operation busted in Arizona** . . . Brad Tuttle, "The $40 Million Counterfeit Coupon Caper," Time.com, July 19, 2012.

54 **Couponer Sybil Hudson** . . . Heather Pilkington, "Woman arrested for stealing newspaper coupons," *Gainesville Daily Register*, June 29, 2011.

54 **Another chit filcher from northern Arkansas** . . . "Extreme Couponer Charged with Stealing Newspapers," 4029tv.com, August 5, 2011.

54 **So bad has the coupon theft become** . . . Justin Graves, "Cash Reward Offered for Conviction in Newspaper, Coupon Thefts," *Cullman Times*, July 31, 2011.

54 **The Detergent That Cleans Away Dirt and Crime** . . . All quotes and reporting unless otherwise noted are from three days spent knee-deep in coupon pros at the ACP conference in Nashville, TN, April 24–26, 2012. The city is a honky-tonk retort to Hollywood, as one local joked. "In LA, every waiter wants to be an actor, but here, every waiter is a songwriter hoping to be discovered."

56 **In 2007, IOS CEO Chris Balsiger** . . . For more on the compelling, almost thrillerlike story of this CEO, see Robert Gray, "Balsiger and IOS: 5 Years Later," *El Paso Inc.*, April 8, 2012; and David Kesmodel, "The Coupon King," *Wall Street Journal*, February 16, 2008.

56 **The feds believe his true identity** . . . David Andreatta, "Alleged Coupon Counterfeit Clipped by Beds," *Rochester Democrat and Chronicle*, May 12, 2011.

57 **Everyone at the ACP remembers the Vryl Mkt** . . . Susan Kelleher, "Hacked Coupons Create Million-Dollar Mess," *Charleston Gazette*, August 29, 2008.

58 **They could do worse than draw inspiration** . . . Rod Taylor, "Cleans Away Dirt and Crime," Promo, April 1, 2006. The charming couponing vet Earl Ellsworth is a natural raconteur, and filled in much of the color in this story through firsthand anecdotes, April 25, 2012, author interview.

3

61 **The World of Coca-Cola is a fountain of pop culture** . . . I spent a day trawling through this museum-cum-store, January 17, 2012. The name of the shop clerk has been changed, for obvious reasons. For the record, I'm with Vanessa.

62 **The English word for** *discount* . . . Defined by *Merriam-Webster*, http://www.merriam-webster.com/dictionary/discount.

63 **Until the French Revolution** . . . Michael B. Miller, *The Bon Marché: Bourgeois Culture and the Department Store 1869–1920*, (Princeton, NJ: Princeton University Press, 1994) pp. 21–2.
During World War II, though. . . Jan Whitaker, *Service and Style*, p. 39; and author interview, January 19, 2012.

63 **As part of Le Bon Marché's reopening** . . . Per interview with pricing guru Jon Manning, January 22, 2012. For more on Boucicaut, see Miller's terrific history book.

64 **Two men have a viable claim** . . . Marilyn Much, "R.H. Macy's Store Cashed In; Make the Sale: The Company's Founder Directed the Way for Transactions and Ads", *Investor's Business Daily*, July 5, 2007; Michael Lisicky, retail historian, January 10, 2012, author interview.

64 **White sales also originated** . . . Jean Bond Rafferty, "Does less + luxe = more?" *France* magazine, Winter 2002–03.

64 **In 1927, five years after his death** . . . Whitaker, *Service and Style,* p. 285.

64 **The scene is a carpet warehouse** . . . I spent a day on set on August 13, 2012. There was a post-euphoric hangover blanketing the city. Even the weather, which had been gloriously sunny for the previous fortnight, turned ashen and gray overnight.

65 **The actor's foul mouth** . . . The source for much of my background on HGS is Lindy Woodhead's gallopingly good, gossipy bio, *Shopping, Seduction and Mr. Selfridge* (also the basis of Piven's show). Nancy Koehn's *Brand New: How Entrepreneurs Earned Consumers' Trust from Wedgwood to Dell* was also invaluable.

66 **Since Field left a fortune** . . . Woodhead, p. 17.

66 **"Marshall Field had a knack . . ."** Woodhead, December 9, 2011, author interview.

66 **Intriguingly, it's to Chicago that we owe** . . . Lisicky, January 10, 2012, author interview.

67 **"He gave them glamour . . ."** Woodhead, December 9, 2011, author interview.

68 **A Mrs. Valerie Ranzetta reminisces** . . . "Memories of a customer shopping in 1926," by Mrs. Valerie Ranzetta, supplied courtesy Lindy Woodhead and originally sourced from the Selfridges Archive.

69 **Jealous competitors at first** . . . Daniel Cohen, "Grand Emporiums Peddle Their Wares in a New Market," *Smithsonian,* March 1, 1993; Lisicky, January 10, 2011, author interview.

69 **"This sale has come from your eyes . . ."** *Mr. Selfridge,* Season 1, episode 8. Originally broadcast in the United Kingdom on February 24, 2013.

70 **When Coca-Cola was invented** . . . Much of this information is from Ted Ryan, Coca-Cola company archivist, January 17, 2012, author interview.

70 **To feed it, he off-loaded** . . . History of Coupons, and Coupon Clearing, NCH press materials

70 **"[Candler] was a strict, teetotaling Methodist . . ."** Ted Ryan, January 17, 2012, author interview.

71 **Between 1886 and 1920** . . . Ryan, author interview.

71 **8.5 million glasses drunk gratis** . . . Megan Geuss, "Prototype: Coca-Cola and the Birth of the Coupon," *Wired* magazine, November 2010.

71 **Notably, Harry Gordon Selfridge** . . . Information provided by Ted Ryan via e-mail, August 2012.

71 **Post cereals was typical** . . . History of Coupons, and Coupon Clearing by NCH, NCH press materials.

71 **As US retail sales halved from $48.5 billion** . . . Jan Whitaker, *Service and Style,* p. 36.

72 **Companies started printing coupons** . . . Matt Hickman, "Back to Basics," *Mother Nature Network,* February 26, 2010.

72 **Prompted by the emergence** . . . Eileen Smith, "Burlington Twp Kmart to Close Doors," *Courier-Post,* Cherry Hill NJ, June 24, 2009.

72 **One of them was Earl Bartell.** . . . Much of the story is drawn from my talk with Earl Bartell, January 25, 2012, author interview.

74 **Ten years of falling sales later** . . . Alice Z. Cuneo, "CODEBLUE; Kmart turns on the light: One day in the battle to bring a brand back to life", *Advertising Age*, April 9, 2001.

75 **In 1969, longtime CEO Manfred O. Lee** . . . Jeffrey L Rodengen, *The Legend of VF Corporation*, (Fort Lauderdale, FL: Write Stuff Press, 1998) pp. 88–93.

75 **Eventually, the discount mall would turn** . . . Katherine Rizzo, "City's 'Chic' Spells Success for Outlet Malls," *Reading Eagle*, August 28, 1983.

75 **Certainly, factory-direct stores had existed** . . . Stuart and Scott Anderson, January 27, 2012, author interview.

75 **M.O. ordered his machinists** . . . These details are drawn from interviews with Steve Fritz, January 31, 2012, and Rich Maloof, February 17, 2012.

76 **"In the beginning, things were . . ."** Maloof, author interview.

76 **Almost forty years later, one Ralph Lauren** . . . , May 21, 2012, author interview.

77 **"There's no question there were bribes . . ."** Maloof, author interview.

77 **"That was a time when . . ."** Maloof, author interview.

77 **This was all thanks to a rise** . . . Fritz, author interview.

78 **By 2012, there were almost one hundred eighty.** . . Linda Humpers, EIC Value Retail News, March 13, 2012, author interview.

78 **Ninety percent of the stock** . . . Fritz, author interview.

78 **The townhouse in which Clive Dunn** . . . I spent a fascinating wintry afternoon with Dunn and Humby, who were charming hosts and served especially delicious biscuits. The account of their rise owes much to this meeting, February 6, 2012, author interview.

79 **S&H Green Stamps** . . . "S&H Green Stamps," Wikipedia entry.

79 **Theirs was a mammoth task** . . . Dunn and Humby, author interview.

80 **Profits skyrocketed from $860 million** . . . Rebecca Thomson, "Terry Leahy—Clubcard—Putting the Customer at the Heart of the Business," *Retail Week*, March 18, 2011.

80 **Initially, the envelope-opening rate hovered** . . . Dunn and Humby, author interview.

80 **"People thought . . ."** Dunn and Humby, author interview.

81 **Diapers are Clive's favorite** . . . Dunn and Humby, author interview.

81 **There are some intriguing inequalities** . . . "As It Pushes into Finance, Tesco's Clubcard Gives It a Competitive Edge," *Economist*, November 5, 2011.

82 **"Stimulating sales through offers . . ."** Dunn and Humby, author interview.

82 **In 2012 a smaller British supermarket chain** . . . Nils Pratley "Morrisons Disloyalty Card Risks Upsetting Regular Shoppers," *The Guardian*, November 14, 2012.

82 **The doubters were proven right** . . . Dunn and Humby, author interview.

83 **After a few weeks, Edwina's number whispering** . . . Dunn and Humby, ibid.

4

85 **"It's a classic look that's not going out of style . . ."** Mollie Fitzgerald, August 29, 2011, author interview.

85 **French cobbler Vivier invented the stiletto** . . . "The Paris Review," *WWD*, March 7, 2011.

86 **"I get a gorgeous engraved . . ."** Fitzgerald, author interview.

86 **Calling the subterfuge . . .** , April 8, 2012, author interview.

87 **"I suppose it makes me feel . . ."** Fitzgerald, ibid.

87 **Ralph Lauren, for example** . . . Alexandra Rowley, November 25, 2011, author interview.

88 **"Of course we did private sales . . ."** , author interview.

88 **One former floorwalker confides** . . . June 8, 2012, author interview.

88 **Clothing boutique Intermix** . . . Confirmed via email by Jennifer Talbott, former public relations head, Intermix, July 16, 2012.

88 **Such restrictions aside** . . . June 8, 2012, author inteview.

89 **One freelance personal shopper** . . . May 20, 2012, author interview.

89 **And Bloomingdale's has a bargain program** . . . Confirmed via email by Marissa Vitagliano, OVP National Media Relations, Bloomingdale's, June 11, 2012.

89 **One fashionista reported**   Valerie Steele, Director and Chief Curator, museum at FIT, January 23, 2012, author interview.

89 **Another wrangled a spontaneous deal** . . . John Melick, December 2, 2012, author interview.

90 **Meeting Shelly and Renée in person** . . . Unless otherwise noted, the stories and quotes in this section are drawn from several hours spent with Shelly Antebi and Renée Salem, June 19, 2012, author interview.

92 **Soiffer Haskin is a similar** . . . Rosemary Feitelberg, "Clamping Down on Sample Sale Shoplifters," *WWD*, December 12, 2006; Fawnia Soo Hoo, "Navigating the Fray: Play Nice, Ladies: A Shopper's Guide to Sample Sale Etiquette." New York Racked.com, February 23, 2011.

92 **The most exclusive operation** . . . Yale Breslin, "Marjorie Gubelmann on Her Favorite Secret Sample Sale Society," New York Racked.com, November 4, 2011; "USPTO issues trademark: Shopsecret," *US Fed News*, May 27, 2011.

93 **His gowns are still sold** . . . Frank Pulice, Head of PR, Carmen Marc Valvo, June 6, 2012, author interview.

93 **However the product may vary** . . . April 5, 2012, author interview.

93 One longtime visitor to St. Barts was staggered . . . January 25, 2012, author interview.

94 According to industry insiders . . . January 6, 2012, author interview.

94 In the past, the merchandise was often shipped . . . Elizabeth Cline, *Overdressed*, p. 135.

94 *Real Housewife* Ramona Singer . . . Her company is called RMS Fashions. See Felix Gilette "Hot Housewives of Manhattan," *New York Observer*, February 19, 2008.

94 The arrival of secondhand clothes . . . Cline, *Overdressed*, p. 135.

94 One world-famous brand . . . June 8, 2012, author interview.

94 "For years, I heard Chanel . . ." Alysa Lazar, June 7, 2012, author interview.

95 Alysa Lazar was out in the Hamptons one day . . . Unless otherwise noted, stories and quotes in this section are drawn from Alysa Lazar, June 7, 2012, author interview.

96 Foremost among them today . . . Unless otherwise noted, quotes and anecdotes in this section are from Izzy Grinspan, August 17, 2011, author interview.

97 Carrie Bradshaw's beloved Manolo . . . Maureen Dowd, "Women on Pedestals," *New York Times*, November 5, 2011.

97 "It's tables in all sizes . . ." June 6, 2012, author interview.

97 It was what one veteran wittily dubs . . . June 19, 2012, author interview.

98 Such is the frenzy around sample sales . . . Izzy Grinspan, "New Jersey Ferragamo Sale Reportedly Ends in Chaos, Arrests" New York Racked.com, November 15, 2011.

98 The risk of fisticuffs . . . June 20, 2012, author interview.

99 Two ubiquitous divas duel . . . I spent an entire evening watching the frenzy at the Gilt City Sample Sale on May 18, 2012, from which all this material is drawn. Full disclosure: Yes, I found some too-hard-to-resist bargains despite swearing not to spend a dime—four pairs of shoes, in fact.

100 The hoary story of Gilt's founding . . . Lauren Sherman, "By Invitation Only," *Forbes*, February 25, 2008; Andrew Riche, "What's a Dress Worth?" *New York* magazine, February 10, 2010.

100 The e was added to convey . . . It was actually Alexandra's idea. Alexis Maybank and Alexandra Wilkis Wilkinson, *Gilt: By Invitation Only*, p. 60.

100 "All I could think was . . ." Riche, "What's a Dress Worth?"

101 His original plan . . . Maybank and Wilkis Wilkinson, *Gilt*, p. 32

102 The pair was so crucial . . . Riche, "What's a Dress Worth?"

102 At the time of writing, the firm is private . . . Maybank and Wilkis Wilkinson, *Gilt*, p. 246.

Gilt is considering becoming public. . . . Nitasha Tiku, "Layoffs at Gilt Groupe Complete: 90 Employees Let Go, Gilt City Closes Offices in Six Markets," Beta-beat.com, January 23, 2012.

102 **Incredibly, Saks, having lost** . . . January 6, 2012, author interview.

103 **Bain Capital estimated that just 25 percent** . . . Riche, "What's a Dress Worth?"

103 **Rival HauteLook.com was smart to accept** . . . Rachel Brown, "Lessons from HauteLook," *WWD*, August 24, 2012.

103 **"It's not that hard to sell things . . ."** Riche, "What's a Dress Worth?"

103 **In 2010 it was estimated that 35 to 40 percent** . . . Riche, "What's a Dress Worth?"

104 **In one instance, Aden and Anais muslin** . . . See sale on Gilt.com, December 15, 2011.

104 **It didn't help that Gilt was valued** . . . Vicki M. Young, "Vente-Privée Said Set to Unveil U.S. Deal," *WWD*, May 11, 2011.

104 **While its revenue that same year hit $500 million** . . . Sherman, "By Invitation Only."

104 **Estimates put yearly losses around $45 million** . . . Garett Sloane, "RED FRI-DAY Alert Gilt's Losses Grow," *New York Post*, November 23, 2012.

104 **Mulpuru worries, too, that Gilt's premise** . . . Sucharita Mulpuru, Forrester, November 1, 2012, author interview.

105 **It's the Friday before Labor Day** . . . This reporting is drawn from a day spent amid the mobs at Woodbury Common, September 2, 2011.

106 **Woodbury Common opened in 1985** . . . Woodbury Commons website, www.premiumoutlets.com/outlets/outlet.asp?id=7, and corresponding Wikipedia entry.

107 **Staggeringly, insiders say that 60 to 70 percent** . . . August 20, 2011, author interview.

108 **"They bring out residue for grand openings . . ."** , August 20, 2011, author interview.

108 **The real estate company that owns Woodbury** . . . From investing.business-week.com.

109 **Since 1995, the amount of square footage** . . . Linda Humphers, EIC Value *Retail News*, August 2012.

109 **When *Consumer Reports* conducted an outlet investigation** . . . "Outlet Shopping Secrets," *ShopSmart*, July 2010.

109 **Ten years later, those same moneymen** . . . Teri Agins's seminal book about the business of frockmaking, *The End of Fashion*, was an invaluable source for much of this section, especially chapter 6, "Gored in a Bull Market," p. 211.

110 **Sometimes, of course, those stats** . . . June 6, 2012, author interview.

110 **In the late 1990s, Gap even boasted** . . . Cline, *Overdressed*, p. 18.

110 **No wonder each American now has 46 square feet** . . . Robin Lewis, April 11, 2012, author interview.

111 **"In every relationship . . ."** *Sex and the City,* Season 6, episode 5. Originally aired on July 20, 2003.

111 **One scene, more than any other, proves Sex and the City's power** . . . Season 3, episode 17. Originally aired on October 8, 2000.

112 **At Bergdorf Goodman, nowhere is that more important** . . . June 8, 2012, author interview.

113 **At one time, the Neiman Marcus Last Call** . . . June 20, 2012, author interview.

113 **A business-savvy Mormon** . . . Unless otherwise noted, quotes and statistics cited come from Ben Hemminger, *Fashionphile,* June 29, 2012, author interview.

5

118 **Groupon promises to help** . . . Examples retrieved from Groupon's website, February 23, 2013.

118 **Such Groupthink-style shopping grew out of founder** . . . Frank Sennett, *Groupon's Biggest Deal Ever,* pp. 31-32; September 5, 2012, author interview.

119 **The firm could make $15.6 million** . . . Sennett, *Groupon's Biggest Deal Ever,* p. 12.

119 **Predicted to be the fastest company ever** . . . Christopher Steiner, "Meet the Fastest Growing Company Ever," *Forbes,* August 20, 2012.

119 **Less than five years after its founding** . . . Oliver Burkeman, "Groupon: The Golden Nugget," *The Guardian,* June 11, 2011.

119 **A slangy term, *Grouponomics*** . . . See more at urbandictionary.com.

119 **According to Urban Dictionary, Groupon Anxiety** . . . Ibid.

119 **CBS developed (then shelved) a sitcom, *Friend Me*** . . . Lisa de Moraes, "CBS announces return date for 'Rules of Engagement,' sets 'Golden Boy' on Friday nights," washingtonpost.com, December 6, 2012.

119 **A crucial market, as 54 percent of households** . . . Brad Tuttle, "Daily Deals: More for the Rich Than the Poor, More About Spending Than Saving," Time. com, October 27, 2011.

119 **One behavioral economist even conducted** . . . Dan Ariely, "How Online Companies Get You to Share More and Spend More," *Wired,* July 2011.

121 **On average, 92 percent of passengers** . . . Larry Robinson, PricePoint Partners, March 13, 2012, author interview.

121 **The same seat has usually** . . . Eduardo Porter, *The Price of Everything: Solving the Mystery of Why We Pay What We Do,* p. 36.

122 **Back then, there were just four rates** . . . George Hobica, Airfarewatchdog. com, January 30, 2012, author interview.

122 **Prices were as genteel** . . . Taken from my own article, "Come Fly with Me!" *Departures* magazine, March/April 2008.

122 **United CEO Richard Ferris** . . . Kristina McQuaid, "Delta and Northwest File for Bankruptcy: Is It Time to Ground a Major Airline?" *Houston Journal of International Law*, March 22, 2007.

122 **But American Airlines CEO Robert Crandall** . . . "Our favorite air lines," Economist.com, December 22, 2011. The original quote was from 1971.

122 **Regulations abounded over more than just fares** . . . Ellwood, *Departures* magazine.

122 **But given that just three** . . . Severin Bornstein, "All Things Considered," NPR, December 16, 2011.

124 **One senior executive at Hampshire** . . . June 23, 2011, author interview.

124 **"There must be fights in the lobbies . . ."** May 2, 2012, author interview.

124 **The Hoxton Hotel in East London is known** . . . Timothy Barber, "A Fancy Hotel Is the Answer if You're Stranded by Snow" *City AM*, December 21, 2010.

124 **Iconic hotelier Ian Schrager mimicked** . . . Watch for the next batch to be released at http://www.publichotels.com/chicago/dollar/.

124 **Airline fares, for example, change three times a day** . . . Hobica, author interview.

125 **Sometimes, though, such automation can backfire** . . . "United Airlines booking bungle lets customers buy FIRST CLASS flights to Hong Kong for just 33 reward miles," Mailonline, July 20, 2012.

125 **One senior staffer at Starwood** . . . July 23, 2011, author interview.

125 **No wonder that the company declared very healthy** . . . Data from marketwatch.com.

126 **Spirit Airlines was pilloried** . . . "Just in time for the holidays! Spirit Airlines to charge up to $100 for carry-on luggage," Mailonline, November 7, 2012.

126 **Tellingly, such nickel and diming** . . . Aaron Smith, "Spirit Air to charge up to $100 for carry-on bags," CNNMoney.com, May 3, 2012.

127 **In Starwood's case, the Preferred Guest Program** . . . Confirmed via email by Starwood PR team, October 23, 2012.

127 **These programs certainly shore up** . . . Hobica, author interview.

128 **During the 2008 recession, for example** . . . January 6, 2012, author interview.

128 **In 1992, American offered a JFK–LAX** . . . Edwin McDowell, "American Air Cuts Most Fares in Simplification of Rate System," *The New York Times*, April 10, 1992.

129 **Others followed, which pushed** . . . David Field and Mark Pilling, "A Simpler Life," *Airline Business*, February 1, 2005.

129 **In 2005, then-Delta CEO Gerald Grinstein** . . . Rich Thomaselli, "Reinvention: Delta Sets the Stage for a Marketing War; Pits Itself Against Low-Cost Carriers with Price Cuts," *Advertising Age*, January 10, 2005.

129 **"While you're sitting here talking . . ."** John Helyar, "Why Is This Man Smiling?" *Fortune,* October 18, 2004.

129 **No one sums up the problem better** . . . Al Ries, Marketing Consultant, January 10, 2012, author interview.

130 **Once a grubby East Village crossroads** . . . Unless otherwise noted, quotes and observations from this section were drawn from the morning I spent with the Town team, June 15, 2012. Thanks to Wendy Maitland for helping wrangle my attendance and for her kind hospitality. I was dazzled.

131 **The change dates to 2005** . . . Bradley Johnson, "No-Haggle Pricing Climbs Higher, Finds Fans Among Affluent, Educated; Cars, Electronics, Homes at Fixed Prices; but More Feel They're 'Negotiating,'" *Advertising Age,* August 1, 2005; Eduardo Porter, *The Price of Everything,* p. 30.

132 **Unfortunately, a new study suggests that** . . . Grace Wong Bucchianeri and Julia A. Minson, "Listing Behaviors and Housing Market Outcomes," working paper, April 19, 2011. Thanks to Jed Kolko, Chief Economist and Head of Analytics at Trulia.com, for pointing this out.

132 **It holds true for homes, too** . . . Jonathan Clements, "I Have Issues . . . Do You?" *Wall Street Journal,* June 15, 2008; Manoj Thomas, Daniel Simon, Vrinda Kadiyali, "Do Consumers Perceive Precise Prices to Be Lower Than Round Prices? Evidence from Laboratory and Market Data," Cornell University Johnson School, September 2007.

133 **Many homes are put on the market** . . . Jed Kolko, Trulia, September 25, 2012, author interview.

133 **Not every homeowner might put faith** . . . Thanks to Ashley Cox, a real estate agent based in Dallas, Texas, for this tip-off, September 26, 2012, author interview.

134 **An icon of the industry is** . . . John Kalish "Screenwriter Finds New Career 'Staging' Houses for Sale," Reuters, December 28, 2000; Mark Oppenheimer, "The Story Seller," *The New York Times,* October 25, 2009.

134 **"I might think: This is an heiress . . ."** Meridith Baer, video interview "Staged for Sale," nytimes.com, October 22, 2009.

135 **"I want it to look like someone just . . ."** Baer, ibid.

135 **Baer's career wouldn't even have** . . . Barb Schwarz, StagedHomes.com, August 30, 2012, author interview.

135 **One real estate maxim** . . . Candy Evans, candysdirt.com, September 4, 2012, author interview.

135 **Scuffed kitchen cabinets can be** . . . Karen Eubank, home stager, September 20, 2012, author interview.

135 **The only difference is when stagers** . . . Jonathan Miller, Miller Samuel, September 28, 2012, author interview.

136 **One agent in California examined 2,772 homes** . . . Beth W. Orenstein, "Staging for sale; Professional put a house in its best light to broaden is appeal," Morning Call Allentown PA, November 28, 2004; Ann Brenoff, "Behind the Scene; Sellers Are Turning to Professional Stagers More Than Ever to Give Their Homes a Look that Will Hook Buyers," *Los Angeles Times*, March 16, 2008.

136 **Real Estate Staging Association (RESA)** . . . Shell Brodnax, President, RESA, September 24, 2012, author interview.

136 **Another metric even claims** . . . National Board of Realtors study, cited at www.spectacular-spaces.com/staging/.

136 **Resulting lowball offers** . . . Matt Kelton, COO, ShowHomes, October 1, 2012, author interview.

137 **Show Homes even personality tests** . . . Kelton, ibid.

137 **One Dallas-based TV producer** . . . That producer, a TV media sales vet, is Stephen Giles. "That short film on the house? You can put it out virally on Youtube," he enthuses. "But it's also great for the owner as a keepsake." Since that owner is detached enough to have sold the home, it seems a strange souvenir. October 8, 2012, author interview.

137 **Several years ago, Chicago's Smell and Taste Research** . . . Dr. Alan Hirsch, September 25, 2012, author interview.

137 **Firms like D.R. Horton** . . . James Vlahos, "Scent and Sensibility," *The New York Times*, September 9, 2007.

137 **A quick digression into the strange** . . . Kiran Yadav, "Scent of Success," *The Financial Express*, January 24, 2010; John Madigan, Meggitt, January 9, 2013, author interview.

138 **But in normal conditions, most experts** . . . Ashley Cox, author interview.

138 **Real estate agent and blogger** . . . Ardell DellaLoggia, October 8, 2012, author interview.

139 **Then again, you could just sign up** . . . Lew Sichelman, "Redeem at Closing," *Chicago Tribune*, October 16, 2011; Katherine Tarbox, "The Groupon of Housing," Realtor magazine blog, August 2, 2011; John Caulfield, "Online Vouchers Offer Home Buyers Deep Discounts," *Builder*, August 2, 2011; Lew Sichelman, "New Housing-Related Websites Aimed at Buyers," *Los Angeles Times*, October 2, 2011.

139 **Groupon itself trialed** . . . "Save $1,000 on Real Estate Purchase with Groupon," Walletpop.com, April 10, 2011; Michele Lerner, "Group coupon craze comes to real estate," Bankrate.com, June 29, 2011.

140 **Shares that sold for** . . . "Groupon Fails to Meet Expectations," Reuters, November 8, 2012.

140 **Professional goof-offs, such as** . . . Sennett, *Groupon's Biggest Deal Ever*, p. 9; Matt Schwarz, "The Coupon Rebellion," *Wired*, December 2010.

140 **Typical was the faux PSA** . . . Sennett, *Groupon's Biggest Deal Ever*, pp. 114–118.

140 **Mason's unprofessionalism was never more** . . . Kara Swisher, "Exclusive: Groupon's Mason Tells Troops in Feisty Internal Memo: "It Looks Good," Allthingsd.com, August 25, 2011.

140 **Perhaps the founders should have** . . . Kevin Kelleher, "The Checkered Past of Groupon's Chairman," *Fortune*, June 10, 2011.

141 **Eventually, it wasn't madcap antics** . . . Cyrus Farivar, "Groupon CEO Andrew Mason fired after ridiculously poor earnings," arstechnica.com, February 28, 2013.

141 **The mattress world** . . . "Mattress Store Experiments with Non-Blowout Sale," *The Onion*, February 1, 2008; Ken Schmier, May 9, 2012, author interview. Nothing sums up the ickiness of the all-sale environment that we're forced to sleep on than Geoffrey Arend's mattress salesman in *Devil*. "What makes me good at selling mattresses is I can look at a person's clothes and know exactly how much they can afford to spend," he smarms to one schlubby woman, "And you, lady, you're no supersleeper."

141 **McKinsey Consulting has** . . . Robert A. Garda and Michael V. Marn, "Price Wars," *The McKinsey Quarterly* , Number 3, 1993.

141 **Take one Santa's Grotto, deluged** . . . John Bingham, "Elf Resigns and Fairies Sworn at as Groupon Mix-up Spells Trouble in Santa's Grotto," *Daily Telegraph* (UK), December 3, 2011.

142 **There have been other splashy problems** . . . Bonnie Kavoussi, "Back Alley Waffles, D.C. Restaurant, Blames Groupon's 'Shocking Business Practices' for Its Demise," Huffington Post, July 23, 2012.

142 **The margins are only going down** . . . Lauren Etter "Groupon Therapy," *Vanity Fair*, August 2011.

142 **The UK arm has been so overeager** . . . Sennett, *Groupon's Biggest Deal Ever*, p. 69; Sean Poulter, "Gunning for Groupon: Watchdog tells discount site to ditch misleading offers," Mailonline, March 16, 2012.

143 **LivingSocial has carved out** . . . Nielsen data supplied by LivingSocial, February 16, 2012; "Demographic Differences between Groupon and LivingSocial," orbitalalliance.com, June 22, 2011.

143 **One psychologist even believes** . . . Kit Yarrow, June 6, 2012, author interview.

143 **The five-hundred-plus competitors have helped** . . . Kunur Patel, "Think Consumers Are Tired of Deals?" *Advertising Age*, September 19, 2011.

144 **Businesses risk committing** . . . All these negative neologisms were kindly coined and defined by urbandictionary.com.

144 **There's even a blog, The Bad Deal** . . . Thebaddeal.com is run by Ryan Sutton, the NY food critic for Bloomberg news, no less.

144 **Some Harvard economists have also** . . . Benjamin Edelman, Sonia Jaffe, and Scott Duke Kominers, "To Groupon or Not to Groupon: The Profitability of Deep Discounts," working paper, *Harvard Business School*, August 2, 2011.

6

145 **The impasse was down to** . . . Thanks to Alex Benblock of *The Hollywood Reporter* for much of this analysis, February 14, 2012, author interview.

146 **So there was a mold-breaking move** . . . Nikki Finke, "UPDATE: Hollywood's Desperate Discount! Lionsgate-Groupon Deal for $1 Movie Ticket to 'The Lincoln Lawyer' Opening Weekend," Deadline.com, March 18, 2011; Ben Fritz, "Groupon sells 190,000 tickets to 'Lincoln Lawyer,'" *Los Angeles Times* blogs, March 18, 2011.

146 **It was illegal for a supplier.** . . . The full story of this battle of handbags at dawn is extraordinary. See Maria Halkas, "Antitrust Fight Takes Local Man to Washington," *The Dallas Morning News*, March 25, 2007; Linda Greenhouse, "Justices Hear Arguments About Pacts on Pricing," *The New York Times*, March 27, 2007; Joan Biskupic, "Who Has Say in How Much You Pay? States Try to Counter Minimum-price Ruling," *USA Today*, December 22, 2010.

147 **A few things are obvious** . . . I spent a few hours skulking in the American Girl Store in midtown Manhattan, eyed suspiciously the entire time, on June 16, 2012.

148 **American Girl was founded** . . . Judy Newman, "Breaking the Mold," *Wisconsin State Journal*, November 13, 2011; Christopher Borelli, "The American Way," *Chicago Tribune*, December 22, 2011.

149 **When two BFFs, one black and the other white** . . . Borelli, ibid.

151 **A few years before the Euro** . . . Story relayed by , June 19, 2011, author interview.

151 **The practice dates back to the 1970s** . . . Dana Thomas, *Deluxe*, pp. 35–37.

152 **In 2005, at the height of luxury's new** . . . Christina Passariello, "Louis Vuitton Tries Modern Methods on Factory Lines," *Wall Street Journal*, October 9, 2006.

153 **"Its entire history . . ."** April 8, 2012, author interview.

154 **In 2012, twelve years after Nespresso** . . . Julian Liew, Nespresso public relations, June 21, 2012, author interview.

154 **"This store grosses more per square foot . . ."** Walter Isaacson, *Steve Jobs*, p. 421.

155 **Poached from Target** . . . Isaacson, ibid, p. 416.

155 **The first Apple Store** . . . Alec Klein, "At Tysons, Apple Takes First Bite of Retail Pie," *Washington Post*, May 16, 2001.

155 **Johnson can take credit** . . . Isaacson, *Steve Jobs*, p. 417.

155 **Apple is said to spend around $200** . . . James Dion, Dionco, January 31, 2012, author interview.

155 **Laptop screens are** . . . Carmine Gallo, "How Apple Store Seduces You with the Tilt of Its Laptops," forbes.com, June 14, 2012.

155 **But his solution was even more** . . . Isaacson, *Steve Jobs*, p. 420.

156 **The results are impressive** . . . Dion, author interview.

156 **Elsewhere, Vuitton flagships have been** . . . Marion Hume "Anatomy of a Maison," *Australian Financial Review*, November 25, 2011.

157 **The biggest stores originally** . . . Kate N. Grossman, "American Girl dolls offer a Barbie alternative," Associated Press, February 22, 2000.

157 **To celebrate its twenty-fifth anniversary** . . . Newman, "Breaking the Mold".

158 **Vuitton so admires this gesture** . . . The fashionistas' favorite inker, Scott Campbell, has worked on Marc Jacobs. The designer then hired him to collaborate on the catwalk. See examples of the neck spatters at http://www.refinery29.com/louis-vuitton-neck-tattoos-by-artist-scott-campbell.

158 **The label isn't always so forgiving** . . . Luis Gispert, May 22, 2012, author interview.

159 **The cost of many luxury goods** . . . Cline, *Overdressed*, p. 113

159 **Thorstein Veblen was** . . . Cline, ibid. p. 77; Bryce J. Jones, II and James R. Turner, "The Fall of the Per Se Vertical Price Fixing Rule," *Journal of Legal, Ethical and Regulatory Issues*, July 1, 2010.

159 **When students paid full price** . . . "Price Tag Can Change the Way People Experience Wine, Study Shows," Stanford University press release, January 15, 2008.

160 **In yet another scenario** . . . Dan Ariely, "Predictably Irrational," p.181.

160 **American Girl's current dollmaker-in-chief Ellen Brothers** . . . Newman, "Breaking the Mold."

161 **She just wants to offer** . . . Liew, author interview.

161 **More than half of the firm's** . . . Liew, ibid.

161 **Thank Ron Johnson again** . . . Isaacson, *Steve Jobs*, p. 421.

162 **"All that the [traditional] salesman . . ."** Isaacson, ibid, p. 413.

162 **A sizable chunk of the warehouse** . . . Borelli, "The American Way."

163 **In 2007, Stanford business school grad** . . . Evelyn M. Rusli, "Stores Go Online to Find a Perfect Fit," *The New York Times*, April 11, 2012.

163 **After years of tweaking bonobos.com** . . . Stephanie Clifford, "Once Proudly Web Only, Shopping Sites Hang Out Real Shingles," *The New York Times*, December 18, 2012.

164 **Staffers are loath to** . . . December 1, 2011, author interview.

166 **Ron must have been horrified** . . . "J.C. Penney gets rid of hundreds of sales," Associated Press, January 25, 2012; Phil Wahba, "Penney clears out clearance with new pricing plan," Reuters, January 25, 2012.

166 **The idea of sales, even the very word, was banned** . . . Kim Bhasin, "Ron Johnson Admits He Was Wrong and Will Bring Back the Word 'Sale' To JCPenney," www.businessinsider.com, June 5, 2012.

167 **He promised these would be 40 percent less** . . . Anne d'Innocenzio, "Penney's tries to simplify pricing" Associated Press, January 26, 2012.

167 **"And the word I kept hearing . . ."** Ron Johnson, Bloomberg TV interview, January 25. 2012.

167 **"It's the dumbest thing in my lifetime . . ."** C. Britt Beemer, ARG, April 13, 2012, author interview.

167 **In fact, it was less than six months after** . . . Anne d'Innocenzio, "J.C. Penney says President Francis is leaving," Associated Press, June 18, 2012.

168 **In 2001, Kmart's then-CEO announced** . . . "After Refilling Shelves, Kmart Copes with Empty Aisles," Associated Press State & Local Wire, August 27, 2002.

168 **When Macy's bought four hundred stores** . . . Michael Barbaro, "Given Fewer Coupons, Shoppers Snub Macy's," *The New York Times*, September 29, 2007.

168 **"People love these coupons . . ."** WWD Fashion Scoops, April 27, 2012.

169 **A fresh CEO was brought in** . . . Lewis and Dart, *The New Rules of Retail*, p. 201; David Snyder and Peter D Waldstein, "Sears: Why the Last Big Store Must Transform Itself, or Die," *Crain's Chicago Business*, July 11, 1998.

169 **An estimated 30 percent of staff at headquarters** . . . April 10, 2012, author interview.

169 **"They were hiring and firing . . ."** March 20, 2012, author interview.

169 **Such corporate roiling** . . . Aaron Task, "J.C. Penney Is the New Sears: Ron Johnson Has Done 'Incalculable Damage,' Davidowitz Says," finance.yahoo.com, May 16, 2012; James O'Toole, "J.C. Penney and Ron Johnson still struggling in turnaround effort," CNNmoney.com, February 28, 2013.

169 **Stock that had hit $43.18** . . . Ronald Thomas CFA, "Dropping the Dime on J.C. Penney," Minyanville.com, June 11, 2012; Lauren Coleman-Lochner and Chris Burritt, "J.C. Penney Reports First-Quarter Loss Amid Sales Slump," May 16, 2012.

170 **Such pummeling was a little unfair** . . . Natalie Zmuda, "Ellen Proves Key as JCP's No-Sale Tack Is Tested," *Advertising Age*, April 2, 2012.

170 **"I wouldn't assume they like . . ."** Anne d'Innocenzio, "AP Interview: JC Penney CEO talks about the chain," Associated Press, January 30, 2012.

170 **"We want our pricing to be fair and square . . ."** Meredith Galante, "The 6 Ways Ron Johnson Plans to Transform JC Penney into 'America's Favorite Store,'" *Business Insider*, January 26, 2012.

170 **Johnson clung to his EDLP strategy** . . . James Covert, "It's 'timber!' time: CEO Johnson swings ax to cut Penney" *New York Post*, May 15 2012

170 **Since Ron Johnson was unlikely to fire** . . . Dana Mattioli, "Penney ousts President" *Wall Street Journal*, June 19 2012

170 **By mid-May, just fifteen weeks or so since** . . . "Penney resurrects the word 'sale' in advertising" *Bloomberg Business Week*, June 5 2012

170 **A year after his arrival, in January 2013,** . . . Zoe Chace, "Sales Are Like Drugs. What Happens When a Store Wants Customers to Quit?," npr.org, March 01,

2013; "The J.C. Penney sale is BACK! Struggling retailer attempts to lure back lost customers after axing executive behind failed alternative pricing plan," Mailonline, January 28, 2013.

171 **His biggest champion had been activist** . . . James Covert, "Penney takes a clip – Coupon cut kills", *New York Post*, May 16, 2012; Andrew Ross Sorkin "A Dose of Realism for the Chief Of J.C. Penney", *New York Times*, November 13, 2012.

171 **Having handpicked Johnson to perform** . . . . Max Nisen, "You Know Ron Johnson Is In Trouble When Even Bill Ackman Is Criticizing Him" *Business Insider*, April 8, 2013.

171 **After snapping up a chunk of Target stock** . . . Andrew Bary, "Ackman's Target Campaign is Off-Target", *Barrons*, May 25, 2009.

171 **No wonder, given that Johnson had presided over a staggering annual loss in 2012: $985 million** . . . J.C. Penney press release, February 27, 2013.

171 **while its credit ratings slalomed junk status** . . . Abram Brown "J.C. Penney: Moody's Junk Downgrade Doesn't Spoil Rare Rally" Forbes.com, October 8, 2012; Nathalie Tadena, "Fitch cuts J.C. Penney rating", *Wall Street Journal*, February 22, 2012.

171 **In response, the board finally junked Johnson** . . . James Covert, "Ron John's gone JCP fires CEO, turns to former chief Ullman", New York Post, April 9, 2013

172 **In the EU, Vuitton was the single largest** . . . "Anti-Brand Counterfeiting in the EU," Università Cattolica del Sacro Cuore, Università degli Studi di Trento, working paper, December 30, 2012.

172 **Susan Scafidi is a Fordham professor** . . . Susan Scafidi, September 17, 2012, author interview.

173 **"Not every woman on the street . . ."** Scafidi, ibid.

174 **In 2012, there were two thousand** . . . Michael Tonello, June 27, 2012, author interview. See also Thomas, *Deluxe*, p.174. "From 2000 to 2004, Hermès created 1,230 new jobs, including adding more than six hundred leather artisans . . . By early 2006, Hermès had fifteen hundred leather artisans . . ." Four hundred more were added to the roster in 2011, according to Rupert Neate in, "Hermès Cannot Meet Demand for Luxury as Profits Leap to £257m," *The Guardian*, August 31, 2011.

174 **"Hermès pays them around . . ."** Tonello, *Bringing Home the Birkin*.

174 **In 2012, French police busted** . . . "French police bust fake handbag ring," Agence France Press, June 15, 2012.

174 **Superfakery is spreading faster than ever** . . . Peter Nitz, handbag reseller, June 28, 2012, author interview.

175 **In fact, in early 2013, there were heavy-** . . . April 17, 2012, author interview.

175 **The Japanese mafia, or** *yakuza*, **has** . . . Paul Pluta, Louis Vuitton collector, June 21, 2012, author interview.

175 **The Middle Kingdom has always been** . . . Melanie Lee, "Fake Apple Store in China even fools staff," Reuters, July 21, 2011. The stores were originally unearthed by an amateur blogger, whose account of the stores and the subsequent worldwide viral spread is a rollicking read at http://birdabroad.wordpress.com/tag/fake-apple-stores/.

7

178 **In that short time, the country has rocketed** . . . World Bank GDP data is accessible at http://data.worldbank.org/data-catalog/GDP-ranking-table.

179 **Freer markets for China's goods** . . . Orley Ashenfelter, "Comparing Real Wages," NBER Working Paper No. 18006.

179 **China became a rapacious rival** . . . Gil Rudawsky, "As Cotton Prices Approach 15-Year High, Clothing Prices May Increase," dailyfinance.com, August 17, 2010.

179 **In the United States, the net worth** . . . Paul Harris, "The Decline and Fall of the American Middle Class," *The Guardian*, September 13, 2011.

179 **There's even a new marketing buzzword** . . . Harris, ibid.

179 **In China, yearly earnings have increased** . . . Annalyn Censky, "China's middle-class boom," CNNmoney.com, June 26, 2012.

180 **"Normally Americans are not terribly . . ."** Sarah Maxwell, April 17, 2012, author interview.

180 **She initiated a study.** . . . This study is explained in detail in Sarah Maxwell's book, *The Price Is Wrong*, pp. 155–164.

182 **Sites such as Teambuy.com.cn** . . . "Shop Affronts," *Economist*, June 29, 2006.

182 **"It was great. We just bought . . ."** Ibid.

182 **Hong Kong has even systematized its discounts** . . . April 10, 2012, author interview.

183 **Groupon flouted the Massachusetts** . . . Brendan Coffey, "Groupon Has a Drinking Problem," Forbes.com, March 16, 2011.

183 **In France, rules go further** . . . Geraldine Baum, "French Pay a Price for Rules on Sales," *Los Angeles Times*, January 31, 2008.

183 **Until 2001, coupons in Germany** . . . David Wessel, "Capital: German Shoppers Get Coupons," *Wall Street Journal*, April 5, 2001.

184 **In 2004, another restrictive rule** . . . "Germany: Competition and price regulations," EIU ViewsWire Select, August 16, 2011.

184 **Twofer deals on steins** . . . Wessel, "Capital: German Shoppers."

185 **One study of the world's economic center** . . . Danny Quah, "Global Economy's Shifting Centre of Gravity," Global Policy, Volume 2 Issue 1, January 2011.

185 **A staggering 72 percent of GDP growth** . . . Pankaj Ghemawat, IESE, October 16, 2012, author interview.

185 **No wonder China overtook** . . . Alex Lawson, "China Becomes World's Largest Grocery Market," *Retail Week*, April 4, 2012.

185 **"They have a sense of confidence . . ."** Yuval Atsomon, McKinsey, October 5, 2012, author interview.

185 **Premium prices are reassuring** . . . Yuval Atsomon, Peter Child, Richard Dobbs, Laxman Narasimhan, "Winning the $30 trillion decathlon: Going for gold in emerging markets," McKinsey & Co, August 2012 p. 94.

186 **A recent McKinsey study** . . . Atsomon et al, ibid, p. 35.

186 **Former *Wall Street Journal* columnist** . . . Robert Frank's book-length examination of this idea, "The High Beta Rich," is delicious: voyeuristic and hubristic in equal measure.

186 **In the Great Recession of 2008–2010** . . . Frank, ibid, p. 44.

186 **Tokyo is a schizophrenic city** . . . Unless otherwise noted, quotes and reporting in this section are taken from the wet, warm day I spent strolling around Gotemba, June 2, 2012. Frustratingly, it wasn't worth buying anything. The markdowns simply countered the markups on retail price, bringing much of the merchandise down to normal prices stateside.

187 **According to the *Economist*, 85 percent of the** . . . "LVMH: the Empire of Desire," *Economist*, June 2, 2012.

187 **Vuitton items here** . . . Amanda Kaiser and Kelly Wetherille, "Paying More in Japan: Luxury Prices Higher Even as Demand Ebbs," *WWD*, August 11, 2010.

187 **Brands did it "because they can"** . . . Kaiser and Wetherille, ibid.

188 **"In Japan, we don't go . . ."** Ron Sternberg, CS Advertising, June 1 2012, author interview.

188 **These were so crucial a retail** . . . "Annual 'Lucky Bags' Coming to Japanese Apple Stores on January 2," Macrumors.com, December 26, 2012.

188 **Japan's aging population doesn't help** . . . "Japan population to shrink by one-third by 2060," BBC News Online, January 30, 2012; Justin McCurry, "Japan's Age-Old Problem," *The Guardian*, April 17, 2007.

190 **(remember the $25,000** . . . "Ridiculous Gifts for Ridiculous Prices," *Palm Beach Post*, December 20, 2009.

192 **Turkey has been an economic bright spot** . . . Atsomon, Child, Dobbs, Narasimhian, "Winning the $30 trillion decathlon," p. 30.

192 **It expanded at 7.5 percent between 2002 and 2006** . . . Zoe Wood, "Turks Look to Mobile Technology to Change Bazaar Cash Customs," *The Guardian*, November 19, 2011; "Background Notes: Turkey," State Department Documents and Publications, September 7, 2007.

192 **Just off Istikal Caddesi, the main** . . . Unless otherwise noted, quotes and reporting in this section are taken from my visit to Istanbul, May 22–28 2012.

194 **"My soul clears here," she sighs** . . . Nirvana Asaduryan, May 25, 2012, author interview.

194 **"It's all handmade . . ."** Asaduryan, ibid.

195 **In January 2012, a new fine** . . . Joe Parkinson, "Please Be a Little More Quiet When Shouting at Your Customers," *Wall Street Journal*, May 13, 2012.

195 **By the end of 2013, it's estimated** . . . Simon Packard, "Turkey's Young Shoppers Choosing Malls Powers Development Boom," Bloomberg.com, January 19, 2012.

196 **The former charmingly calls them** . . . Ferhan Istanbullu, EIC Marie Claire Turkey, May 23, 2012, author interview.

196 **In April 2011, Nirvana recalls** . . . Asaduryan, author interview.

196 **The police raided 137 stores** . . . Constanze Letsch, "Turkey Cracks Down on Counterfeit Goods," *The Guardian*, October 17, 2011.

196 **One report claimed there was widespread unhappiness** . . . Richard Lloyd Parry, "Shops plagued by big spenders, little manners," *The Times of London*, October 19, 2010.

197 **Selfridges—Harry Gordon's legacy** . . . Peter Walker, "Britain's Stores Tempt Chinese Shoppers," *The Guardian*, December 27, 2011.

197 **Rival Harrods already keeps** . . . Walker, ibid.

197 **True Brit brand Burberry pegged** . . . Andrea Felsted, "Burberry Targets Chinese Consumers," *Financial Times*, September 19, 2010.

197 **No wonder, since the average** . . . Harold Tillman, "Harold Tillman: Chinese Tourists Can Save the High Street—if We Let Them," *Independent*, February 15, 2012.

198 **Chinese milk firm Yili** . . . Rachel Hunter, "The Great Wall of Spenders," *Property Week*, August 24, 2012.

198 **Luxury menswear brand Bosideng has** . . . Luke Leitch, "Mencyclopaedia; Bosideng China's First Fashion Invader Makes Its Mark on London," *Daily Telegraph*, August 3, 2012.

198 **One penthouse apartment in Dorset** . . . Genevieve Roberts and Sheri Hall, "Working for the Yangtze Dollar!" *Independent on Sunday*, July 1, 2012.

198 **UK tourism chiefs were so keen** . . . "Queen 'Lookalike' Gets Chinese into Diamond Jubilee Mood," *The Telegraph*, May 25, 2012.

198 **It's a lucrative strategy, since** . . . "Few Hate Shopping For Clothes, but Love of It Varies By Country," Harris Interactive press release, June 24, 2011.

199 **"This is a return to the normal . . ."** Ghemawat, author interview.

199 **In 1820, China was responsible** . . . Maddison Historical GDP data and IMF GDP data supplied by Ghemawat. One theme park in Guilin, China . . . Alice

Yan, "Short-skirt Prices Draw Crowds Amid Sexism Row," *South China Morning Post*, August 6, 2012.

199 **The catch-up is happening at warp** . . . Atsomon et al, "Winning the $30 trillion decathlon," p. 6.

199 **By 2025, 60 percent of the one billion** . . . Ibid, p. 8.

200 **Bicester Village, a short drive from the city** . . . Unless otherwise noted, quotes and reporting in this section are from my day spent rifling the racks at Bicester, February 9, 2012.

200 **In 2010, average annual sales** . . . Lydia Slater, "Bye bye Bond Street. Hello . . . er, Bicester: The small market town with designer labels at High Street prices," Mailonline, June 22, 2011.

8

203 **The last days of the giant Filene's Basement** . . . reporting based on a very depressing afternoon spent strolling around the moribund Filene's flagship, December 29 2011.

204 **Its demise, in September 2012** . . . Spotted by author, September 23, 2012.

204 **It was similarly momentous in February 2013** . . . Mathew Katz, "Barneys Warehouse Sale to Move as Fashion Retailer Closes Chelsea Store," DNAInfo.com, January 23, 2013.

205 **A traditional luxury markup is 7.5** . . . Josh Stevens and Colin Fernandez, "Produced for £60 in an East End factory, the Posh frocks stars snap up for £1,500," Mailonline.com, December 23, 2011.

205 **As long ago as 1997** . . . "Stores Agree to Change Ads on Furniture," *Palm Beach Post*, March 19, 1997.

205 **TJX had annual revenues of $21.9 billion in 2011** . . . Data from Fortune 500 ranking; , June 8, 2012, author interview.

206 **Best Buy has 19 percent of the US electronics market** . . . "Best Buy Is a Great Value Play," www.buylikebuffett.com, March 1, 2011.

206 **In 2007, it installed** . . . David Lazarus, "Best Buy Kiosks Not Connected to Internet," *Los Angeles Times*, December 23, 2007.

207 **On December 10, 2011, Amazon announced** . . . "Amazon Price-Check App Draws Fire," *Chattanooga Times Free Press*, December 11, 2011.

207 **Retail consultant Nikki Baird says** . . . Nikki Baird, RSR Research, December 20, 2011, author interview.

207 **Especially as Smartphone penetration** . . . "comScore Reports September 2012 U.S. Mobile Subscriber Market Share," comScore press release, November 2, 2012.

207 **Those products are often . . .** "Who Makes Trader Joe's Food? Our Taste Test Results," Huffington Post, February 12, 2013.

208 **When Trader Joe's enters a new market . . .** Beth Kowitt, "Inside the Secret World of Trader Joe's," *Fortune*, August 23, 2010.

208 **In fashion, Kohl's and Macy's rely on . . .** Lewis and Dart, *The New Rules of Retail*, pp.125–126.

208 **Research firm NPD has tracked . . .** Ibid, p. 78.

208 **Store brands in supermarkets . . .** Matthew Boyle "Why Grocers Are Boosting Private Labels," *Bloomberg Business Week* November 23, 2011.

208 **And Target, so snitty . . .** Ann Zimmerman, "Target Sends Letter Vendors Asking for Help to Combat," *Wall Street Journal*, January 23, 2012.

209 **Meanwhile, rebate giant Parago launched . . .** Juli Spottiswood, CEO Parago, January 12, 2012, author interview.

209 **Shopkick deals usually involve a discount . . .** "Old Navy Joins Shopkick to Bring Mobile Rewards Deals and Offers to Shoppers at All Its Nearly 1,000 U.S. Stores," Gap Inc Press Release, November 9, 2011.

209 **Walmart calls the program . . .** Ann Zimmerman, "Can Retailers halt 'Showrooming'?" *Wall Street Journal*, April 10, 2012.

209 **More tellingly, the chain trialed . . .** Lisa Baertlein, "Walmart.com test stores hint at Web shopping fight" Reuters, November 10, 2011.

210 **Piperlime, the online subsidiary of Gap . . .** Stephanie Clifford, "Once Web Only, Shopping Sites Hang Real Shingles," *The New York Times*, December 19, 2012.

210 **When San Francisco clothing start-up Everlane.com . . .** Michael Preysman, CEO, Everlane, June 30, 2012, author interview.

211 **Belgian boutique HonestBy.com . . .** Tamsin Blanchard, "Bruno Pieters's Honest By: The only way is ethics" *Daily Telegraph UK*, March 9, 2013.

211 **It's the same thinking that led . . .** "Interview with Michael Dubin, Dollar Shave Club, socalTECH.com, March 22, 2012."

211 **In fiscal year 2011, it continued to hardily . . .** Claire Smith, "Consumer Watch: Partnership the key to success as John Lewis bucks trend" *Scotland On Sunday* July 8, 2012.

212 **Those figures remained . . .** "John Lewis Partnership plc Results for the year ended 28 January 2012," JLP PLC Press Release, March 7, 2012.

212 **"It's part of a broader trend . . ."** Oren Etzioni, Decide.com, April 17, 2012, author interview.

212 **That's the reason Uniqlo offers . . .** Bryant Urstadt, "Uniqlones," *New York* magazine, May 9, 2010.

212 **Dr. Jinhong Xie, a University . . .** Jinhong Xie, April 5, 2012, author interview.

213 **"A seller has two strategies . . ."** Ibid.

214 **At swimoutlet.com, its TYR Grab Bag** . . . See www.swimoutlet.com/product_ p/1623.htm.

214 **German Wings, a European discount** . . . See http://www.germanwings.com/ skysales/BlindBooking.aspx?culture=en-GB.

215 **Gilt Groupe tried its own version** . . . Rachel Strugatz, "Another Record Monday: Cyber Sales Hit New High," *WWD*, November 28, 2012.

215 **"Over the last couple of years . . ."** Lauren Sherman, "Moda Operandi's Aslaug Magnusdottir Talks Isabel Marant, Layaway for the Elite, and Why LSD Was Her Top Choice for a Partner" *Fashionista* March 14, 2011.

215 **Given that the average spending** . . . Eric Wilson, "Retail Site Raids a Big Closet," *The New York Times*, November 9, 2011.

216 **The idea that became Moda Operandi** . . . Robert Sullivan, "Lady and the Trunk," *Vogue*, January 2011; Leah Chernikoff, "Moda Operandi's Founder Talks Strategy, Taylor Tomasi Hill, and Average Transaction Price Per Customer (Hint: It's Over $1000)," *Fashionista*, January 13, 2012.

216 **Moda levies a 50 percent deposit** . . . Marc Karimzadeh, "Site Brings Trunk Show Concept to Web," *WWD*, February 16, 2011.

216 **"None of the buyers had picked . . ."** Sherman, "Moda Operandi's Founder Talks."

217 **"I've heard that . . ."** Ibid.

217 **And Magnusdottir's entrepreneurial instincts were** . . . Erin Kutz, "Moda Operandi Founder, HBS Alum Talks Fashion Curation, Data, and Fit," xconomy.com, June 6, 2012.

217 **Though Moda Operandi launched only.** . . "Aslaug Magnusdottir," Drapers, August 5 2011.

217 **Another endorsement is that it's already** . . . Bianca London, "The most lavish proposal EVER?" Mailonline, January 22, 2013.

217 **Moda Operandi buys its stock** . . . Karimzadeh, "Site Brings Trunk Show."

217 **Another on-call acolyte: Project Runway** . . . " Nina Garcia Is Really In Touch," Michael K, Michael Kors, dlisted.com, August 4, 2012.

218 **In March 2011, Gap quietly trialed** . . . Jessica Wakeman, "Gap Introduces Gap My Price, A Puzzling New Name-Your-Own-Price Feature" Thefrisky.com, May 14, 2011.

218 **"Americans may finally learn that . . ."** Herb Cohen, January 12, 2012. author interview.

219 **As soon as the economy cratered** . . . Sean Gregory, "In the Recession, Shoppers Are Becoming Hagglers," *Time* magazine, August 10, 2009.

219 **More tellingly, six months later** . . . Ibid.

219 **A 2010 *Consumer Reports* survey** . . . Matthew Hathaway, "Recession-Weary Consumers Find Haggling Success," *Pittsburgh Tribune Review*, March 29, 2010.

219 **This is the impulse that has** . . . Sylvia Rector, "Panera's Pay-What-You-Can Cafes Inspire Others; They've Proved That They Work, and the Model Is Spreading," *USA Today*, February 27, 2012.

219 **One company, Pricing Prophets.** . . . Jon Manning, Pricing Prophets, January 22, 2012, author interview.

219 **Take Nancy "Negotiation" Fox** . . . Nancy Fox, January 4, 2012, author interview.

220 **"You can inject humor, too . . ."** Ibid.

220 **Another well-known negotiation coach is Ed Brodow** . . . Ed Brodow, June 28, 2012, author interview.

220 **"If you go into Bloomingdale's . . ."** Ibid.

221 **"It's a subliminal thing . . . "** Ibid.

221 **Michael Sloopka, another negotiation** . . . Michael Sloopka, June 28, 2012, author interview.

221 **"You run into an obstacle . . ."** Ibid.

222 **"It was the Olympics in 1996 . . ."** Kevin Mitchell, Professional Pricing Society, March 12, 2012, author interview.

222 **Three years after the Atlanta games** . . . Constance L. Hays, "Variable-Price Coke Machine Being Tested," *The New York Times*, October 28, 1999.

222 **He has trawled** . . . Confirmed via e mail, Ted Ryan, February 13, 2012.

222 **Every January, the NRF commandeers** . . . Reporting from January 16, 2012.

223 **The company is based in France** . . . Guillaume Portier, SES, February 20, 2012, author interview.

223 **The industry leader, though, is emoticon-loving** . . . Nils Hulth, VP Business Development, Pricer, March 22, 2012, author interview.

224 **In one notorious case in 2000** . . . David Streitfeld, "On the Web, Price Tags Blur; What You Pay Could Depend on Who You Are," *The Washington Post*, September 27, 2000.

224 **"It was done to determine consumer . . ."** Ibid.

224 **Nonetheless, an Annenberg Center study** . . . Anita Ramasastry, "Web sites change prices based on customers' habits," CNN.com, June 24, 2005.

224 **Users have reported that some sites** . . . Thorin Klosowski, "Leave Items in Your Online Shopping Cart to Get Random Coupons from Retailers," Lifehacker.com, November 6, 2012.

225 **Delivery from easyPizza was cheaper** . . . "What If Flicks Go the Easy Way?" *Bristol Evening Post*, May 24, 2003.

225 **To ease congestion, the SFPark project** . . . "Hold Onto Your Seats, Sports Fans: SF Giants to Try Airline-Style," *Wall Street Journal*, December 9, 2008.

226 **The automated cab-calling app** . . . Nick Bilton, "Disruptions: Taxi Supply and Demand, Priced by the Mile," *The New York Times* Blogs (Bits), January 8, 2012.

226 **According to Shauna Mei, the Tracy Flickish** . . . Shauna Mei, AHALife.com, September 15, 2010, author interview.

226 **There are convenience stores in Frankfurt** . . . Edmundo Braverman, "Is Dynamic Pricing the Wave of the Future?" wallstreetoasis.com, April 16, 2012.

226 **Some vending machines in Japan have enacted** . . . Constance L. Hays, "Variable-Price Coke Machine Being Tested," *The New York Times*, October 28, 1999.

226 **According to Pricer** . . . Hulth, author interview.

227 **"Dynamic pricing done for the retailer . . ."** John Ross, Inmar, May 16, 2012, author interview.

227 **ICA Vanadis supermarket in Sweden** . . . "Dealer Chic," trendwatching.com, November 2011.

227 **Brazilian department store Magazine Luisa** . . . Laura Gurski, A.T. Kearney, April 20, 2012, author interview.

228 **Oren Etzioni's Decide.com claws data** . . . Etzioni, author interview.

228 **No wonder Whalesharkmedia.com.** . . . Lizette Chapman, "WhaleShark Media: We Have Six More in Acquisitions Pipeline," *Wall Street Journal*, May 12, 2012.

228 **Uniqlo launched its London flagship in October 2011** . . . "Uniqlo makes Regent Street Happy!" Uniqlo Press Release, October 5, 2011.

228 **Virgin Holidays sold premier package** . . . Spotted on Oxford Street, London, by author, July 28, 2011.

228 **Supermarket Carrefour staged a Hora Magica** . . . "Dealer Chic," trendwatching.com.

229 **Struggling online travel agent Orbitz.com** . . . Dana Mattioli, "On Orbitz, Mac Users Steered to Pricier Hotels," *Wall Street Journal*, June 26, 2012.

229 **"In many cities, customers are . . ."** "Orbitz Worldwide CEO—Interview," *Analyst Wire*, June 26, 2012.

229 **Within a week of the story breaking in August 2012** . . . Data from marketwatch.com.

230 **John Ross is a former Home Depot VP** . . . Ross, author interview.

231 **Sales have become so constant** . . . See Mark di Vicenzo, *Buy Ketchup in May and Fly at Noon*.

231 **Deal site data points** . . . Data supplied by shopittome.com, February 6, 2013.

Selected Bibliography

Agins, Teri. *The End of Fashion: How Marketing Changed the Clothing Business Forever.* New York, NY: Morrow, 2000.

Ariely, Dan. *Predictably Irrational: The Hidden Forces that Shape Our Decisions.* New York, NY: Harper, 2010.

Berns, Gregory. *Satisfaction: The Science of Finding True Fulfillment.* New York, NY: Henry Holt, 2005.

Brennan, Bridget. *Why She Buys: The New Strategy for Reaching the World's Most Powerful Consumers.* New York, NY: Crown Business, 2011.

Cline, Elizabeth L. *Overdressed: The Shockingly High Cost of Cheap Fashion.* New York, NY: Penguin Portfolio, 2012.

Conley, Lucas. *OBD: Obsessive Branding Disorder: The Illusion of Business and the Business of Illusion.* New York, NY: PublicAffairs, 2005.

diVincenzo, Mark. *Buy Ketchup in May and Fly at Noon: A Guide to the Best Time to BuyThis, Do That and Go There.* New York, NY: Harper, 2009.

Eisenberg, Lee. *Shoptimism: Why the American Consumer Will Keep Buying No Matter What.* New York, NY: Free Press, 2009.

Finlay, Victoria. *Color: A Natural History of the Palette.* New York, NY: Random House, 2003.

Finney, Kathryn. *How to Be a Budget Fashionista: The Ultimate Guide to Looking Fabulous for Less.* New York, NY: Ballantine, 2006.

Frank, Robert. *The High Beta Rich: How the Manic Wealthy Will Take Us to the Next Boom, Bubble and Bust.* New York NY: Crown Business, 2011.

Isaacson, Walter. *Steve Jobs.* New York, NY: Simon & Schuster, 2011.

Iyengar, Sheena. *The Art of Choosing.* New York, NY: Twelve, 2001

Klaffke, Pamela. *Spree: A Cultural History of Shopping.* Vancouver, BC: Arsenal Pulp Press, 2003.

Koehn, Nancy. *Brand New: How Entrepreneurs Earned Consumers' Trust from Wedgwood to Dell.* Boston, MA: Harvard Business Review Press, 2001.

Lehrer, Jonah. *How We Decide.* Boston, MA & New York, NY: Mariner, 2010.

Lewis, Robin, and Michael Dart. *The New Rules of Retail: Competing in the World's Toughest Marketplace.* New York, NY: Palgrave MacMillan, 2010.

Levitt, Steven D., and Stephen J. Dubner. *Freakonomics: A Rogue Econimist Explores the Hidden Side of Everything.* New York, NY: Morrow, 2009.

Lindstrom, Martin. *Buyology: Truth and Lies About Why We Buy.* New York, NY: Broadway, 2010.

Maxwell, Sarah. *The Price Is Wrong: Understanding What Makes a Price Seem Fair and the True Cost of Unfair Pricing*. Hoboken, NJ: Wiley, 2008.

Maybank, Alexis, and Alexandra Wilkis Wilkinson. *By Invitation Only: How We Built Gilt and Changed the Way Millions Shop*. New York, NY: Penguin Portfolio, 2012.

Mnookin, Robert. *Bargaining with the Devil: When to Negotiate, When to Fight*. New York, NY: Simon & Schuster, 2011.

Mohammed, Rafi. *The 1% Windfall: How Successful Companies Use Price to Profit and Grow*. New York, NY: HarperBusiness, 2010.

Montague, Read. *Why Choose This Book?: How We Make Decisions*. New York, NY: Dutton, 2006.

Newlin, Kate. *Shopportunity: How to Be a Retail Revolutionary*. New York, NY: Collins, 2006.

Porter, Eduardo. *The Price of Everything: Solving the Mystery of Why We Pay What We Do*. New York, NY: Penguin Portfolio, 2011.

Poundstone, William. *Priceless: The Myth of Fair Value (and How to Take Advantage of It)*. New York, NY: Hill & Wang, 2010.

Ruppel Shell, Eileen. *Cheap: The High Cost of Discount Culture*. New York, NY: Penguin Press, 2010.

Schwartz, Barry. *The Paradox of Choice: Why More Is Less*. New York, NY: Harper Perennial, 2005.

Sennett, Frank. *Groupon's Biggest Deal Ever*. New York, NY: St Martin's Press, 2012.

Stern, Remy. *But Wait . . . There's More!: Tighten Your Abs, Make Millions, and Learn How the $100 Billion Infomercial Industry . . . .* New York, NY: Collins Business, 2009.

Thomas, Dana. *Deluxe: How Luxury Lost Its Luster*. New York, NY: Penguin Press, 2008.

Thompson, Damian. *The Fix*. London, England: Collins, 2012.

Tomsky, Jacob. *Heads in Beds: A Reckless Memoir of Hotels, Hustles and So-Called Hospitality*. New York, NY: Doubleday, 2013.

Tonello, Michael. *Bringing Home the Birkin: My Life in Hot Pursuit of the World's Most Coveted Handbag*. New York, NY: Harper, 2009.

Underhill, Paco. *Why We Buy: The Science of Shopping—Updated and Revised for the Internet, the Global Consumer, and Beyond*. New York, NY: Simon & Schuster, 2000.

────── *Call of the Mall: The Geography of Shopping by the Author of Why We Buy*. New York, NY: Simon & Schuster, 2004.

Walker, Rob. *Buying In: What We Buy and Who We Are*. New York, NY: Random House, 2010.

Whitaker, Jan. *Service and Style: How the American Department Store Fashioned the Middle Class*. New York, NY: St Martin's Press, 2006.

Woodhead, Lindy. *Shopping, Seduction and Mr. Selfridge*. London, England: Profile, 2007.

Zukin, Sharon. *Point of Purchase: How Shopping Changed American Culture*. New York, NY: Routledge, 2005.

Index